D1590192

dancing on water

PUBLICATION OF THIS BOOK
IS SUPPORTED BY A GRANT FROM
Jewish Federation of Greater Hartford

Northeastern
University Press
Boston

Elena Tchernichova
with Joel Lobenthal

DANCING
ON
WATER

A LIFE IN BALLET,

FROM THE KIROV

TO THE ABT

NORTHPORT PUBLIC LIBRARY
NORTHPORT. NEW YORK

Northeastern University Press
An imprint of University Press of New England
www.upne.com
© 2013 Elena Tchernichova and Joel Lobenthal
All rights reserved
Manufactured in the United States of America
Designed by Eric M. Brooks
Typeset in Whitman and Filosofia
by Passumpsic Publishing

University Press of New England is a member of the
Green Press Initiative. The paper used in this book meets
their minimum requirement for recycled paper.

For permission to reproduce any of the material in
this book, contact Permissions, University Press of New England,
One Court Street, Suite 250, Lebanon NH 03766;
or visit www.upne.com

Library of Congress Cataloging-in-Publication Data
Tchernichova, Elena.
Dancing on water: a life in ballet, from the Kirov to the ABT /
Elena Tchernichova with Joel Lobenthal.
p. cm.
ISBN 978-1-55553-792-0 (cloth: alk. paper)—
ISBN 978-1-55553-824-8 (ebook)
1. Tchernichova, Elena. 2. Ballerinas—Russia (Federation)—
Biography. 3. Ballerinas—United States—Biography. 4. Dance
teachers—United States—Biography. 5. Leningradskii
gosudarstvennyi akademicheskii teatr opery i baleta imeni S.M.
Kirova. 6. American Ballet Theatre. I. Lobenthal, Joel. II. Title.
GV1785.T395A3   2013
792.802'8092—dc23   [B]   2012046385

5 4 3 2 1

For my son,

ALYOSHA

~ CONTENTS ~

PART 2

THE NEW

Illustrations follow

page 144

~ PREFACE ~

I know exactly the date that I met Elena Tchernichova. It was November 21, 1981, in the studios of American Ballet Theatre at Nineteenth Street and Broadway in Manhattan. ABT was then in the process of reviving George Balanchine's 1949 *Bourrée Fantasque*, which had been dropped by New York City Ballet over a decade earlier. I was twenty-two and just starting to write about dance. I hadn't yet had anything published on the subject, but audaciously I decided that I wanted to write a book on Tanaquil Le Clercq, who had been one of *Bourrée*'s original stars.

I called ABT and spoke to Florence Pettan (you'll meet her in this book). After repeated phone calls, I was finally told that I could attend a single run-through of the ballet. Tchernichova was sitting at the front of the studio watching the rehearsal with several others on the artistic staff. I recognized her from the pages of *Vogue*, where she'd been profiled in 1980. At the end of the rehearsal, I mustered my courage and went over to her: "Would she mind—" if I continued to watch her rehearsals of *Bourrée*? "Oh, I think so, I think so," she said. For a moment I was befuddled. Did she indeed mind, or was she thinking that yes, it would be okay? But then, fortunately, she added, "No problem."

It was a many-cornered route that brought me to ABT that Saturday afternoon. British author Wendy Neale had written one book on ballet and her second was on its way. She was working in the late Daniel Moynihan's Senate office at the time, where my brother was a summer intern. He put us together for lunch. Neale told me how much she admired David Howard, who then had his own ballet studio near Lincoln Center. She advised me to go and watch Howard's classes. I subsequently did. ABT's Cynthia Harvey was one of the professionals who frequently took class there. I overheard Harvey discussing the revival of *Bourrée* in which she was going to dance.

And I continued to watch ABT's rehearsals of the ballet, including another full cast run-through attended not only by Tchernichova but by then-ABT artistic director Mikhail Baryshnikov as well as most of the coaching staff. On that day Balanchine himself was coming in to watch and work with the dances.

"Have you been watching rehearsals?" Pettan asked me suspiciously in a hallway at the studios. "Yes, Elena said it was okay." And that settled that. I was fortunate that it was Tchernichova whom I had approached, because probably no one else on the coaching staff had the clout or the readiness to grant such a request. Years later I asked her why she had said yes. She told me that it was a tradition in Russia for critics routinely to watch rehearsals, which is certainly true. But that was just as certainly not customary in America.

I thought I would try to write something about the revival and suggested an interview with her. She invited me to eat at the Red Baron restaurant on Sixty-ninth Street and Columbus Avenue, a favorite hangout of hers, just across the street from her apartment. Her bluntness about ABT, its repertory and dancers, was startling. But as it turned out, I never did write the piece. Right after that, ABT left for its annual four-month tour of the United States. By the time they returned in the spring, I was working at *Dance Magazine* as a photo assistant. I thought maybe I'd try to do a piece on her.

I quickly was party to some of the rigors of her work when she invited me to watch her rehearse on a Sunday, a week into ABT's long Metropolitan Opera season. In one of the Met's basement studios, days before her New York debut as Odette/Odile in *Swan Lake*, Susan Jaffe was rehearsing with her partner, a slightly inebriated and heavily argumentative Alexander Godunov. Tchernichova tried her best to keep the peace and make some progress at the same time. I watched more of her rehearsals during that Met season and sometimes watched performances with her from a lighting booth at the back of the auditorium, the preferred observation deck for many on the ABT staff.

Later that summer of 1982, Tchernichova was rehearsing a small group of ABT dancers for a tour to Israel she had organized, which was eventually cancelled because of the war with Lebanon. Sometime around then she told me that she had been encouraged by friends to write a memoir, after sharing anecdotes about her school days at the Vaganova Institute in Leningrad.

That was the beginning of my adventures with her on three continents, during which I personally witnessed a lot of what is recounted in this book. I received from her such a great education in how ballet is put together: it was a unique, invaluable exposure. Today, unfortunately, coaching is something of a lost art in ballet. Ballet production has become above all a matter of cutting corners, making do. It's all the more difficult for me to accept the frequently slapdash performances I now see on stage, after watching how creatively and painstakingly she prepared the dancers.

Glasnost made my perspective on the Leningrad ballet experience and culture so much richer. With travel to Russia now much less complicated to arrange, I stood with her more than once on the stage of the gilded old Mariinsky Theater. I met and sometimes interviewed many of the colorful and passionately opinionated performers she recalls in this book. They were indeed just as she had described them.

My life has been enriched knowing Tchernichova and watching her work. I hope the reader will feel the same way about this book.

JOEL LOBENTHAL

~ ACKNOWLEDGMENTS ~

I want to thank Helen Atlas for her hospitality and her abiding interest in seeing this book come to fruition; Elena Vostriakova for locating family photos, Marvin Hoshino and Dmitri Strizhov for their help in transmitting photos, and Marina Ilyacheva for retrieving photos from our shared past; Remi Saunder for her encouragement, and Nina Baren for always going beyond the call of duty.

E.T.

I would like to thank Natasha Bar for her help retrieving some names and dates, Kevan Croton for his computer assistance, Ann Kjellberg and the estate of Joseph Brodsky for permitting us to use his essay; Marvin Hoshino for his untiring assistance with all matters photographic.

On the agenting front: Joan Brookbank for her advocacy of this book in its early stages, and Kathleen Anderson for staunchly enabling it to come to fruition; Nina Alovert, Valentin Baranovsky, Tom Brazil, Natasha Razina, Martha Swope, Marc Hom (and Nadja Conklin), and the Getty Research Institute (and Kathlin Ralston Knutsen) for retrieving photos from their archives and allowing us to publish them; the Library for the Performing Arts at Lincoln Center and its staff, an indispensable resource; Joseph, Shirley, Lydia, and Nicholas Lobenthal for being tough but loving critics; Stephen P. Hull at University Press of New England, whose astute editing approached the book from a different perspective than Elena's and mine, which I found stimulating; and production editor Bronwyn Becker and copy editor Lindsey Alexander, who kept the ball rolling with alacrity; the members of Soka Gakkai International for their inspiration.

J.L.

1

A WORLD NOW LOST

~ 1 ~

leningrad

If I could bring back anyone, it would be my father. I barely knew him; he disappeared when I was three, midway through World War II. I never had more than bits and pieces of information about him. Born in Russia of German parents, his name was Philip Kittel. (Had he not earlier dispensed with the aristocratic particle "von," he would not have survived as long as he did.) He was a military engineer who oversaw a munitions plant in Leningrad.

So much about him is murky, and yet somehow I seem to clearly remember well the last time I saw my father. Leningrad was being strangled by the German blockade. Lying on my parents' bed, I was dwarfed by a green satin folding screen that seemed to scrape the ceiling. My father faced the window, warming his hands in front of a wood stove. His face was shadowy. I didn't know that he'd been summoned by the KGB, but I distinctly remember him muttering, "I don't want to go; I just don't want to go!"

My mother, Maria Karusina, was a free spirit born caged, in the wrong time and place. She was beautiful: sculpted cheekbones and a high forehead gave her a slightly Tatar look. She had light brown hair, chestnut eyes. Her figure was as sleek as a ballerina's. Heads swiveled wherever she walked, admiration and bewilderment following in her wake, for she never distinguished between party clothes, business clothes, kitchen clothes. They were all costumes in a private, personal theater, and what the audience thought didn't matter. Picking through the ravaged streets of wartime Leningrad, helping to excavate the rubble of buildings, searching for unexploded German shells, she still wore a silk dress, lipstick, and high heels. She sailed into the kitchen of the apartment we shared with many other families, stirring pots in her crepe de chines, and to our neighbors she might have descended from the moon.

At eighteen my mother had been studying acting at the Leningrad

Theater Institute. She met my father when her class toured his plant. He was twice her age and wanted her all to himself, so she dropped acting, turning her ambition to the home. She liked to bake, do needlepoint—and of course dress flamboyantly. Our apartment was like a film set, the decorating scheme eclectic escapism. In our rooms an antique European redwood table faced two eighteenth-century bronze sconces flanking an art deco mirror. That dark green satin screen I found so towering sheltered an enormous bed—one Jean Harlow could have frolicked in—topped by an antique brass headboard. Around it, Persian carpets hung on the wall and covered the parquet floors.

We lived a few steps away from the Lomonosov, a bridge spanning the Fontanka Canal, one of many tributaries of the River Neva flowing through Leningrad. Our building dated back to the late nineteenth century, when the district was popular with artists and performers working in the imperial theaters nearby. Before the Revolution, my father's family had been well off; they had owned our building and two others on the Nevsky Prospect, the Fifth Avenue of Leningrad.

My father indulged my mother unstintingly. During the thirties, Russia enjoyed an abundance of consumer goods not known since before the Revolution. Luxurious fabrics were expensive but available. My father was one of the first delegates Stalin sent to America. He returned with a stack of New York fashion magazines. My mother ran to a local tailor, who outfitted her in the latest Manhattan styles. Somehow I don't think my father was too pleased. Her standing out from the Soviet herd made him uneasy. And he was very possessive.

My father never returned home from his meeting with the KGB, and at first my mother feared he'd been ambushed. It was only later that she learned of the summons that he had received. Perhaps, she thought, he was killed for his fur-lined leather coat, which he wore every day for the walk across freezing Leningrad. No buses ran during the war. "I told him not to wear it," she told me later. She called and called, badgered every municipal agency she could. Day after day, she went to the morgue, until she was convinced he had to be alive, somewhere.

While the war raged on, I sat crowded in my grandmother's apartment—my mother sent me to her mother's after a shell sliced off a corner of our building. Sharing one long, narrow room were my grandmother, also named Maria, me, my mother's sister Zoya and her daughter Nina, and my mother's younger stepbrother Leo. The apartment was filled with crags and corners that made it seem to fit into the building's façade like the lining of a glove. We taped the windows so shells wouldn't shatter them; we stuffed paper in every crack to save heat. I passed the time by counting the corners in the apartment again and again.

Government rationing had dwindled to one scrap of bread a day. We were forced to eat anything we could snatch, uproot, or improvise. We crowded around my grandmother as she fried pancakes from a batter of rice-based face powder mixed with water. They tasted just like the chalk that later, in the still-hungry years right after war, friends and I stole from our kindergarten classroom to gnaw on. Anything that could even simulate food was coveted.

Sometime later, I was back living with my mother when a friend of hers got hold of a horse and sled and drove us someplace in the country hours away, trekking all day and into the night. Friends there had saved a sack of potatoes for us. I can't imagine what my mother gave them in exchange. It was very late and we were groggy by the time we headed back. My nose, my feet, and my hands blanched. "Don't sleep," my mother kept saying, breathing on me, pulling me back from hypothermia. Bundled in blankets, I was nearly frostbitten and so were our potatoes. The moment we arrived back home we shot into the apartment to thaw out our cargo.

Now there was a frequent visitor in the apartment, slim, well-dressed Victor Balobanovich. His apartment was on the same floor as ours. He and my father had been best friends. He was director of some kind of public works. His wife and teenaged daughter had been evacuated at the beginning of the war. But not long after, a telegram came: their train had been bombed and Victor's family was reported dead.

I think he had long harbored a secret attraction to my mother, and it was now that Victor came courting. I liked him: he was friendly and attentive, and sometimes brought me gifts. My mother liked him, too, but no more than that. Still, he could help us to survive. So before long, we were going back and forth between his place and ours. Victor's apartment wasn't communal like ours; it was completely private.

One night in our room the windows were draped in black to deter enemy bombers. Suddenly my mother was in my room, gently shaking me awake. I smelled something wonderful. "Here, eat some," she urged. Beneath a cellophane cover was an entire salmon, cooked with its own red caviar. Victor brought it for us, because the government gave valued employees weekly food bonuses. In this city without bread, we ate caviar in the dark.

I imagined my father existed somewhere, but didn't think much about him. My mother never discussed him, as if words would dispel hope for his return. All that remained was a framed picture on the bureau, which brought back to my mind two bright flashes, his last day with me, and one time when he came home from work with a surprise box of chocolates. He had been in high spirits; he lifted me on his shoulders and I towered above the world.

Sirens regularly announced the approach of enemy planes. Once we heard them, we extinguished all the lights and hurried to the basement. One night I wore a chocolate-brown crepe de chine pinafore with a black velvet yoke, feathers down the front. My mother had made it out of one of her evening gowns. I loved it so, I kept it until I left Russia thirty years later. That night I wanted to make the sad faces around me smile, and I started singing a German Christmas song my father taught me. Crouched around us were dirty, weary people . . . and I wore silks and trilled the enemy's language!

It may have been treason, but my little diversion drew cheers. "*Bis!*" they yelled, "Again!" I gave encore after encore. Someone played waltzes on a harmonica and I danced, raising my skirt to my sides like butterfly wings. In its folds I caught tiny sugar cubes—a day's rationing—that they tossed. (This must have been toward the end of the war, when America was aiding us and more staples became available.) I can say without hesitation that their tribute was the most money I've ever been paid; that's how precious those cubes were.

We were living with Victor when victory was declared in May 1945. The evacuated returned, but my father didn't. Finally my mother asked Victor to investigate, because he could access classified information. "Do you really want to know?" he asked.

Victor eventually told mother that the authorities claimed they were protecting my father by keeping him in prison, for should the Germans take Leningrad, they would surely execute him as a traitor to his own population. He spoke several languages, he had a photographic memory, his head was stocked with plans and inventions. He was a precious resource the Russians wanted to hoard. When the German blockade lifted, he could be released and would take up his old job again.

However, at a precarious moment during the war, the Soviets killed prisoners indiscriminately, not bothering to check who was who and on what charges they were rotting in jail. They assumed that the Germans, should they prevail, would liberate the prisons, and the Soviets wanted to forestall the possibility of a fifth column.

That's how Victor explained it to my mother. That's undoubtedly what he was told, for he was too kind to deceive. But who could really know for sure? Eventually my mother received an official paper stating that her husband was still missing.

Soon after the war's end, Victor was invited to move to Moscow and head a government ministry. He wanted to go and take us with him, having already asked my mother to marry him. Then a letter came: his wife and daughter were alive. Communications had been destroyed because of the blockade; they'd been sent far away to Tashkent in Asia Minor. But Victor was adamant. He would leave his family the apartment and cut loose from the past.

But my mother wouldn't hear of it. A creature of extremes who loved fashion, parties, and make-believe, she was puritanical at her core. She ordered Victor back to his family. He decided to remain in Leningrad—at least he would be close to my mother. His wife and daughter returned, and he must have told them everything. To his family, we were personae non gratae—that was clear.

Once, when Victor called at our apartment, I hung behind my mother when she went to the door. She wouldn't let him in. He tried to pass her a sheaf of bills. "We don't want any help," she said. She dropped them at his feet and slammed the door shut.

So now, for the first time, she had to support herself. The administration of my father's factory came to our rescue. They gave her a job managing a warehouse that stored first-aid and cleaning supplies. Her small biweekly salary was supplemented with a bottle of methyl alcohol. This was a precious commodity on the black market. One couldn't buy liquor for love or money, and the thirsty citizens of Leningrad mixed wood alcohol with water and poured this poison down their throats.

Alcoholism was an epidemic, an escape from horror and privation. The desperate gulped perfume or medicine; they rubbed lacquer off furniture, mixed it with water. There weren't bars to sit and fraternize in. Instead people drank at their homes or at a friend's until their brains were almost paralyzed.

At first my mother sold her rations of alcohol, and we lived a little more comfortably. But then she started to drink herself, first with girlfriends from work, then at home alone. Drinking unloosed her despondency. "We're a very unlucky generation," she said. "We will never find ourselves again. We'll never recover." For one, two, three days at a time I wouldn't see her. She was stigmatized by our neighbors. Most Russians still lived by the strictures of the Church. I heard their grumbling. She was a whore, a disgrace. I should be in an orphanage, they whispered. I loved her so much and was determined to protect her. Sometimes neighbors came to our door, bringing a little bread or milk. "No, I'm not hungry," I assured them.

Once I poured a bottle of spirits down the sink and my mother beat me for the first and only time. But I would not cry. Finally she broke down. She sobbed, she apologized over and over. I begged her not to drink. She promised to try, but life was so difficult—"You're lucky, you don't understand."

Every year toward the end of the summer, a fair was held in a large city square. Farmers brought their fresh crops to sell in the open air. The war wasn't long over and there was nothing much to offer, but still, market produce started appearing again. Clowns entertained and it was like an outdoor fiesta. My mother promised to go with me one Sunday, but when that day came she was not to be found. So I decided to go alone. I picked up a bill, the only money I found in our room, to buy ice cream. It was five rubles, I thought; but it was really fifty. A fifty-ruble note was the same size as five rubles. Only the extra digit told the difference. In old Soviet currency it would be about fifty American dollars.

Near the square, a gypsy woman sat caked in dirt, cradling her child. She asked for change and I didn't have any, so I handed her the fifty rubles.

Of course she realized right away that I didn't know what I was doing. "I will pray for you," she said, and ran off with her baby.

Walking through the door, my mother's voice hit me between the ears. Did I take the money? How dare I—like a criminal! And where was the change? I told her what happened. She was still angry, but then she asked, "Did you buy any ice cream? Okay, here's twenty kopeks. Go and buy some for yourself and for me."

She was ashamed of her life, a life her own mother couldn't understand. "We're all suffering, but it will pass," my grandmother told her. "Life is like sand in the bottom of the river, moving, changing all the time." But my mother was impatient; she didn't want to suffer; she had no endurance. She had to pick apart her misery, analyze it, plumb its depths. She turned deaf ears to what my grandmother was saying; instead she raged at her mother's stoicism.

It happened that one afternoon I sneaked out of school. Something told me I was needed at home—immediately. When I arrived, I found my mother sitting in front of her bedroom mirror. "Why are you home?" her voice lashed at me. "You're not supposed to be here. Go away!"

She pushed me out and closed her bedroom door. I was hurt, baffled. Off went my coat and I barged back into her room. She had slashed her wrists.

She returned from the hospital several days later. I had saved her; I wanted and needed to be treated like a heroine, but suicide was considered a sin by both the Church and the Soviet ideology—not something to be mentioned out loud. There was only humiliation on both our parts, silence ramming against silence.

Psychiatrists tell me if a person tries to kill himself and fails, sometimes it will be as if he has been reborn. Even if his life really is miserable, he appreciates waking up in the morning and breathing. But once my mother cut her wrists, she injured her mind and body irrevocably. She wasn't reborn. She did not fight for her life.

She was theatrical always, never more so than when planning her final curtain. A year later, in March 1948, when I was nine, my mother threw a party to celebrate her thirtieth birthday . . . her farewell gala. Somehow she managed to drum up a festive spread of food and drink. She found a ham and served it with Russian potato salad. A large cake was an un-dreamed-of treat. Her friends dug in as if it were ambrosia.

That night, screams awakened me and I ran to her room. "What hap-pened? Are you sick? Should I call the doctor?"

"No," she said, "don't do that. I took poison and I will die. I'm so sorry. It's better this way."

I ran down a long hall to the phone and dialed frantically.

"Hang up!" The hospital staff thought I was playing pranks.

"Hang up!" Three tries and then they warned, "Once more and we'll call the police."

I ran to our neighbor in the apartment, a nurse. She summoned an ambulance. They came and pumped my mother's stomach and took her away.

It wasn't long before a swarm of neighbor-buzzards carted away any-thing they could. My mother was a pariah. Our neighbors disliked her clothes, her makeup, her behavior. Most didn't even try to make excuses to me, but some showed a little shame. "Your mother owes us money," they explained, or, "She borrowed this from us." My mother's wedding ring was a marquise diamond set amid tiny diamond chips. It was worthless on the black market during the war, when all transactions were barter. She often left it on the table, and I'd tried it on many times, bewitched. "Someday it will be yours," she told me. But I never saw it after her death.

Through empty streets I ran to my grandmother's, on the other side of the city. I didn't know her exact address; like an animal, I homed in. I thought she would die of shock. "How did you get here? Alone? You found me by yourself?" We ran to the hospital, but my mother never recovered.

Soon after, my aunt Zoya insisted on dragging me to identify my mother in the morgue. Row after row of tables ranged across a freezing basement. Numbers stuck out from under sheets. The newest bodies waited at the far end of the room. Someone pulled back a sheet. "No," I screamed, turned my eyes away, and ran. My shoes clattered on the flagstone floor—weren't they, those strangely disembodied sounds, really spirits of the dead? In my hysteria, it was if those phantoms had leapt off their biers . . . they chased me . . . they were breathing down my back. I threw open the door and found my grandmother. My aunt appeared. "You didn't even see your mother!" she scolded. My aunt lived into old age, well into Glasnost in once-more St. Petersburg, and only in recent years could I find it in my-self to forgive her.

That day haunted me for years. In dreams I fled the ghouls, running underwater, in slow motion. Sometimes a scream came from nowhere, until I realized it was me. I woke and dreaded the dawning day. But other times I suddenly realized, "Oh, I can fly!" My arms began churning. I soared high, higher still. The phantoms were far below me. Above the green forests and the blue sky I floated. In the morning, I jumped out of bed; I couldn't wait to start the day—and whenever I think back it seemed as though on those days something good always happened.

We buried my mother in a lakeside cemetery an hour's train ride from the city. Years before, she'd asked to be buried there. Her burial plot was at the bottom of a ravine, but I lingered on the hill above. Friends and relatives called me to come and kiss her: in Russia we place a kiss on the forehead of the deceased. I stayed where I was and they were shocked, murmuring, "This child has no heart."

"Come and tell your mother good-bye," they ordered.

"It's not my mother," I said. "She left already." Several years later I saw the ballet *Giselle* for the first time and felt as though I were watching my own story. Giselle's grave is on a desolate fringe of the cemetery, her head turned away from the church. She was a madwoman, an infidel. So was my mother, a suicide.

A year later, my grandmother begged the priests in the graveyard church to perform a special mass, since no service could be held for a sui-cide in the orthodox faith. After palms were greased they agreed to hold the service, so long as it was outside.

I was embarrassed to tell other children what really happened. I claimed that it had been food poisoning, something she'd eaten at her birthday feast, and I hid the death certificate. In bed at night I wept; at night I still think of my mother sometimes: always rewinding the same film loop but freezing now this frame, now that, things she said, choices she made. She was spoiled and irresponsible . . . maybe she would have stopped drinking if she'd lived . . . maybe things would have gotten better . . .

Grief doesn't respect schedules, but my mother's mother really had no time to mourn. She was also Maria, Maria Chiukova. I called her Ba-booliah, for grandmother. She never opened herself up completely, even to friends, family. She was so different than my mother and most Russians, who were guarded by political hazard, but nevertheless were so often impulsive, voluble, and forthcoming among friends. Whereas my grandmother talked only when it was necessary. My mother's voice raced up and down the octaves, but my grandmother's was low and soothing. When she was angry she retreated: her huge brown eyes became even darker. Her spirit was uniquely feminine, nurturing. Invisibly, seemingly by magic, she did whatever those around her needed to be satisfied. Her personality was warm and soft but her face was rugged, revealing her country upbringing. To support me, she began working a double shift at a textile factory, returning home from work at one in the morning.

She had never gotten any formal education. My mother was a great reader; how was it possible, I wondered, that her own mother couldn't read? But my grandmother's mother was born a serf and bore my grandmother in a field. "It's so easy to read. Look at this letter," I drilled her. "Say it." She pronounced each one in turn. "Now just put them together." She tried dutifully, but she didn't have much interest in reading. Instead, she was a fount of folklore and wise sayings, each one exactly right for the moment. They were maxims that let me stand back sometimes, think philosophically, and they helped me survive.

Fifteen was the age when peasant families sold their daughters to husbands, but my grandmother wasn't pleased with her parents' choice. Having moved with her husband to St. Petersburg, she ran away from him by jumping out of a second-floor window, barefooted and wearing a nightgown, so she told me. But life in St. Petersburg had been easier then than it was now in Leningrad, she recalled. The czar's children had faces like angels. People were pious; they went to church dressed splendidly. At Christmas glorious celebrations ensued. "We are now living in an evil age that must pass," she believed.

On her day off we went to see movies together or took walks in the Summer Garden, along the Neva River. It was years before we talked much about my mother, a phantom neither my grandmother nor I wanted to acknowledge. Nevertheless, once a year we visited her grave. "Elena's been a very good girl," she told her daughter, and we put pussy willow branches on the wooden cross.

Since my grandmother was already past fifty, old in Russia at that time,

I'd been registered on a list of orphans. A government agency showed photo albums to prospective foster parents. An older woman and her two unmarried daughters agreed that I was the little girl they wanted. They were one of the most privileged families in Russia. Evgenia Vecheslova-Snetkova was a noted instructor at the state ballet school in Leningrad. Her older daughter, Evgenia Vecheslova, was a brilliant scientist; her younger, Tatiana Vecheslova, was a ballerina in the Kirov company—one of the two greatest in the Soviet Union.

They invited my grandmother and me to dinner late in the spring of 1949. I'd never seen an apartment like theirs. Filled with antiques and a grand piano, their living room flowed toward a magisterial balcony. They even had a cook: our dinner was scrumptious and elegantly served.

At dinner Tatiana wore a neat suit and high heels, but her eyes were those of a provocative gypsy, dark fiery brown, never quiet. She had pale olive skin and ebony hair. Energy flew from her, and joie de vivre. Over dinner she joked, made us comfortable; they all were very convivial. The three wanted to adopt me, and what did my grandmother think about it? She told them it would be my decision, not hers. "Of course, we understand," they said diplomatically. Tatiana asked if I'd like to audition for the *Choreographitschka*, the state ballet school in Leningrad. "Yes," my grandmother replied for me, "her mother always wanted her to study there." My mother and I had passed the school almost every day, gazing down Rossi Street, a magnificent vista crowned by the Pushkin Theater, flanked by two long colonnades. "In two years, I'll take you there," she had promised.

When we returned home, my grandmother asked me if I'd like to live with Snetkova and her daughters. They were well off. Tatiana and Evgenia were young, and my grandmother's health wasn't terribly robust. She could die soon. I told her, "As long as you're alive I'll be with you," and there were tears in her eyes. She called and told them. "Fine," they said, "we understand. We like her very much and we'd like to see her whenever she wants." So I lived with my grandmother but went to visit them frequently.

I regaled my friends: the Vecheslova family lived in a palace popping with gold and diamonds. "Tatiana is a *ballerina*," I told them. "She dances on her toes." Having already been to the ballet with my mother, I felt very smart and special.

"Could you get us some of her shoes?" my friends asked a couple of weeks later. They'd never seen ballet shoes. "Of course, no problem." Then I started to worry. Maybe these shoes were very rare, very expensive, and I didn't like asking anybody for anything. Finally I told Tatiana how much I needed them. She was delighted and turned over a trove of used pointe shoes. They were way too big for us, but no one cared. These slippers were as magical as Cinderella's, and they were shredded before my girlfriends stopped shuffling around in them.

Thinking back more than sixty years, I clearly see the silver fox boa that Tatiana used to sling around her shoulders. I pitied the poor dead beast. When she came home she'd clamp his mouth on a light bulb and let him dangle. Whenever I was there, I was preoccupied by the gagging fox.

One Saturday Tatiana invited me to sleep over and spend the morning with her, her mother, and sister. They fussed over my hair, trimmed my fingernails, and baked special cookies for me; they were starved for a child to dote on. They put me to sleep in their guest bedroom. The next morning they sat down to bowls of buckwheat kasha; it gave you lots of energy, Snetkova told me. But I hated it. "You will sit at the table until you finish," they insisted. Everybody drifted off and it seemed I'd been sitting there for hours. Finally, I filled my mouth, ran to the bathroom, spat it out, and flushed the toilet. Two or three runs later, the plate was empty. Busy in the other room, they hadn't noticed. I came to Snetkova. "Oh, good girl; now you can have dessert!"

They expected me to visit frequently, but each time I came I had to behave myself, not squirm or jump, listen to them, and keep a polite conversation going. I was too rambunctious for their museum. I wanted to run and jump in the courtyard with other children. And I didn't want to eat kasha!

I came to see them before I left Leningrad to spend the summer at a state-run camp. It was open to everyone; price varied according to the family's income. On her vacation, my grandmother would join me, and work in the camp's kitchen. Snetkova said to be back by July 1, but camp didn't finish until the end of August. "No, if you want to go to the *Choreographitschka*—you must be here."

We didn't come back till the end of August, but we called the Vecheslovas right away and they invited us over. "Why did you come so late?" Snetkova asked. There were only a few days until the school term began.

"Everything's already booked, but I'll take you anyway." I was ten. The next year they were starting an experimental class for girls older than nine, the traditional entry age. I could start then. "We'll go and check if you're qualified."

Snetkova steered me through a lobby fraught with tears and disappointment. A long audition process was ending. Some children had been told to try again next year, some to forget all about dancing. In several days a few would embark on their ballet adventure.

Snetkova took me to the office of Nikolai Ivanovsky. He was a character dance teacher and an important school administrator. He had been a favorite student of Mikhail Fokine before the Revolution and was now in his late fifties.

My name sounded German, he bantered.

"Yes, my father was German."

He simply stared. "Okay, let's see," he began his inspection. "She has beautiful legs. Let's see your arch. Point your feet," he said. "Where did you learn to do that?"

"Nowhere, myself." I was always pointing my feet, idly massaging my arch while I read or passed the time. My mother's feet were beautiful, and I wanted mine to look like hers.

Ivanovsky pushed me down into a plié. I pushed back. "Just relax," he said.

"But it hurts!" They laughed and I thought, Why are they so happy it hurts? I asked them why they were checking my legs.

"Because to dance you have to have good proportions." So this school was for dancers! I was a little disappointed. For somehow, to me, *Choreographitschka* had initially evoked some type of singing or music academy.

"I like her," Ivanovsky said. Now I would take an academic examination. He took me to the school library and found a teacher who later taught me literature. I wrote dictation and computed numbers. Grades in hand, I walked through the corridors looking for Snetkova, peeking in this room and that. I opened one door. There was that same Ivanovsky. He took me to the doctor's office. They measured me standing up and sitting; they measured my hips and chest and head. And that was that: they handed me my papers and told me to tell my elementary school that, rather than waiting another year, I would be transferring to Rossi Street immediately.

~ 2 ~

make-believe

I find it daunting to try to explain the Vaganova Institute to Americans, whose children are so much freer than I could have remotely imagined being when I was a student. For our school was something like a cross between a naval academy and a British public school, with a bit of Dickens peeking around the edges of our ruthlessly regimented lives. Punishment followed misbehavior as inevitably as night follows day; once there had been corporal punishment, but it had been abolished by the time of Revolution. Our teachers weren't really cruel, but oh, were they tough!

In addition to classical ballet technique, we were taught acting, piano, historical dance, character dance, make-up, as well as all of the standard academic disciplines. Of equal importance was the syllabus of decorum in which we were indoctrinated. In and out of the classroom or ballet studio, our manners had to be impeccable. When we sat our legs snapped shut; we could never sprawl. We bowed to our teachers every single time we passed them in the hallway. We looked straight into their eyes whenever they spoke; when they scolded, we dared not evade their angry glare. When we talked we could not use our arms too freely. That, we were told, was an unruliness suitable only for peasants, and it was clear that, classless society or not, we were to aspire to a higher station altogether. We learned to express ourselves using the fewest, most economical gestures.

Naturally we tried again and again to break the laws, to seize a piece of freedom any way we could, cutting classes or stirring up food fights in the cafeteria. We knew we would be punished, and still we went ahead. But in spite of ourselves, we absorbed everything the school taught as completely as if it were mother's milk. Since our forks and knives were to be placed in parallel position, anything else eventually came to look to my eyes as graphic as splayed limbs.

The school was headed by Agrippina Vaganova, the most renowned ballet teacher in Soviet Russia. Vaganova was born in 1879. She had been a soloist of the Imperial Ballet and then, shortly before retiring in 1916, was promoted to the rank of ballerina. At the time, the Russian school had been a blend of French and Italian influences. Starting to teach right after the Revolution, Vaganova eventually codified the curriculum and synthesized a national system. Perfecting her method, she enlisted her contemporaries Vecheslova-Snetkova and Maria Romanova. By 1949, they were a legendary triumvirate at the school. Snetkova taught the first division, Romanova the intermediate, and Vaganova the senior girls. For a while Vaganova had directed both the school and the Kirov Ballet, but by my time she was working only in the school. Yet she had trained a constellation of great ballerinas and she continued rehearsing her former students.

Each year, the school admitted twenty-six girls and thirteen boys chosen from the vast reaches of the Soviet Union. It was mandatory that children from each republic be recruited. The boys in my class were taught ballet by Boris Chavrov, while Natalia Komkova and Lidia Tyuntina taught thirteen girls apiece.

Fidgeting in our regulation white dresses, we waited for Tyuntina to appear on our very first day. Our families had starched our skirts so they wouldn't stick to our legs. The tops were sleeveless, with little straps and a square neckline. We wore white socks and soft white ballet shoes, for we would not put on tights until our fifth year at the school.

Tyuntina entered: a middle-aged woman wearing a white-gray silk skirt with a red windowpane pattern and a short-sleeved white silk shirt tied up the front. She told us her name and that she would teach us classical ballet for the next nine years. "Let's start," she said. Tyuntina told us to face the barre, she turned our heels out into first position, and we were off.

After graduating from the school in 1922, Tyuntina had been a soloist at the post-revolutionary Leningrad ballet, dancing ingenues as well as young revolutionaries in the new Socialistic Realism balletic repertory. As a young woman Tyuntina had something of the same look as her classmate Alexandra Danilova, who became a great star in Europe and America. Both had large eyes and a cameo-shaped face, but Tyuntina's features were more delicate. In class, her hair was held with an elastic, rolled to the side and back in what we called a "bagel." Then and for the rest of her life, Tyuntina was invariably perfumed, her lips daubed with red lipstick, her face powdered, her nail polish impeccable.

By contrast, when I saw Vaganova herself walking the halls, she impressed me with her large head, eyes that were X-rays, and a severe mouth. She always wore a dark suit set off by a light-colored blouse. She never smiled in my presence; rather her face was somber and philosophical. Passing her I felt brushed by an electromagnetic force. "Keep your chin up," she commanded me once. Her own chin seemed weighted by thought. But she didn't need to say a word to instill fear and reverence. She reminded me of Tchaikovsky's Pique Dame, a fearsome old matriarch, but above all she was an immaculate deity. I could no more picture her going to the bathroom than I could Stalin or Lenin.

Of all the teachers Vaganova had trained, Tyuntina was her favorite. Now she had entrusted Tyuntina with a new experiment: rather than teaching the three-year elementary grade, Tyuntina would be our teacher for the entire nine-year course of study.

Although Vaganova was absolute monarch of the school, in her frequent visits to our class she never usurped Tyuntina's authority. She never gave us corrections directly or contradicted Tyuntina. She sat very quietly, occasionally whispering to her former student. Tyuntina was the youngest teacher on the staff. Vaganova called her "Liditchka," but Tyuntina always used the formal "Agrippina Jacovlevna." Tyuntina was solicitous with her, without being in the least obsequious. Watching them I felt that Tyuntina was expressing respect, affection, politeness. I was thrilled one day when Vaganova told the class that my port de bras was the best, and then asked me to demonstrate some positions.

Almost every day we discovered a new step or detail, and the next day Tyuntina would quiz us on the proper French pronunciation. In the middle of the first year, she demonstrated to us relevé in second position. We gripped the barre with both of our hands. We were given eight counts to slowly raise our leg high, eight more to hold it as high as we could, and four more counts to lower it to the ground. I started raising my leg, but by count six or seven I knew I wasn't made for this. By count nine or ten my muscles were in spasms, and I was whimpering. We were really too young to be able to hold a developpé for eight counts. Our abdomens and lower backs just were not strong enough.

Tyuntina rushed over to me. "Hold it, hold it, hold it!" she yelled. Finally my legs crumpled to the ground and I started to bawl. "What's wrong with you?" she asked.

"It hurts!" I cried. "I can't hold it. It hurts!"

"Well then, you're in the wrong profession," she said. "It will hurt for the rest of your life!"

Those were harsh and discouraging words to use with a child, and I think that for me they turned the idea of ballet into something torturous. I didn't want to get hurt. I didn't want to live the rest of my life in pain. Gradually I learned how to cheat: my leg would rise so slowly that it was still moving up a couple of counts after I should have begun holding my extension. "Faster, faster, do it faster!" Tyuntina would scream.

§ ₰

Tatiana Vecheslova was more cerebral than most ballerinas. I often found her in her apartment immersed in poetry. I knew, too, that she was a friend of our great poet Anna Akhmatova. One day she produced a book that she wanted me to read. I had read many of the books remaining in my father's library, taking down anything from the shelves willy-nilly. Now I was happy that someone was going to point a way for me.

Tatiana had selected a biography of the great Russian actress Maria Yermolova. I started the biography immediately, and I couldn't put it down. Yermolova's career had spanned two epochal periods in Russian theater: the realism of Stanislavsky and the symbolism of Meyerhold and his contemporaries. Like many privileged Russian performers, Yermolova had become radicalized by the Revolution, convinced that the new order would improve the lot of the Russian people.

One day a teacher took us on a trip to the Leningrad theater museum, housed in a building adjoining our school. In one room was displayed a floor-to-ceiling painting of Yermolova. We gathered around our teacher. "I want to introduce you to a great, great Russian actress," she intoned with an evangelical hush.

A voice piped up: "Yermolova!"

"Who said that?" she asked. "Come here. What is your name?"

"Elena Kittel."

"How did you know that?"

"I read about her."

"Is your mother an artist?"

"No, I don't have a mother."

"What about your father? Who is your father?"

"I don't have a father, but he was an engineer. I live with my grandmother."

"What about your grandmother? What does she do?"

"She's just a nice lady. She never went to school."

She turned to the class. "This girl should be an example to all of you. It's amazing. She didn't come from an artistic family but already she knows about artists." I was too proud to mention a word about Tatiana. But satisfied that I had absorbed Yermolova's life story, Tatiana then selected for me a biography of the great Russian basso Fyodor Chaliapin. At this time, he was officially invisible, since he had left Russia after the Revolution, but Vecheslova was not overly concerned with things like that.

Ballet teachers at the school were a royal family. Their studios were fiefdoms, in which they could do whatever they wanted. Snetkova liked to grab me in the corridor, pull me into her class, and command me to point my feet or try to raise my leg in an extension. She complimented my extension, but I still didn't like quatrième devant any more than I did in Tyuntina's class. Snetkova's students cooled their heels while she kissed me, smoothed my hair, plied me with candies and cookies. "Come back on your next break," she'd tell me, but I tried to avoid it and she'd have to catch me in the corridor.

Snetkova and Tatiana were angry when I evaded them, thinking that I was an ungrateful child. But I was embarrassed by their special treatment. My fellow students imagined that Snetkova was really my grandmother and resented the favoritism. They teased me, accused me of speaking Russian with an accent. Probably I did, given that my father's Russian must have been German inflected, but at the time I was dumbfounded and angry.

Yet to us students, foreigners were veritable Miraculous Mandarins since we so rarely encountered any. In the 1950s the school began hosting Roumanian and Hungarian students, and even they were mysterious to us. The teachers were less strict, less harsh with them: throughout my life

I saw that Russians would forgive foreigners for things they would never accept from their own people.

It was during my first year at the school that I made my stage debut, in *The Red Poppy*, a ballet in which Tatiana scored one of her greatest triumphs. After the earlier bloodbaths of World War I and the Revolution, the old-fashioned classical ballet had been stigmatized. *Swan Lake, Sleeping Beauty*, all those ballets that reeked of princesses and courtiers were branded decadent, fit only for the old society. A genre of ballets emerged, often constructed to conform to Socialist Realism, relying heavily on realistic pantomime, and usually displaying an appropriate political moral. These were the *dramballets*, and they thrived alongside the old classical ballets, which were themselves tweaked to align with the new political orthodoxy.

The Red Poppy is considered the first ballet to project the new Soviet doctrine and aesthetic. It was originally choreographed in 1927 for the Bolshoi in Moscow by Laschcillin and Vasily Tikhomirov, the latter a great star then at the end of his performing career but who nevertheless choreographed for himself the starring role of the Soviet captain. The red poppy was an emblem of the longed-for freedom won by the downtrodden Chinese. The ballet showed rich imperialists controlling the native laborers until Russians rescued them from eternal oppression. At the Kirov we were now dancing a new *Red Poppy* restaged in 1949 by Rotislav Zakharov, one of the primary architects of the Soviet *dramballet* since the 1930s. Tatiana danced the heroine, Tao-Hoa, an entertainer in a Shanghai waterfront dive.

Tyuntina was in charge of rehearsing the school's children when they performed in ballet or opera. All of the children were dying to be included, but Tyuntina gave preference to her own students. For my part, I couldn't wait to taste life on the stage.

At six in the evening a special bus came to the school to drive us to the theater. (How envious we were when we learned that in the czar's time transport was a horse-drawn carriage!) Snetkova met me at the stage door since she was going to take me to see Tatiana before the performance. She led me up a few steps and then Tatiana faced us in a silk robe and Madama Butterfly–style makeup. An Oriental hairpin speared her coiffure. She looked magnificent.

Her dressing room was spotless, the light soft and warm. A mirror nearly covered one wall, mirrored panels flanked it; a panel on the opposite wall completed the crossfire of reflections. On her table a powder puff sat in a huge pink-and-white porcelain dish. It was my first exposure to the special allure of Russian ballerinas' dressing rooms. They are pockets of femininity, filled with the smell of powder, for every dancer swabs her body as well as her face.

Preoccupied with the performance ahead, Tatiana wasn't her usual fizzy self, but she had danced *The Red Poppy* many times and was very sure of herself. "I'm going to do my warm-up now, but look around at whatever you want." I looked around, stroking the pointe shoes Tatiana had selected for the performance; lined up in formation, pink satin ribbons spilling over the table's edge. I'd never seen clean new pointe shoes in all their shiny, impudent glory. Their sleek satin hides and spangly ribbons put to shame the drab cotton ballet slippers that I wore in class.

Snetkova was waiting for me in the narrow corridor outside Tatiana's room. In a moment Snetkova took me to the makeup room to be made up for the performance. My cheekbones were made higher and my eyes longer and rounder. I was fitted with a short dark wig. We children hadn't been given any rehearsal, because we weren't dancing steps in *The Red Poppy*; we were just part of the crowd. "Stay close to your 'parents' on-stage," was all I had been told by Tyuntina.

Tao-Hoa's cabaret was run by Li Shanfu, a spy for the imperial government. He kept her as his slave, his concubine. An enormous boat steamed into the harbor and a platoon of Russian marines disembarked. One of them visited Li Shanfu's cabaret and he commanded Tao-Hoa to dance, showing the Russians his prize. She performed with two fans given to her by an old lady in the crowd, a confidante to Tao-Hoa. Then Tatiana signaled to the old lady, who put a set of mandarin finger guards into my hands. She gave me a little shove toward Tatiana and I stumbled toward her, my heart in my mouth. Everything was unpredictable here, just like life.

Then Tatiana was dancing again, starting with hands pressed against her chest, raising one finger, then two, then fluttering both hands, while doing little steps around the stage with a mincing Chinese flavor that required a difficult coordination between hands and legs. She explained in pantomime to the visiting Russians how poorly the Chinese lived. "Look," she gestured, "the children, the people—all of them suffering." Improvising some extra business to make me feel more included, she plucked me from the crowd and brought me center stage: "Look at this poor girl!"

And then it was if all hell broke loose. The Chinese were forbidden from talking to foreigners. Now police swarmed onto the docks, cleaving us from the Russians. Shanghai was a treaty port, and so American, British, Russian, and Chinese personnel fanned around the waterfront. The Chinese soldiers pushed and prodded the cowering crowd, while our elders tried to shield us. I stared down the barrel of a rifle, leveled by a guard with a surly expression. I was sure if I moved, he'd shoot me dead. His back was to the public; I faced the audience. He saw me cringing and finally winked and gave me a little smile. But then his face turned hostile again. By the dock the workers started unloading cargo from the Russian ship. A sadistic foreman whipped their backs. Some fell to the ground and struggled up again. Be whipped raw or shot dead: the choice was mine!

Across the stage, Tatiana saw me grow wide-eyed. She improvised some mime passage to allow her to come over and give me a hug. "Everything's fine," she whispered.

During intermission, we were to be debriefed in the wings. I was trembling, paralyzed by all that had transpired onstage. Finally a dancer pulled me from the stage. "You were wonderful," Tyuntina told me. "You did everything right, your acting was perfect." I don't think she realized that I'd hardly been acting at all!

Tailed by Li Shanfu in act 2, Tao-Hoa drowned her woes in an opium den, where she nodded off in a reverie populated with her religion's nature and spirit gods. During the dream scene, Tatiana as Tao-Hoa danced a taxing classical divertissement with three birds and their partners. In her dream Li Shanfu appeared as a dragon; here Nikolai Zubkovsky danced a virtuoso solo with two knives that was magical, sinister, the air thick with green and red smoke.

In act 3, Tao-Hoa attempted running away with her Russian marine. Li Shanfu apprehended her. A shot reported. Tatiana collapsed and blood was smeared on her hands. Her friends mourned, but I was hysterical with grief. They carried her off and she hung from their arms like a limp stag. And thus sparked a revolution: the exploited proletariat killed Li Shanfu and overthrew the capitalist warlords.

The curtain fell and Tatiana was resurrected, smiling and joking with her fellow dancers. "How was it?" she asked, and accepted their congratulations. I was dumbfounded. Moments ago she'd been so sad and then so dead and there was such grief on the stage! In front of the curtain, Tatiana bowed and bowed and bowed. I hung back in the wings, until she walked over, patted my head, and asked, "How did you like it?"

"Very much."

She saw my glazed eyes and wet cheeks and asked, "Did I impress you?"

"Yes, I was very afraid for you."

"My daughter is a great artist," said Snetkova, who was suddenly at my side. "She can make anyone cry."

"I tried," Tatiana told me, "I did this performance for you."

At the school we accepted it as a fact of life: *we* were something special and *they* were normal human beings. It wasn't even snobbism on our part. We didn't dream there was any other way. In the courtyard my friends tagged passersby.

"Who's that girl?"

"She's from the ballet."

"And who's that one?"

"Oh, she's just a girl."

We felt proud walking in the street, wearing our uniforms. We were stared at and we were on stage. Our pulled-back hair, our turned-out-feet duck waddle, our skinny bodies made us instantly recognizable. A "Vaganova girl" had a mystique. The school wasn't just the foremost in Russia; it was almost the only one. The Bolshoi in Moscow was not as renowned during these years. After the war, Perm and Kiev were developing excellent schools, but the Vaganova still was beyond compare. So our indoctrination was bred in the bone, and the professional dancers felt like a race apart, too. Alla Shelest, who was one of our greatest, was embarrassed to step into a toilet stall in front of anyone. If someone saw her, she'd look at herself in the mirror and pretend she was just there to primp. She was a ballerina; she wasn't supposed to engage in any earthly functions.

We children were never allowed to watch any part of the ballet that we weren't in. Chained to our dressing room, our confinement was sweetened with pastries and tea. A chaperone herded us onto the bus and guarded our dressing room. She had cylindrical legs, beady eyes, and no less than three chins. We called her the Bulldog. "Oh, she's barking again," we whispered.

And she barked constantly. "Don't talk! Don't run in the corridor! Don't leave the dressing room! Get dressed quickly as soon as the performance is finished! Take off your costume immediately! Don't put your dirty fingers on it!"

"Stay here. Don't move," she warned whenever she had an errand on another floor. The moment she was gone we debated what gruesome torture would be justice for her.

So we didn't have any contact with the ballerinas at the theater, even when we shared the stage with them. Our dressing rooms were on another floor, and our bulldog of a chaperone never let us stray. But the Kirov took class and rehearsed in studios at the school. Their professional realm was connected to ours via a balcony overlooking the largest studio, named in honor of Vaganova after her death in November 1951. We weren't allowed in their wing until we got into the company. We were dying to cross this threshold but felt too much respect and fear even to walk across the balcony.

To me the door was like the border from Russia to the West, a passage to a hallowed land. What was in there? How did they live over there? Goddesses in long robes appeared, silk scarves wound around their heads. Their pointe shoes were in their hands, their noses in the air. Some barely deigned to answer our reverential hellos. My first year I didn't even know who was who: they were interchangeable, images of the glorious life of a ballerina.

We didn't have glossy magazines so we turned to the ballerinas for a glimpse of high fashion and fantasy. We discerned who was who in the passing parade and talked about how each one dressed, how much makeup she wore or didn't wear, what kind of earrings dangled that morning—as though it were the most important conversation on earth.

Toward the end of my first year at the school, I made my opera debut, dancing in Rimsky-Korsakov's *The Snow Maiden* at the Maly Theater across town from the Kirov. This was Leningrad's number-two destination for ballet and opera, a beautiful theater that was smaller than the Kirov and even older. It was superbly situated on Arts Square by the Russian Museum and the Philharmonic. Tyuntina also rehearsed the children for Maly performances.

In *Snow Maiden* we girls were spring's act 4 entourage of birds, dancing many different types. I was a robin redbreast. The costume was a big round balloon, a metal skeleton covered with fabric and feathers. Stepping into this sphere was like being strapped into a cage. My toothpick legs stuck out through two holes, and my arms slipped into wings ending in fingerless mitts. All of us birds wore similar contraptions; encased like astronauts, locked in the scaffolding, we couldn't scratch, drink, eat, or urinate.

Naturally the Maly Theater staff made sure we children were ready early. Way before our call, we were taken down to the stage, where we sweated out an interminable wait. When the urge to scratch or brush pastry crumbs off our face was too strong, we punched holes for our fingers in the mitts, balling our mitts into fists to hide the finger holes from the wardrobe mistress.

Right before we went onstage, we pulled on helmets made of papier-mâché. They were hard and thick and heavy, so cumbersome that one's head had to make a complete revolution in order to take in any peripheral sights. We couldn't put on the helmets until the last minute or we'd risk asphyxiation from the foul-smelling glue. The helmets were made like bird's heads, with beaks that opened and closed. Inside the beak was a piece of net so we could breathe without the public seeing our faces.

We had had many rehearsals, in the studio and onstage, because there were some real steps in our little dance. But we had never had a stage rehearsal with scenery. Instead, minutes before the curtain rose, Tyuntina walked us around the stage. In the middle stood a huge tree stump. "Look, little girls," she said over the buzz from the audience, "you have to be careful of this tree. The singer will appear; she will stand on the tree stump while you dance around her." Coiling around the stage, the roots were all different lengths. Tyuntina warned us: do not dance too close to these roots.

During the performance the mezzo-soprano singing the spring fairy snuck to the center of the stage so that she suddenly appeared as if she had just landed from the skies. A Junoesque diva, she was perfectly equipped to suggest spring's rebirth. Standing in a dress festooned with flowers, her long blond wig threaded with more flowers, she was enthroned on a desolate stump: a once-magnificent tree burned to warm perpetual winter. She was the apex; we were the base of a gorgeous tableau. She was singing, we were jumping in sauts de basque in and out across the stump's twisting roots.

I thought I was doing beautifully, and then disaster struck. Turning to the front of the stage, I stepped on a gnarled root and fell flat on my stomach. I was bull's-eye in the middle of the stage. Because the costume was shaped like a swollen melon, my legs and arms couldn't touch the floor, but that was all I could see; my face locked in place by the helmet. I foundered, flailing my wings and feet. Straining into the stage boards, I was immobilized. I was perspiring heavily, breathing with difficulty.

Laughter rumbled around me. The mezzo's notes were wobbling; it seemed as though none of the singers could control themselves. Finally one member of the singing chorus gave me a heave-ho and I rocketed into the wings. The audience burst into applause. Giggling, light-headed, I skidded straight to the feet of our "bulldog" chaperone. "Who's this?" she asked, "Who's this?" as she pulled off my helmet. Then I saw Tyuntina standing behind her. Her face was a gorgon's, her left cheek on fire. Whenever Tyuntina was nervous or angry, she developed this strange tic: her full face didn't flush, only her left cheek, while the right stayed pale.

As Tyuntina's students we had the privilege to be in every performance; at the same time, she was especially hard on us, as if we were her own children. She stood me back on my legs and started to take my headpiece off. "Of course, I knew it would be you! Who else?"

When aroused, Tyuntina could all but inject you with anger without betraying any agitation. From a distance she seemed to be tilting her head affectionately, her hands resting on your shoulder, but really her eyes were drilling into you—her long red fingernails, too.

"Do you understand what you did?" she hissed. "The singer couldn't sing! You spoiled the whole scene. You're responsible for this mess."

When the act finished, the curtain came down, and everyone on stage applauded me. But my bulldog took me by the scruff of the neck and I shrank back to my room, sure I'd never again be allowed on stage. But some of the adult performers came to console me. "Thank you, it was a *great* pleasure to take part in this performance," the spring muse said mischievously. "I never laughed so much!" Need I add, however, I was never again included in that opera.

After every theatrical performance in Russia at that time, the director, stage manager, ballet masters, and theater staff met to recap the evening's proceedings. They entered into a special journal anything noteworthy that happened: which famous visitor came backstage, which scenery flap fell down inopportunely. It was called the "five-minute meeting." This night they all had a good laugh, and as I later learned from Tyuntina, my mishap had been recorded for posterity in the journal.

§ §

By early 1950 my grandmother and I had moved back to my mother's old apartment, so that I could live only five minutes from school. We had been away a year. Our first night back I couldn't sleep. In our room, wind fluttered the curtains . . . was that my mother visiting? I ran to the kitchen and waited for my grandmother to return from work.

Every day my friends in our courtyard waited for me to come back from school: I'd perform for them, spinning tales, acting out what happened that day. They wanted to hear me retell my misadventure in *The Snow Maiden* nearly every day. I decided to stage *Cinderella* with these children. We worked for several weeks to put it together. I drilled them in their lines and told them what their faces were supposed to look like as they said their lines. I guess my life as a coach had begun.

I cast a girl named Gala, angelically blond, as Cinderella. Gala had played a baby duck in my first production a couple of years earlier. She was a little younger than I was. I played the king and Cinderella's father and a page apprenticed to a magician. I kept telling her, "I am not a magician; I am only studying to be one." It was a sentence from a Cinderella book that I had at home.

Our opening was early evening after school. I turned the furniture upside down in our room and put up a curtain, dividing the space in two. I covered the chairs with a dark green blanket. They became grassy hills, and I strewed silk flowers around the room; they had been chic in the thirties. Everything in one curtained-off section of the room became one stage. When we needed location scenes, we moved to our green chairs.

The castle was near the mirror covering a small table, and I put candles there to maximize their reflected gleam.

I opened and closed the curtain, in addition to acting my multiple roles. Everybody from our building was invited. Tickets were ten kopeks. The spectators all screamed "Bravo!" and asked for a repeat, so we scheduled an encore Sunday matinee. After that performance, I had no energy to strike the set and I fell into bed. My grandmother came home from work to an apartment that had gone topsy-turvy. "Did we have a battle here?" she asked the next day.

"No, there was a theater," I said proudly. We pooled the takings and had a party and nearly died from the amount of ice cream consumed.

My grandmother and I enjoyed more privacy than most of the other residents of the enormous old apartment, because we reached our room via a little hallway that was like a cul-de-sac. But each year the population grew in our communal facilities. As families raised their children, their children married but kept on living with their parents because of the housing shortage in Leningrad. Eventually over forty people were sharing one toilet, one shower. The residents became fierce about protecting their patches of space. Our kitchen dinned with chopping and clanging rising from eleven little tables and several stoves. After disputes neighbors put foul things into each other's cookware, until all the residents took to locking up their own pots and pants. It was a zoo and I hated it, and it bothered me to see people cooking on plates they had stolen from my mother.

Sweeping up from our apartment lobby was a large marble staircase, broad enough that it was possible to pass someone on the stairs without greeting him or her. Whenever my mother's former lover Victor Balobanovich and I happened to meet each other this way, we exchanged no more than hello. But once when I was thirteen or fourteen, Victor stopped me. He told me he was so happy that I was doing well. I looked a lot like my mother, and if I ever needed anything, he would like to help me. I remembered him cheerful and ebullient when he was with my mother. Now he looked dejected, beaten. He lived into old age with his daughter and his wife, but it was clear to me that life had somehow passed him by.

~ 3 ~
facts of life

Our exercises at the barre were long, slow, and grueling. They demanded a titan's stamina, and whenever I pushed myself too hard in ballet class, I fainted. Sometimes I'd get through the barre but collapse at the end of class, when we worked on jumps. Perhaps our diet was to blame. In the cafeteria we were raised on starch: kasha, mashed potatoes, potato pancakes with sour cream, bland purées—dumplings were an infrequent delicacy. Protein was supplied by fish, ground meat cutlets, and sausages. Cabbage was our one vegetable, and it appeared on our tables only rarely. For dessert we were served dried apples, pears, and plums, stewed to a drab dirty brown.

But perhaps I was responsible: while my classmates seemed to gobble as much as they could, I never had much appetite. I drank tea and nibbled. In fact I don't think I have ever had a normal appetite. Yet outside class I always had more than enough energy. But when the pain of exertion began creeping through my muscles, it was as if they began to panic. As a result, I began working half-force in class, conserving my strength. The teachers thought that I was merely lazy. They didn't realize how terrified I was of fainting, and how that prevented me from fully committing myself in class.

Vaccine injections made me faint, too. Needles reminded me of my mother's bandaged wrists. Broken skin made me sick. Every year we were given vaccinations, and every year I pleaded, "I can't! I can't! Whenever I see needles I faint!"

"Oh, come on," the school doctor scolded. "Don't be a baby." They went ahead, and as promised, I hit the deck. The school's medical staff was determined to wash out this thin-blooded sensitivity. I had to be strong! A real proletarian! The staff thought that they could train me out of my complex by enlisting me to help the first-year students. I was instructed to hold their hands as they received their inoculations. "It's very simple," a nurse assured me, "it doesn't hurt them. You shouldn't be afraid." I tried.

I didn't watch, and by the second or third girl I was once more flat on the floor. Finally I was allowed to take all my vaccinations in pill form. The other students were jealous, and the teachers teased me. "Princess, princess," they cooed. "She's so sensitive."

We arrived at school at 8:30 a.m., and left at 6 p.m., Monday through Saturday. In the depths of Leningrad's winter, I might not see the sun for weeks, for on Sundays I slept into the afternoon. Direct sunlight streamed only into the school's ballet studios, not into our classrooms or our room at home. Ballet class, however, was in the morning, and Leningrad stayed dark until 11 a.m. on the shortest days of the year. Sometimes I would just have a fit, running out of a class and out of the building while a teacher screamed, "Where do you think you're going? Don't you realize that class isn't over yet?"

"I have to see the sun!" I cried, and threw myself into the street.

But the theater itself was always a refuge. Often I watched performances sitting in the aisle of the top balcony. Whenever children danced in a Kirov production, each of our names was kept on a list maintained at the stage door. But when Natalia Dudinskaya was going to dance, Tyuntina made sure the name of every girl in her class was included. She was a great fan. "Did you watch last night?" she would nudge us the morning after a Dudinskaya performance.

In act 2 of Petipa's full-length *Don Quixote*, the Don's fantasies take him to a dream world where the village girl Kitri is transformed into a celestial princess.

I was eleven when I danced a cupid in the dream scene, and was thus able to study Dudinskaya at closer range. We girls were wrapped in gray-blue tunics trimmed in silver. Armed with tiny bows, we fell in behind the adult corps as they ballonnéd around the stage, while we squinted in the glare of spotlights banked in the wings. While Dudinskaya danced Kitri's dream variation, two girls and I lay on the floor in a semicircle opening toward the audience. Our heads were supposed to stay vised into place; our eyes unflinchingly trained straight ahead. But no matter what, I had to see the great Dudinskaya! As discreetly as I could, I shifted my eyes like a periscope. She still wasn't in sight. I swiveled my head upstage left: there she was, about to begin a diagonal of scissory jumps followed by dives into arabesque. She finished in front of my eyes; I snapped my head back into position; then she whipped around the stage in a circle of turns, a blur of pink lightning. We went into the wings and there was Tyuntina, fuming, grabbing me, shaking me. "Girl, you didn't buy a ticket to watch!" she screamed. "You have to stay still!" When I was a child people told me my eyes were saucer sized. "Don't you know when you turn your eyes the whole audience sees?" she said.

"But I couldn't miss it. It was *Dudinskaya*!" That saved me.

"Well," she huffed, "this is the last time!" But she was so pleased.

Dudinskaya was by now almost forty but still commanded a high jump and a wonderful bravura technique. She would dance ten more years; to the end she could peel off five pirouettes on pointe easily, and even today that is rare. She hit the jackpot every time, but her methods were her own and no one else's. Her foot cranked in as she turned; any moment I expected her to trip and break her legs. But instead she spun like a top. Probably my eyes weren't just following her, they were bulging, my mouth hanging in disbelief.

Dudinskaya was not only one of Vaganova's favorite pupils, they were also personal friends. She was in addition the common-law wife of Kirov danseur and artistic director Konstantin Sergeyev. And so she enjoyed privileges not entirely warranted by talent; she virtually owned the role of Giselle, for example, despite the fact that she was very wrong for it. On the other hand, her right to prima status was unquestionable. No ballerina had a more electric communication with her public. A few years later, in *Sleeping Beauty*, I was one of the children dancing the act 1 Garland Waltz and Dudinskaya was Princess Aurora. By then I'd seen her rehearse in the studio many times. There was a lot about her body and her technique that didn't fit my ideal. But after running off stage with the other children, I stayed in the wings to watch Dudinskaya's Aurora make her entrance from the opposite wing.

The courtiers onstage waited to greet their princess. The music leapt higher and higher, and then Dudinskaya, a frosted bonbon, was descending a staircase from heaven, her hips swaying ever so slightly to Tchaikovsky's swift, pattering notes. The audience saw her flirtatious little steps, and then their cheers drowned out the music throughout her entire entrance variation. I stopped questioning, analyzing: joy rocked the theater and I was swept along in the tide.

On other nights the Aurora was Lubov Voichnis, who had graduated from Vaganova's class and joined the Kirov in 1942, when they had been evacuated to Perm.

Voichnis was a ballerina who could both dazzle and wring tears. Dudinskaya was perpetually a coquette: she glittered with happiness, vitality, determination. But in *Beauty*, Voichnis was a bona fide princess whose body almost seemed to shed an amber light. She was a little slower than Dudinskaya, who moved as fast as a flame, but on the other hand, applied to Aurora, a dewy young princess, Dudinskaya's attack was perhaps a little too much.

Dudinskaya excited us by revealing the naked force behind what she did: "Look, I am *jumping*!" her leaps seemed to be saying. Voichnis jumped like a cat. She took an effortless preparation, no more than a lazy stretch into the ground—and then she was sitting in the air. Voichnis's Aurora, jumping from happiness at being young, at appearing in front of the court—I'll remember the sight as long as I live.

Onstage, I could be whatever I imagined. What I lacked in reality I could have in theatrical fantasy. One Christmas, I stood in the crowded wings of the theater before a performance of *The Nutcracker*. A woman in nineteenth-century costume approached and laid a firm hand on my shoulder. "Hello," she greeted, "I am your mother."

She called me "my little boy," and I whispered "mama." I was dressed as a boy because I was much taller than most of the girls in my class. My hair was parted and tucked under a beret. My "mama" was Maria Halina, an outstanding character dancer. Her son, Konstantin Rassadin, who also became one of our leading character dancers, was two years ahead of me in school.

Onstage we strolled around the Christmas tree. "Look how beautiful it is; look at all the presents," Halina prompted me. Her face wore the serious, instructing look that signifies "parent" in Russian tradition. But her voice was mischievous. "Wait here," she said, "I'll bring you something good to eat." I stayed close to the tree and waited; on stage we always did what our elders told us to do. She returned to my side and handed me a lavishly wrapped candy. "Here is a chocolate-covered plum," Halina told me, "with a nail." I opened it and to my disappointment realized that it was only a wood facsimile.

Most of the Soviet Union may have been poor, yet it was still possible for us to become wealthy children, dressed splendidly in Zakharov's *The Bronze Horseman*, strolling with our nannies in the St. Petersburg of 1830, watching politely as street entertainers tried to catch our attention. I had more fun, however, on those nights when I was cast as a street urchin, picking pockets and pinching girls.

§ ?

Agrippina Vaganova died in November 1951, eight months after Vladimir Ponomaryov, who had been administrative director as well as one of the finest men's teachers the school ever had. Now Nikolai Ivanovsky was promoted to a leadership position almost equivalent to Vaganova's, while Valentin Shelkov, an ex-dancer now in his fifties, became what might be called administrative or executive director. No two directors could have been more dissimilar. Ivanovsky was an old-world gentleman, obviously adept at wielding power, but nonetheless soft-spoken and velvet toned. On the other hand, everything about Shelkov was grating. He was a dyed-in-the-wool bureaucrat, yet he didn't rule straight by the Communist playbook but rather by his own quasi-military code.

Shelkov liked to remind us students that he had once danced Siegfried in *Swan Lake*. "He was a prince? How is it *possible*?" I wondered. A round face, a bald, moon-shaped head, and stocky body packed into a dark suit: in Shelkov's square bulk resided an image of implacable authority. We students called him "the closet," and we were terrified of him.

From way across the longest corridor in the school, Shelkov might signal me with a curled finger. I knew my break was over before it began. I walked briskly over to him. Running was not allowed, but at the same time no one dared keep him waiting. I bowed and said hello. Then he got down to business.

"Turn around. Did you see that piece of paper?" He referred to a speck on the horizon. Our floors had to be clean enough to eat from, and he watched like a hawk. "Go back, pick it up, and throw it in the garbage." It didn't matter that I hadn't dropped it; it had to be eliminated. By the time I had walked back, found the piece of paper, and thrown it out, the break was over and the bell for class had rung.

A nurse who lived in our communal apartment had helped me call an ambulance for my mother, and she continued to keep her eye out for me. In the evenings, my grandmother away at work, I would visit her room. In her spare time, she knit sweaters and sold them privately. They were beautiful, unlike anything we could find in stores in those days. For me she once made a bright blue cardigan with white pompons at my neck. But at school, we weren't allowed to wear anything except our uniform: a chocolate-brown dress and black apron. Yet I loved my sweater so much I started to wear it every day. It attracted much attention; some teachers even asked me how they could get one like it. Before long, however, Shelkov summoned me and demanded an explanation.

"I don't feel well," I whimpered. "It's too cold in here."

"Take it off!" he snarled.

Each of us at the school was privileged to share a piano teacher with only one other student. It was like having a private coach. "My name is Maria Dmitrievna Shostakovich," my piano teacher had told me our first week in 1949.

"Are you by any chance related to the great Russian composer?" I asked officiously. She was taken aback. A child was talking about the greatness of a brother no one could mention. For Shostakovich had fallen out of official favor. I think at that moment many Soviets were embarrassed to even pronounce his name.

Maria Dmitrievna's eyes misted over: "How did you know him?"

"I heard his music on the radio."

"Did you like it?"

"Oh, yes, very much."

"Which piece?" The oratorio *Song of the Forests* and several polkas Shostakovich had written for children. "I'm very flattered that you know him. Yes, he is my brother."

"How lucky I am to have not one but two Elenas!" Maria Dmitrievna exclaimed one day. Elena Shatrova and I were studying together. I was fair, she was dark. "I'll call you 'white Elena,'" she told me, "and you 'black Elena.'"

For Maria Dmitrievna, a plump babushka, with a face like a warm, yeasty piece of fresh bread, I could do no wrong from the moment I praised her brother. But Tatiana Vecheslova was less forgiving. We had no piano at home, and so I would go to her apartment to practice. I had trouble remembering the notes and was forced to count them out every day. One day I decided to write them on the piano keys. Needless to say, my playing improved rapidly. I was plunking away one afternoon when Tatiana came home. "Brava!" she cheered. "Finally! You're playing very well!" But then she came over to the piano and saw my ink marks scrawled across the keys. "How dare you?" she screamed. She wasn't mad I'd defaced her piano, but that I had cheated art. "You must remember them all by yourself. Get a rag and wipe them off immediately!"

Some time later, Maria Dmitrievna told us that if Shatrova and I promised to work diligently, she would arrange for us to play Shostakovich's polka for him personally. "You'll both play for me first. I'll turn away, but I'll know who is who by your mistakes. So if you want to fool me, you've got to play perfectly."

I knuckled down and spent long hours practicing. When we sat for Maria I played as well as I could, but I couldn't resist dropping one or two of dark Elena's usual flubs to fool our teacher. Elena on the other hand played very well all the way through. "Well, it wasn't so difficult; that was Shatrova and that was Kittel."

"Wrong!" I chirped. Several months later, Maria Dmitrievna did take me to play for her brother at her apartment, across Nevsky Prospect from the Kazansky Cathedral.

When the great composer heard me he actually cried and exclaimed, "Oh, what a talented girl!" I was surprised that such a great composer couldn't tell that I didn't have the talent to become a pianist. But later I found out that Shostakovich wept frequently when he heard his music played. He particularly couldn't resist the sight of a child wrestling with the mighty keyboard. And furthermore, he knew that I was supposed to become a dancer. Even with his endorsement, he realized that I would never get the chance to degrade his own art form.

Intermediate-level literature was taught at the school by Zoya Strakhova, whose appearance was stern and severe, her face blinkered by big glasses. Right off the bat most of the class disliked her and probably I did more than anyone else, because I adored literature. How, I wondered, could such a stiff, dry woman teach a subject so beautiful? Her daughter Gala was in our grade and was also in her mother's class. As the weeks went on, I made Gala the butt of my resentment. But Gala didn't deserve anyone's anger. She never talked, was completely withdrawn, and was a very dedicated student.

In our class were two girls from the Arctic regions of the Soviet Union, bordering Alaska. Between themselves they spoke their native language, but in class they answered in Russian that wasn't textbook perfect. We were nice to them; we pitied them. But they hardly said a word to us; they always seemed to be huddling in corners. I've forgotten one of their names, but I'll remember the other, who was called Rosa, for the rest of my life. She was only eleven when her period started. She was bleeding in the dressing room, screeching and crying. Oh my God, she's sick, we thought. Our stomachs turned; we were afraid to sit near her. Was it contagious?

Rosa and her friend cried to each other, while we whispered behind their backs. They felt completely ostracized. The school staff realized that something had to be done. One day Zoya told us that she would talk to us after classes finished for the day.

This was only for girls; the boys could go free. The boys ran out and we girls looked at one another, baffled.

Zoya closed the door, looking like she was about to divulge some appalling secret. She spoke so clinically that I wanted to vomit. She didn't tell us about the beauty of maturity and childbearing and perpetuating life. "It's nothing to be ashamed of," she said. But she shouldn't even have mentioned "ashamed," because this was a country where anything to do with sexuality was shameful. Pornography was illegal, even kisses were proscribed in films.

How horrible, I thought. Everybody would know we're supposed to get this. The boys would know. How embarrassing for us.

Zoya told us that menstruation usually happened when girls were thirteen or fourteen. However, it could happen earlier: for instance in the Central Asian regions, women grew up faster, Zoya continued, in Georgia as well as in Italy. Immediately Rosa became to me disgustingly premature.

A door had been opened, but it led nowhere. We were still in the dark, given only half an explanation. I felt as though something had been stolen from me. I couldn't live freely anymore; I would only be waiting for this curse to descend. Zoya had given a death sentence to our youth and the class decided to punish her—or rather I decided for them. We were all going to boycott her class one day. I turned to Gala. "And if *you* tell anyone," I warned her, "you will be in *trouble*." The other kids obeyed me. I was never afraid of teachers or directors and they respected that.

We scouted a hiding space. I knew they would search the showers, dressing rooms, bathrooms, cafeteria. But behind the huge wooden doors to our school theater was a vestibule, a sliver of space just big enough. We squeezed in and waited. Frantic footsteps tapped down the hall and doors slammed. "Maybe they're in the bathroom!"

"No, I just looked." Then the footsteps were gone.

After two hours—literature was always a double period—we tumbled out. Sweat was dripping off us; steam poured out of the room. We scrambled into the bathrooms and washed up.

Back in her classroom, Zoya was hyperventilating. We were rounded up: "You have to tell us where you've been. We were afraid there was a Bermuda Triangle in our school. You have to tell me!" she thundered. "Who did it?"

"I can't," Gala whimpered.

Then Shelkov visited the class to call us on the carpet. He pointed at one trembling face: "Was it you?" He jabbed at another. "You?"

"I smell somebody," he told us, "but I want to hear it from her. If you don't tell me, no one in here is going to camp." He had rattled the right saber. We looked forward to that all year: skiing and ice-skating for two weeks during our January recess.

"I did it!" I confessed.

"I knew it!" Shelkov chimed. "Everyone is free. She will stay." He launched into an endless lecture. I wouldn't be going anywhere that January.

Then Gala missed three days of classes. She came back to school with a bruise on her face, exactly the shape and size of five fingers. She kept shielding it with her hand. I took her into the dressing room. "Your mother hit you, didn't she?"

"Don't touch me," she cringed. "I won't tell you anything."

I spread the news throughout the school that Gala had been beaten. It was rash on my part because her mother might have only punished her more harshly. But Shelkov must have confronted Zoya, because if it happened again, it was never apparent to us. Gala slowly began to open up to her fellow students. She must have forgiven me; when we both danced in the Kirov later on we were friendly. She was a very hard worker, very honest, a lovely person.

I continued to understand that menstruation, like death, existed but never thought it would happen to me. Even after Zoya's lecture, we girls didn't discuss these things. It was all too embarrassing. We never traded stories or speculation. In the dressing room we primly covered our bodies as much as our libido all the way into adulthood. One of the girls liked to walk naked around the dressing room, and most of the others were horrified. "My God!" we clucked. "She has no shame."

~ 4 ~

disillusionment

Stumbling back to life after the war, Leningrad had found solace in Hollywood escapism. Returning from Berlin, our troops had brought a cache of American films seized from the Nazis. There was little capital in the Soviet Union available to produce new films, but Hollywood productions became the perfect antidote to our reality. Throughout the 1940s and '50s, the same films were screened over and over and over again. The city flocked to see them. In her last years, my mother had dyed her hair platinum, inspired by Marlene Dietrich and Betty Grable, the celluloid pinups we all adored. When I was little, I all but lived at the movies, cutting class so that I could follow Chaplin, Pickford, Disney, Jeanette MacDonald, Nelson Eddy, Errol Flynn, and Olivia de Havilland from theater to theater, seeing the same films time after time after time. Sad endings devastated me. Each time I watched Garbo's *Camille* I hoped Armand would somehow manage to save her. But I was prepared for her death from the very beginning of the film, especially since I had already heard *La Traviata*. *Waterloo Bridge* was totally unfamiliar, so somehow more upsetting. The beauty of Vivien Leigh and Robert Taylor was mesmerizing. I wept at the final scene, when Taylor finds Leigh's amulet on the bridge and imagines that he might somehow see her once more. I must have seen *Waterloo* two dozen times, but I'd always run away before the end, not wanting to put myself through this ordeal once more.

Inna Saygel, my French teacher, was a brilliant, sophisticated woman whose brother became a famous movie director after Soviet film production ramped up again during the mid-1950s. She was bracingly sarcastic and a lot tougher on the girls than the boys, but I nevertheless adored her. She was very thin, with short hair styled like George Sand's, always dressed in a jaunty skirt and jacket. To me she stood out like a Renaissance heroine.

She buttonholed me once on the street. "Which movie was it today?"

There was no point in blathering about doctor's appointments, all the other alibis that I had already exhausted. I confessed that it was once again *Camille*. "How many times have you seen it so far?" she demanded.

"Um . . . eleven."

"Well then, maybe it's time to come back to class."

Somehow reality was so far from my own imaginative world that I was twelve years old before I realized that my city had once been named St. Petersburg. Reading Gogol's *Nevsky Prospect*, I was enthralled by his description of the city's elite swanning down the Prospect. Someday I would live there, I thought. St. Petersburg immediately became my dream city. "Well, don't you know that you *are* there?" my grandmother said. And there forever went my dream.

But I was convinced that everyone in America lived the way they did in those films. The longing to move to the West had taken hold.

Every day at school in between periods, a designated student was delegated to open each classroom's windows to air it out. Each day a different student was entrusted with this patrol. One day it was Elena Shatrova's turn. But I didn't want to leave; I wanted to stay and read whatever novel was engrossing me at the moment. It was too noisy in the hallway to concentrate. When Elena started to get a little authoritarian, I responded by mimicking her stutter. She burst into tears and sobbed that it wasn't her fault that she stuttered. Word of our confrontation spread throughout the school. Everybody thought it was horrible of me to taunt her that way. Snetkova pulled me into her studio and demanded an explanation. "That's awful," she said. "You must apologize to her."

I said, "I can't, because I hate her." And after that mass hysteria somehow set in. The entire student body was somehow involved in our altercation. Students wept, most without even knowing exactly why it was that they were crying. From then on Thursdays were known as "cry day" at the school. Everybody dreaded this day, thinking something bad would happen.

Mass hysteria on an epic scale set in across the Soviet Union in March 1953, when we heard the news that Stalin was dead. "Our father is dead," people sobbed in the streets. "We'll all starve to death." Sight had been snatched from their eyes. The country was paralyzed. The newspapers wept line after line of pathetic poetry: "The sun has left the sky!" We would live in the dark forever, there would be no food, we wouldn't know what to do, where to go. For a couple of days I waited for the global short-out; each morning when I got up I thought, Is it dark or light?

"Why are you crying?" my grandmother asked that first night after we learned that Stalin was dead.

"What do you mean?" I said, shocked. "We're all crying. What will happen to the country?"

She didn't seem worried. "Finally," she said quietly—we were alone in our room. "The tyrant is gone." Stalin was out of the way. Now the Romanovs could make their belated reappearance. That was undoubtedly what she was thinking. For she believed in her heart that the Soviet period was an aberration, a nightmare that could not endure for too long.

A week later, I was selected as an honor guard to stand at attention by the bust of Stalin in the school lobby. My schoolmates passed by, making faces, trying to crack me up, because I was supposed to stay reverently poker-faced, not allowed to do more than blink. By now the student population was no longer upset. Stalin had been dead a week and still the sun rose and there was food on the table. The minutes ticked by and I started to hate Stalin—but only for the cramp in my legs.

But despite the adoration Stalin was able to coerce from his subject population, there were many like my grandmother who had been born under the Romanovs and assumed that Communism would not last forever. Many in the know considered party members at best nouveau riche, but more truly they thought of them as thugs. They knew that party operatives spied on people, informed on them, destroyed them. What one did to thrive in the party was too horrific; despite the privileges, it just wasn't worth it for many self-respecting Russians. They covertly raised their children on different principles and ideologies.

The older generations knew that not only had the nobility been decimated in the Revolution but peasants and working class as well; so much of the bloodshed was random. That, of course, was not what we were taught in Soviet history class. We students devoutly believed that everyone slaughtered by the Bolsheviks had been a dangerous enemy of the state.

At age ten, we were gradually indoctrinated into the ways of party protocol. At that age all children automatically became Young Pioneers. At the initiation ceremony, the chief slipped a triangular red scarf over our heads, printed with the three-sided insignia of Pioneer/Komsomol/Party, the Soviet trinity, replacing Father, Son, and Holy Ghost. If your grades were good, at fourteen you could progress to the Komsomol, the youth party. Elena Shatrova, me, and a boy who later left the school before graduating were the first members from our class to be made Komsomol members when we turned fourteen. A year later, the rest of our class was admitted. I was a Komsomol junior chief, entrusted with collecting monthly dues, which were equivalent to about twenty-five cents. Once a month we met after classes finished for the day. We were supposed to organize any kind of good works we could think of, prepare a school cleaning on our day off, deliver food to the elderly. But we could take it all seriously, or just slough it off. They didn't lay on the heavy brainwashing—not yet.

Indeed, the school seemed to exist in something of a time warp isolated from Soviet society. The ballet teachers were generally elderly, children of the czar's times, who preserved the old traditions. Our compulsory etiquette preserved a grace and formality that was distinctly old world. Vaganova herself had never joined the party. The school was so private, seemingly a bulwark against Communist reality—but only up to a point. The younger faculty who taught us academics tended to be party members. And it was with them that I would eventually be forced to confront the true dimensions of our society at large.

§ ₰

The word had gone out through the school: Galina Ulanova, Russia's most famous ballerina, prima of the Bolshoi Ballet in Moscow, was coming to Leningrad to dance two guest performances of *The Bronze Horseman* with the Kirov. After she arrived in our city, I stole into the balcony of the school's main rehearsal studio to watch her rehearse.

But after all the fanfare I was disappointed in Ulanova. Why was she so famous? I couldn't see anything exceptionally interesting about her. Ulanova was over forty. Her knees were prominent and her shoulders awfully wide. She never wore makeup offstage; compared to our own ballerinas at the Kirov, her scrubbed-bare face was as plain as a cleaning woman's. Yet I wanted to understand her greatness. I studied her like a legend, but despite the impressive ease to her movement, her dancing didn't touch me in the studio, or onstage for that matter.

Perhaps a year later, in June 1953, a momentous event brought Ulanova back to Leningrad: Tatiana Vecheslova's farewell gala. At forty-three, she was leaving the stage. Vecheslova and Ulanova had been friends since school, for Ulanova was trained in Leningrad and had not moved to Moscow until 1944. Tatiana was still at the top of her form. Both the school and the Kirov lamented her premature retirement, but she was shrewd enough to leave the stage with her reputation intact.

By now we had become somewhat estranged. Two years earlier, Tatiana had decided to have a child. I was embarrassed watching her stomach grow. The Soviets had instituted a cult of motherhood, but in our little world pregnancy seemed like a desecration. She's a ballerina, she is destroying her body, I thought. I avoided her home, and she disappeared from the theater once her pregnancy started. Perhaps she was self-conscious because she wasn't married. Tatiana conceived with Sviatoslav Kusnetsov, a handsome dancer in the Kirov, who was half her age. Like a queen bee, she selected him for breeding. But one day I ran into her on the street, and I gawked as I greeted her. "What are you looking at?" she asked angrily. "Stop that!"

Nevertheless, Tatiana's mother invited me to sit with her and Tatiana's sister Evgenia in their box at the gala. Tatiana cast the dancers herself. Given the chance, many a ballerina—perhaps most—in her situation would have chosen dancers who weren't as good as she was. But Tatiana wasn't afraid to share the stage with the greatest names in Russian ballet. She assigned each ballerina her best and most popular role. Dudinskaya was Kitri in act 1 of *Don Quixote* and Shelest was the Street Dancer. Ulanova and Sergeyev danced excerpts from *Romeo and Juliet*, and finally Tatiana herself danced act 3 of *Esmeralda*.

This time I was truly thrilled by Ulanova. From the audience she did miraculously look like a teenager. She danced the short adagio before Friar Laurence, and then the scene in her bedroom where she decides to visit Romeo's cell and obtains the potion. Her interlude of indecision and then resolution in her bedroom was capped by her legendary run off stage. It was like no other ballerina's in my experience. You saw her beautiful feet flurry across the floor; but all you felt was passion taking flight. She could have winged into the sky and no one would have been surprised. Every dancer who dances Juliet tries to copy her run, and no one I've ever seen has come close to her eloquence there.

In *Esmeralda*, Tatiana wrung our hearts as a gypsy dancer, still in love with the man who betrayed her, cruelly forced to perform for him as he celebrates his wedding. After *Esmeralda* the curtains were opened, and the stage was smothered with flowers. Friends and colleagues presented her with gifts, cards, poetry written especially in tribute. After she retired from performing, Tatiana became director of the Vaganova Institute.

"Be proud, be beautiful," Valentina Ivanova told us, but no more elegant encouragement than her own deportment was needed. She swept across the school studio like one of Chekhov's grand dames, her hair in a top-knot, her skirt brushing the floor, a high ruffled lace collar setting off her gold pendant watch. Ivanova was over forty, but still an eminent character dancer at the Kirov, and now she taught us intermediate-level character dance while still appearing onstage as the queens in *Swan Lake* and *Sleeping Beauty*. Onstage or in the studio, Ivanova didn't walk; she glided, her chin and chest held high and proud. I would almost call her the last of a certain breed. While her blood was indigo blue, by comparison many of her successors' seemed tinged with gold plate.

In classical ballet, raising your arms higher than shoulder level is something akin to screaming. In our sign language it's a gesture reserved only for peasants. A queen never needs to raise her voice. Her nobility is channeled through her back; her arms always stay a little lower than her shoulders. Ivanova showed that to us so clearly. She motioned languidly, compelling the entire stage to watch her, to heed each sentence of mime. Sitting on her stage throne, she never let her back relax the slightest bit. In Russia, we have an expression, a back "so straight it's as though she has swallowed a sword." That was Ivanova.

Her curriculum was intended to tour us through dances of different cultures and continents, but she concentrated on those of the East—all the better to show off her columnar neck, long, sinuous arms, and stately grace. She never made an abrupt or clumsy gesture and she wouldn't let us, either. "Don't move like a lunatic," she'd say. "Respect yourselves!"

Slow movement came naturally to me, and I copied Ivanova's elegant style so earnestly she thought I was her disciple. But we studied about fifteen dances, all quite similar. So the class wasn't very interesting for me. By the end of the year I knew no more than a couple, although our final exam was supposed to test us in five dances. Ivanova, however, told us she would expect to see us perform all fifteen. Her exam was going to last twice as long as the standard hour. During the exam she strolled around being herself, watching us while she admired her reflection, patting her coiffure. She had placed me in the first line, smack in the middle, nose to nose with the examining board of teachers. Tatiana sat in the middle, the director's place of honor. Left, right, my eyes darted, frantically trying to learn the steps of the dances I didn't know. Tatiana saw my face, grim with concentration. "Where are your teeth?" she asked me, using a Russian expression common to ballet and the circus: show your teeth, smile, loosen up! But I'd never heard it used before and was too harried to understand she was kidding. I bared a grisly rictus: here were my teeth, thank you very much.

Tatiana drew herself up haughtily. "This girl has no manners," she told her colleagues. She thought she'd been insulted, and I couldn't understand why she was so angry. Finally I was so frustrated I left the center and stood in the back. Tatiana boiled over: it wasn't enough that I didn't know the steps, I had no discipline! "Get out," she ordered.

My grade was the lowest possible: 1 out of 5.

"Well, what did you expect?" Ivanova asked me serenely the next day. She was too proud of her regal composure ever to raise her voice. But Tatiana was another story altogether. She called me into her office. How dare I insult her in front of the whole class? Did I think because we knew each other personally I had a right to do that? "I didn't mean it," I promised her, "I really didn't." But she thought I was mocking her; she didn't want to accept my apology. She really didn't understand how terribly nervous I had been during the exam. It would be over a decade before the breach between us was resolved.

For my fifteenth birthday, my grandmother gave me a briefcase that might have been every student's dream to possess: it was black leather, oversized, with all sorts of pockets inside and out. I found it mysteriously adult, with its two locks and a little key with which to safeguard all my classified data. No one else at school had one; I had seen bags like this only in store windows or carried by college students. I bustled around organizing all my school paraphernalia, which had been, up to then, completely haphazard. Textbooks, supplies, geometry tools—they had their own special black leather pocket—were installed in what was virtually an ambulatory safe deposit box.

A week later, several girls and I decided to dash out on a school recess to buy ice cream. My briefcase was bulging, so I dropped it near a couch in the entrance lobby.

Mothers and children sat waiting to pick up younger day students. Five minutes later, I was back, but my briefcase was gone. Frantically I searched every nook and cranny until Pasha, the school's doorkeeper, told me to go on to class; she would let me know if it was turned in. But classes finished for the day and there was still no sign of my bag. I walked home feeling so guilty, knowing my grandmother had saved for months to buy it for me. When I told her, she was upset, but she said, "Things come and go; this is only your first, not your last."

The next morning I was surprised by a call from Leontina Karlovna, the new director of the school's dormitory. She lived across the street from me. She was stern and cold; she gave me the impression that she was always turning her nose up at the rest of the world.

"Did you lose something?" Leontina Karlovna asked.

"Yes I did, I lost my briefcase."

"Well, all your books were dropped in my lobby," she told me. "I looked inside and saw your name. If you want, you can pick them up. But I don't have your briefcase, only your things."

My notebooks and textbooks were spread out on a table in her tiny, cramped room. The geometry instruments were missing, so was a little money I'd stashed away in my briefcase. Karlovna looked at me strangely. "What's missing?" she asked tendentiously. Money, geometry tools, I volunteered. "What else?" I leafed through everything again.

"Oh, maybe some pencils are gone," I told her.

Her voice curdled. "*Look carefully!*" she demanded. "It's very important you remember what else is gone."

I took one more inventory; I could notice nothing else. "I don't understand. What's so important?"

"Well," she sniffed, "you could have a better grade for discipline." I gathered my things and went home.

The next day, Pasha stopped me as I walked through the door. "You have to see Shelkov. Somebody turned in your Komsomol book." That was my membership passport for the youth party. "They said they found it in the street." Pasha liked me. "I can't tell you who it was . . . okay," she relented instantly. "It was Leontina Karlovna, but don't tell anybody. She said nobody should be so casual about their most important document."

In Shelkov's office, he and Karlovna stood glowering behind his desk, which for us students represented the mighty cornerstone of the entire school. "How did you lose your book?" Karlovna asked.

"I didn't lose it," I told her. "It was stolen from me with my briefcase."

"We don't believe you," Shelkov said.

"What do you mean, you don't believe me? Leontina Karlovna knows, she gave me all my stuff and books."

"You've shown a terrible example to the other students by being so careless," they told me and sent me out.

Soon after, a notice on the board informed the school that a meeting would be convened the next day to discuss an outrageous case, a shameful incident. Every student was required to be present. The chief of the Komsomol student committee, Solovot Ulaiev, approached me and informed me that it was I who had committed the obscene aberration.

"How?"

"Because of this Komsomol book."

"It's ridiculous!" I protested. I explained the whole story. He said he believed me, but nonetheless an order from Shelkov could not be resisted.

In our school theater the entire student body was assembled. A nine-member committee of students, senior Komsomol members, sat in judgment around a table covered with an appropriately red cloth. I stood. I was on trial in a kangaroo "comrades court." Introductory remarks from the prosecution—there was no defense—told the students that by my carelessness I had betrayed Mother Russia. But I wasn't frightened. I was so convinced that justice was on my side. I couldn't believe that anyone could believe such nonsense.

Karlovna was the éminence grise, setting the whole thing in motion but not appearing herself. Shelkov presided at a table also covered with a red cloth. With him sat members of the jury, including both students and my literature teacher Zoya Strakhova, who was assistant party chief at the school. She rose to denounce me. "Your Komsomol book is the most important document in your life. You must carry it with you all the time. An enemy could use this to spy on us!"

"What secrets can they get from our ballet school?" I asked.

"Don't be smart," she snapped. "They can use it to show that they're a citizen of this country."

"There is my name and my picture and my age," I said. "I don't think they have spies who are fifteen. What was I supposed to do?" I pleaded. "I had to bring it to school. Usually I leave it at home, but this day I took it to get stamped." That sent Strakhova into orbit.

"What do you mean you left it at home? You always have to have it with you. You're *never* supposed to separate yourself from this book!"

"Even in the shower?" I asked. But there would be no end to the preposterousness.

"Well, you have to have a special plastic belt on your body all the time."

"Even in ballet class when we sweat? . . . I'll do it. I will if you show me how."

By now laughter rippled through the audience. "I will make a copy of this belt if you show me one here," I pledged. Strakhova couldn't retreat; she rode out her Red Queen tirade.

"I will find a way to show you," she promised.

"Why not try to check now, while the whole school is here," I asked. "Take off their clothes and show me one person who has this belt." Laughter and applause swept the audience.

"Go away and wait behind the door!" Shelkov ordered, and I left the stage in shock, stunned by the realization that adult figures of authority and rectitude could actually lie without any compunction.

All but one member of the student council voted to expel me from the Komsomol. Only Solovot stood up against the tribunal. "Leaving her briefcase in the lobby isn't immoral, punishing her is." The students in the audience had to vote, too, by a show of hands.

"Come on, come on, be brave," the commission urged in doublethink.

They couldn't find more than ten students to support the council's verdict, but I was suspended from the Komsomol party for one year.

I walked home enraged. No one, even some of my close friends, had the courage to stand up and declare unequivocally that the emperor was simply not wearing a single stich of clothing.

I told my grandmother I was never going back to school. She cried as she saw a secure future for me going up in smoke. For one entire month I played hooky. The school kept calling my grandmother insisting that she send me back. "I can't tell her anything," my grandmother said. "She'll do whatever she thinks is right."

Finally a posse of boys appeared. "Shelkov says we have to bring you even if we have to tie you up." They didn't have to. I'd been having a good time going to movies and museums, reading overtime, but by now I missed my classmates.

In Shelkov's office, however, I poured out to him everything I thought about his proceedings and about my teachers. "Listen, don't be so hard on everybody," he said. "Forget about it all. I love you like my daughter and I want you to be back at school. I think you're very talented and I'm worried about you. You don't have parents, and I want you to have a good profession." What could I say? I was back the next day. But so great was my disillusionment that I don't think I was ever again the same person.

~ 5 ~

rebels

Our new literature teacher, Kirill Poley, resembled Dumas's description of d'Aramis, the cleric Musketeer. His pale skin set off dark hair, a Vandyke beard and a little moustache covering his upper lip, making his cherry-red lower lip all the more enticing to me, especially because he brushed his tongue over it incessantly. I watched and counted while he did it over and over again. During one class I counted no fewer than thirty swipes. Poley is an aristocratic Polish name, and his very long, elegant, nervous hands lived up to the image conjured by his name. Premature arthritis was swelling his knuckles. He cracked them over and over as he lectured. I kept score of that, too.

I was making a telescopic tour of Kirill's mannerisms because, like all the girls in class, I had a crush on him. "I'm not ready," I said each time he quizzed me. "I'll answer in your office." He knew that I was ahead of most of the class; he even called me Socrates because I read so much on my own. In his office, we talked about Chekhov or Shakespeare, which were not in our official program until the final year. His passion was theater, and he acted in amateur dramatic societies around Leningrad.

When, years later, we discovered that he was primarily homosexual, many of the girls were heartbroken. In school, we hadn't a clue, because he was married to Marietta Frangopolo. She directed the school's museum of ballet and taught us its history of ballet—teaching us in her fashion, which was to spill the choicest personal tidbits about immortals of Russian ballet. Before Marietta, the curriculum of ballet history began after the Revolution and included only Soviet loyalists. No one who had left Russia was mentioned. There wasn't a word about school graduates Pavlova or Karsavina or Nijinsky—simply because they'd emigrated to the West thirty and forty years earlier. All but single-handedly, Marietta had created our museum, combing the theater for mementos. She found costumes and shoes worn by the émigrés and tried to rehabilitate their reputations.

We finally saw Fokine's face: even though the Kirov performed his *Les Sylphides*, he, too, was verboten. Marietta had been Balanchine's classmate at the school. She told us that his name was now world-famous, and when foreigners visited it shamed us that he wasn't acknowledged by his own countrymen. She put his photo on the wall of her museum.

Marietta was legendary in the international ballet community. When dancers, specialists, or ballet critics came from the West, they immediately went to her museum and plied her for information. She translated for them, guiding them around the school and the theater. Letters and postcards to her poured in from friends around the globe. She displayed them proudly. She wasn't a member of the party and she was very courageous. "It's amazing they still keep me here!" she said, incredulous but droll. "Every day I think they'll kick me out!" There did come a moment when the school or the party wanted her removed from her position, but her age exonerated her and she was given a reprieve. Finally, they succeeded in routing her from the teaching staff, years after I graduated. They let her keep her museum, but a party stalwart took over the ballet history class.

Marietta was about fifty when I met her, while Poley was about thirty-five. The age difference was quite rare in Russia and very intriguing to us. But Marietta was uniquely attractive, very stylish, her reddish-brown hair twisted artfully into a chignon. Every day she wore a different pastel silk blouse and a different scarf. Marietta wasn't entirely Russian, she'd remind us. She was *Greekchanka*, and inside her coursed "a very, very powerful blood, full of energy and desire for life."

I know now that Marietta herself understood that Kirill was gay. But she truly loved him and wanted to protect his reputation. Nevertheless it wasn't a marriage of convenience, but rather of companionship, and maybe something more, too. Marietta made a great show of advertising their intimacy; anyway, she was as frank about herself as about the titans of ballet. "We're so much in love, Kirusha and I," she told us. "We don't have normal relations like most human beings. We have sexual connections through the piano. When he plays piano, and I listen, I have . . . an orgasm." What was this "orgasm," we wondered—could it be ecstasy, perhaps? Later when someone confided, "I'm having a little flirtation," we'd ask, "How—through the piano?"

"In the winter,"—she paused significantly—"in the winter I love to sleep with Kirusha. I will put my legs between his legs and he will make them warm. It's very pleasant, very special." To be sure, no student ever cut *her* class! She couldn't stop herself, and we certainly didn't want her to. "Oh, my goodness!" she'd exclaim. "I ran out of time again! Okay, read this and this and this yourself at home." Sometimes Kirusha would appear at the end of our class, a faint, sarcastic glimmer in his eyes. He kissed her hand, and she was very proud. "Kirusha, are you finished with your class?" she purred.

She was close to many students, a fount of wisdom and compassion for the lovelorn. Natasha Makarova continued to write her after she defected. We were together in New York when we heard Marietta was dead, in the late 1970s. Natasha wept. "My *padrone*," Natasha called her, thinking of *Romeo*, "my *padre padrone* is dead."

§ ℓ

Every New Year's, Tyuntina presented her students with gifts. One year she wrote on my card she hoped this year Santa would put *staraniya*—ambition, desire, determination—into my stocking. When I was fifteen, she sat me down and told me I was wasting my time, my talent, not even using fifty percent of my potential. "Don't be angry with me," she said. "I love all of you as if you were my own children."

Pointe work was one of my major struggles in class. It was introduced in the second year at the school. But we didn't have very good pointe shoes. They were canvas, not the most comfortable material, and after the war, they didn't have heaters to dry the glue properly. Our pointe shoes were always a little too soggy to support my arch. I could do five pirouettes on half pointe, but on pointe I broke my shoes within a few minutes. We were only allotted one pair of pointe shoes a month—while a ballerina can use more than one pair in an evening.

Each winter students from each class participated in a recital in our little theater. I believe it was December of 1953 when Kasyan Goleizovsky choreographed the girls' recital piece for us. During the 1920s, Goleizovsky had been at the forefront of the new Soviet society's experiments in art. But he fell out of step with the times, for he was a pure aesthete, wanting to create beauty without advancing an overt political message. Eventually he was marginalized, exiled from Moscow's Bolshoi Theater, although he still lived in the capital, occasionally venturing for a stint with some provincial ballet troupe. But Tatiana Vecheslova didn't give a damn about who was in favor and who wasn't, and in her capacity as director of the school she invited him to choreograph for us, undoubtedly knowing what his impact on us would be.

Working with him was unlike anything I've experienced before or since. Unlike most other adults at the school, Goleizovsky never screamed; he was never harsh. Working with him was like working with a priest. He was short and plump, with a barely perceptible neck and a bulbous head; when he sank into a chair, he was nearly hunchbacked. But when he stood to demonstrate, his arms were long and fluid and compelling.

Goleizovsky's was an ensemble piece for twelve girls, twenty-five minutes long, to a suite of Liszt piano pieces. Different episodes and unexpected appearances revealed now three girls, now five, then all twelve. He would play a phrase of music and then show you steps that seemed to flow effortlessly from his imagination, though they looked impossibly difficult to my eyes. Then he instructed us that it was we who would have to fit a certain number of steps into a particular musical phrase. We each had to work it out on our own. The first time I tried, I finished his steps and the music still played. The next time the music was long gone before I had danced all the steps.

"Can you show it one more time?" I asked, frustrated when things didn't work right away. "I can't do it as beautifully as you."

"Oh, you're wrong," he said. "You can't think about yourself like that. Just move. Just be free." He wanted his steps to look improvised. "You're running through the clouds," he told us, "you're trying to catch a bird . . . looking at the water, look down at yourself, swim through the water."

This must have been what Isadora Duncan was like, I thought as we rehearsed. Isadora was still revered in Russia, her enormous portrait reigned over Marietta's museum. But Goleizovsky used more steps than Isadora, and they were on pointe: liquid steps, one combination dissolving into another.

"Try, try, try," he repeated, until finally everything adhered to the musical phrase like a hand in a glove, for he was impeccably musical, and no steps had to be altered to fit the phrase. He tinkered only with a couple of things, late into the rehearsal period, when he thought better of one step or another. Eventually, each one of us girls felt that she had created her own choreography. Once we'd mastered his phrasing, our bodies felt like they were moving independently, without conscious control. The steps that had seemed so daunting now just seemed to flow. Working with Goleizovsky, I understood that when movement is musical and logical, the body can do any kind of technical difficulty comfortably.

"No movement a woman makes can be ugly," he told us. "Women are the most beautiful thing God has created." When this gnomish creature, his small blue eyes twinkling with a child's curiosity, came over to me and spoke in his velvet voice and brushed my arm, everything Marietta Frangopolo said rang true. For Marietta had talked about how many women he had, how many children he fathered. She reported that wherever he choreographed he had a love affair lasting one or two weeks, ending when his work was over. Women were crazy about him. That was perhaps my first understanding of the erotic potency of talent—it can often seduce where mere beauty cannot!

One day Marietta gestured toward one student, Rita, whose mother had been a dancer. "Look at this girl," she commanded, "look at her face!" Then she turned to the bronze bust of Goleizovsky. "And look *here!*" she continued to stage whisper. "Don't you think it's the same face?" she asked conspiratorially. The girl's face, the shape of her head, her eyes, and nose were identical to his. After class we clustered around the newly mysterious Rita, who studied ballet not with us under Tyuntina, but rather in the parallel class of Natalia Komkova.

"Is it true?" we asked.

"I don't know!" she blushed, as confused as we were. Later her mother filled her in, but Marietta was the first to break the news to her.

We sat around Goleizovsky after rehearsal, listening to his stories, for he was an expert raconteur.

"Is it true?" I finally asked him. "Is Rita your daughter?" She wasn't there at the moment, naturally.

"I don't know; maybe," he said.

"How many children do you have?" I asked.

"I never counted: maybe ten, maybe thirty, I don't know," he told us. Our jaws dropped even further.

The next year, we heard that a young dancer in the company was choreographing our annual Christmas recital piece. Yuri Grigorovich had made some dances for amateur theaters. He was talented and intellectual, a maverick who knew what he wanted and was determined to fight his way upstream. He and Kirov ballerina Alla Shelest had recently married.

In Grigorovich's ballet, I was cast as one of six solo girls dancing to Glinka's romantic *Valse Fantasie*. The steps were simple, danceable, and musical. The arms were a little different than what we learned in class: we didn't keep them evenly above our head, one was always slightly lower. Finally, we weren't being screamed at to keep our arms exactly in a classical position. We were excited at being able to break the canons and explore a new style.

In Grigorovich's presence we girls became a flock of nascent Lolitas. We loved being alone with him. We hung on his every word and especially liked when he demonstrated for us, even more when he would come over and correct our positions and thus actually touch us. Sometimes I would deliberately make a mistake, hoping he would set me straight.

But Shelest was parked all the time in rehearsal, smack between Grigorovich and our rampant fantasies. She sat like a little mouse, with dirty blond hair and without any makeup, dressed in a drab skirt and sweater. Why was she sitting here? Whatever did he see in her? It bothered us when she gave him tea or a sandwich, like a mother making sure her son ate. We were jealous of their closeness and annoyed at her attentions: we were creating art, and she was tending to ordinary human needs.

In the middle of one rehearsal Shelest suddenly sprang into the middle of the studio, and now it was if this dowdy woman left the earth behind. "Girls!" she commanded. "Watch your arms! Look at yourself in the mirror! Look at what you're doing!" She turned us and showed us and moved the way she wanted us to. I was struck dumb. I repeated what she demonstrated without thinking, almost as if hypnotized. The more she showed, the more intrigued I became, even forgetting my crush on Grigorovich.

I wanted to see more of her, but it was not all that easy to watch Shelest perform, because at the Kirov Dudinskaya did everything she could to keep Shelest off the stage. Given the fact that Dudinskaya was both an inveterate intrigante and married to the Kirov's artistic director, Konstantin Sergeyev, she would always have the upper hand.

Theater legend had it that Dudinskaya put needles in Shelest's shoes and performed rites of black magic to flummox her. Indeed there was something eerie about the way Shelest's career bumped along, plagued by mishap. Shelest might wait months to dance a full-length role and then so often something would prevent her from getting on stage. One time Shelest was dancing *Sleeping Beauty* when, in the middle of her first act variation, she tore her calf muscle. From the audience I saw the whole muscle retract into a ball beneath her knee. But she was surging with adrenaline and didn't even feel the pain until the variation was over. She took her bow, made her exit, and collapsed in the wings. Ninel Kurgapkina stepped in to finish the performance; she was a dancer who never minded pinch-hitting. And Shelest was out again for six months.

Then, too, Shelest was a hypochondriac. Her dance bag was like a medicine cabinet; she was forever downing special herbs and teas. She could cancel a performance for what would seem the slightest provocation.

But over the next few years I received an education in ballet from her that equaled what I received in the classroom and studio.

There may have been only three or four occasions over a decade when I saw Shelest dance Nikiya in *La Bayadère*, and yet no performance left a more indelible memory. I saw Shelest transform from the vital, passionate young woman of act 1 into a searing figure of tragedy, and finally an aloof goddess. In each act, Shelest was not so much a different character as a different substance, as if one entity could be air and fire and water.

Shelest was shattering throughout the many incidents of the "snake variation" in act 2. Temple dancer Nikiya arrives at the wedding celebration of her beloved, the warrior Solor, to the princess Gamzatti. She tries to leave; the palace guards detain her. She must stay and entertain the court. Shelest danced the opening phrases as if her body were writhing in torture.

Gamzatti's handmaiden Aya presents Nikiya with a basket of flowers, telling her it is a gift from Solor, whispering a duplicitous message: after the wedding Solor will elope with her. At this point, many Nikiyas simply stop furrowing their brows and start to beam openly at Solor, while Shelest, although her face stayed averted from him, was now dancing unmistakably for him and him alone. Every muscle in her body seemed to extend with a new sensuality, as if she was absorbing Solor within herself.

Intent on hiding her relief from Gamzatti and the onlookers, her body could not help but reveal her joy. Her final whirling coda was delirious, the quintessence of ecstasy.

When the snake concealed in Nikiya's bouquet strikes, Nikiya lies stricken as Gamzatti spirits Solor away. The High Brahmin offers an antidote if Nikiya will agree to be his. Usually ballerinas look up at the Brahmin, and we seem to see them think, Better to die than wind up with this old man. But Shelest's Nikiya would have been oblivious to the most desirable creature. Although the Brahmin was practically forcing his vial into her hands, she barely registered his presence. Watching Gamzatti and Solor leave, Shelest's soul seemed to depart with them. She let the vial drop out of her hands and we realized that the prospect of saving herself didn't occur to her. She would neither live without Solor nor let him escape. There was more than a touch of Medea in Shelest's Nikiya. We knew that she would be with him forever. Love was a commitment, a possession for Shelest's heroines; they could only be monogamous.

Thus we were prepared for Nikiya's reappearance in the Kingdom of the Shades, but we were not prepared for her metamorphosis, for feet that with each step toward Solor seemed to promise that all would be well, every wish would be granted. Many, if not most, ballerinas perform the Shades with complete, icy coldness. Presumably they don't feel that they should show any emotion because now they are dead, they are ghosts. But I think that's why the Shades can sometimes be boring to an audience. It's important to remember that this is Solor's opium-induced vision, which would be an elaboration of his fantasies. I don't think Solor could have fantasized about an iceberg as his lover. Shelest's Nikiya had found in transfigured death a new life and a new happiness. There was no more insecurity, ego; there was nothing except joy, as if she was under an opium spell herself. But at the same time, with Solor she remained remote, a goddess smiling benevolently on a subject.

In 1940, Dudinskaya and Vakhtang Chabukiani were filmed in the Shades. Watching them today, Western spectators are amazed that any Kirov ballerina could dance as fast as Dudinskaya. She loved *La Bayadère* and I saw her dance it many times. She was indeed a very musical ballerina, but it's because of that that she chose to dance the Shades in a way that I would call *unmusical* and incorrect. She knew that she didn't have the line, the cantilena, for adagio, and so she danced the Shades faster than probably any other ballerina in history. Everything was con brio: her pirouettes just as clear and bright as if she'd been dancing Kitri in *Don Quixote*. But Shelest could maintain vitality dancing in slow motion. She didn't need to use manic speed to simulate dance energy.

Watching the Shades we need to feel that every movement is a little hallucinogenic, a little smoky, even though the feet are meant to be very clean and the musical accents definite. Shelest's upper body and arms followed her feet by a hair, imparting a wafting illusion. She even managed to retain a whiff of this languidity as she whipped furiously into the chaîné turns in the coda.

Shelest's jump was spectacularly light and fast as well as high. Of all the many Princess Auroras I've seen since Shelest, only Alla Sizova was as quick and brilliant in her act 1 entrance. Sometimes the texture of the role is porcelain; sometimes, unfortunately, it is cardboard. But in *Sleeping Beauty*, Shelest was a human being, a beautiful, noble child. In the Rose adagio, the infinite variety of her phrases was plotted so that every step sketched an adolescent's impetuous, impatient character.

When her leg extended in écarté to her first suitor, she seemed to prolong the phrase, as if she were drawing out the greeting, elegantly, politely, carefully pronouncing each syllable. With the second écarté, her leg repeated her greeting, but it was clear that, for Shelest's Aurora, repetition turned the exchange dutiful. She performed the third and fourth écartés much faster, eager to dispense with this polite formality.

During Aurora's diagonal of arabesques penchés, Shelest's body dipped lower and her leg rose higher with each penché as her happiness mounted, while the orchestral melody also rose higher and higher. As she bourréed round and round downstage before the final promenade balances, Shelest's Aurora was intoxicated with the realization that she was now sixteen, beginning adulthood, courted by four men.

Watching Shelest I learned how important and expressive the position of the neck can and should be. As Aurora she was glimpsing life shyly, her neck tilted slightly sideways but her chin never lowered: she was a princess. As Giselle, Shelest's neck was far in front of her chest and feet, to suggest that as a Wili she was really flying rather than walking; as Myrtha, her neck stayed forward but was now unflinching, a ramrod.

Shelest's Myrtha showed me all but unimagined dimensions of the role. Shelest's entrance incited the audience to screams and applause before she had even finished bouréeing across the stage. Her face was impassive; her feet so swift it seemed as if an evil wind was propelling her. Shelest's jump seemed supernatural; in that period, I never saw Russian ballerinas jump as high. She invested a tragic dimension that was unique among all the Myrthas I've seen. It wasn't one woman's sorrow, for Myrtha is more symbol than individual; it was the tragedy of all women thwarted.

When her myrtle branch fell from her hand, vanquished by Giselle's intervention, Shelest as Myrtha turned away from Giselle and Albrecht, retreating into herself. It was the first time her sovereignty had been challenged. She was broken, but then we saw her recover like a phoenix. The power of the myrtle was lost to her, but what remained was her personal power: she was the Queen of the Wilis. Energy surged from her lower back, through her chest, through that neck. Her back was like a sponge, sucking Giselle and Albrecht under her control. "You will dance," her extended arm told them, and it was a command no mortal or phantom could resist.

Shelest was frequently coached by Elena Lyukom, who had been one our leading ballerinas in the years immediately before and after the Revolution. Lyukom was an angelic presence, her white hair, her china-blue eyes, her soft voice all remain vividly in my memory. But I think Shelest really preferred to work alone, sometimes even without a pianist. She was such a perfectionist that she wanted to polish imperfections even before she went to rehearse with other dancers. She studied every muscle, not only in her body but also in her face. Onstage her plain features became magically beautiful. A long face like hers is always well suited to the stage; Shelest knew how to make up her small eyes so that they opened to perhaps three times their natural size.

She could spend days polishing a couple of details, the way I saw Gelsey Kirkland work years later in the United States. But whereas Kirkland's obsession with details could diminish the natural flow of her performance, Shelest put all the parts back together into one organic whole.

Offstage, Shelest was anything but a temptress, but as the Black Swan she was ineffably seductive. At the performance I recall, she dominated the audience and her Siegfried, Konstantin Shatilov, as if she had put them under hypnosis. Not for a moment did her Odile relax her hold on her prey. Each gesture, every pirouette brought him deeper under her spell. He could be standing across the stage from her, her back facing him, but still she saw him, she manipulated him. It was voodoo, beyond explanation.

As Zarema in *The Fountain of Bakhchisarai*, Shelest composed an altogether different femme fatale. Pushkin's poem and Zakharov's 1934 *dramballet* always fascinated me as a parallel story of two women who have lost love: Maria's husband was killed by the Tatar chieftain Girei; Zarema has been replaced by Maria as Girei's harem favorite.

Tatiana Vecheslova had been Zakharov's first Zarema in 1934, and she performed the role frequently until she retired in 1953. She danced a savage woman whose jealousy drove her out of her senses. The Kirov Zaremas that followed her—even a self-possessed beauty like Inna Zubkovskaya—followed the script Vecheslova had enacted. But Shelest's Zarema was different. She wasn't a siren aflame with spurned fury, heedless of consequence.

When Zarema steals into Maria's chamber, she must, according to the ballet's scenario, be shocked by Maria's beauty. When Shelest's Zarema glimpsed Maria's face, she conveyed instead an aesthetic appreciation. There was no longer any direct rivalry; the harem held no species like Maria. Shelest's Zarema knew, too, that Maria was a victim of her beauty. Seeing her, Zarema now realized, too, that the instrument of her own destruction was before her. After Girei intercepted them, we knew that Shelest's Zarema wanted him to suffer. She realized that her intrusion so enraged him that he was about to kill her. But when Zarema stabbed Maria, it was as though Shelest had sacrificed herself to snuff out an alien presence that was causing dissension in her society. Girei was unable to rule because he was obsessed with Maria.

By now, in the late 1950s, well over forty, Galina Ulanova remained the great romantic heroine of Soviet ballet. Before an audience, she was a beacon of trust and innocence. In romantic roles Shelest, by contrast, was never innocent; she was too complex. And yet for me she provided the most perfect demonstration of those movement principles that define romanticism. The romantic torso flies in front of the legs, which linger behind like a cloud. The upper body should seem almost to be lifting off the legs; Shelest conveyed this illusion as no one else.

Shelest's reactions onstage were never quite those of a "normal" person. In the unreal world of the sylphs, she was in her element; even here, she voyaged to the far edge of fantasy. What would have looked needlessly fey on another ballerina was mesmerizing on Shelest. Dancing the Prelude in *Les Sylphides*, she was the music, an instrumental voice; she was both the conductor producing the music and the listener pausing to absorb the new sounds. Sometimes indeed she seemed to be plucking notes out of the air. Her neck would extend, then her arms and finally her eyes would locate the next sound as it "appeared." In order to truly hear a symphony, you don't crane your neck forward to watch one violinist; you turn away, look inside yourself, and absorb the sound as one complete sensation. And so Shelest, in the Prelude, showed us what it really means to listen.

Watching Shelest in *Romeo and Juliet*, I felt that I saw Shakespeare's heroine come to life more than I had even in Ulanova, for whom Leonid Lavrovsky created the role in 1940. Certainly no one in my experience has been able to recreate Ulanova's run to Friar Laurence, and no ballerina transmitted Juliet's love with more conviction. But Juliet herself is closer to the character Shelest created at the Kirov. For Juliet is strong, stronger than Romeo, almost masculine. Shelest understood Juliet's significance as the first Renaissance heroine, dying not for the Church or God, but for her love and for humanity.

By nature always somehow knowing, Shelest was undoubtedly challenged by Juliet's opening scenes. Years later when I was coaching ballerinas as Juliet, I always thought that they should react with complete surprise to the discovery of their budding breasts. But Shelest played that moment differently: she was musing, contemplating her transition. From that point on, her Juliet started to impersonate her idea of an adult, as if she were now emulating her mother. The spectacle of the mature Shelest playing a fourteen-year-old was then balanced by the sight of Juliet impersonating an adult.

Shelest flew to Friar Laurence on her own special run, her hips and neck rushing ahead of her legs. In the monk's cell and in the later scenes with her parents and Paris, Shelest pleaded, stormed, struggled; she dashed herself to the ground. Yet no movement was ungainly, no pose less than exquisite. Undoubtedly, she had immersed herself in Renaissance art. Like every role she danced, Shelest's Juliet was as much about ballet and art as it was about the character and narrative she enacted.

nureyev arrives

Every summer the school was sent to our own camp outside Leningrad near the village of Ushkova, located in a resort area lush with forest, mushroom patches, and pristine sand beaches on the Gulf of Finland. On clear days we could see straight across to the Finnish shore. This was another country entirely, but so close that we could entertain the fantasy of being able to swim to it. For us those days in Ushkova were idyllic. We would hitchhike rides from passing trucks, and then see a movie in town. Five in the afternoon was teatime back at camp, and in the evenings readings were held in a special room. On some nights we rolled up the rugs and convened our own ad hoc nightclub. The boys had formed a jazz band, using rubber balls for mutes and stuffing newspaper between piano strings to give them a honky-tonk sound. They learned by ear Hollywood soundtracks broadcast over Finnish and Estonian channels. Sultry tangos and lowdown blues were now, in the mid-1950s, the rage among us students.

Igor Tchernichov was two years ahead of me at the school. Soon Igor and I were taking walks together every day. For two years I'd had a crush on Anatoly Nisnevich, a classmate of Igor's who looked like a cherub yet flashed a caustic nihilist wit. But Igor's interest was flattering. He was one of the top students in the school. Not only was he older than I, he already looked adult. He had sensuous lips and teeth like diamonds. Possessed by some thought or idea or obsession, his light gray eyes became projectors.

One day Igor told me we would take a different path on our walk; there was a tree, a certain tree we had to see. I didn't know he was planning a declaration, or that this tree was an anointed place that would bolster his nerve. On and on we trudged until I was exhausted. "Okay, I'm going back," I said.

"No, you have to go there!"

"For *what*? I don't have to do anything I don't want to."

He yanked my arm. "We decided to walk all the way there," he scolded me. "You see, you have no goals. You always change your mind in the middle!" I struggled and broke free. He seized me and gave me a violent kiss. I slapped his face and ran. It was my first kiss, and a not-so-romantic one at that.

A spy by profession and a yenta by nature, Evgeny Statskevich taught us the history of Russia and was also party chief at the school. A very tall, handsome Jewish man with dark hair and large blue eyes, he had taught previously at a teen reformatory. He was tough as nails, but behind his flintiness there did lurk some human qualities. He was forever eavesdropping in the boys' dressing room, a fly on every wall. "Oh," he'd say slyly, "I know what you did yesterday," a cunning smile playing around his face.

Prowling around the grounds one night, Evgeny had watched me jump out my window to walk with Igor. Caught by Evgeny's flashlight, Igor hurried into the bushes. "What are you doing here?" Evgeny said to me. "How dare you be out at night?"

"I'm going to see the fireflies," I told Evgeny. "How can I see them in the daytime?" He liked the fact that I could think on my feet, so much so that it was with a smirk on his face that he ordered me, "Go back to your room right now!"

A Cuban girl named Menia Martinez had joined our class. She was older than the rest of us, very sexy and uninhibited, always dressed scantily, with big hair and enormous dangling gold hoop earrings. Evgeny Statskevich was just as titillated as we were. "We have to watch where she spends time in the evenings. She's an American spy," he cautioned. (Batista still ruled Cuba.) "You can check. Here's how: insult her in Russian. Watch her expression; that'll give her away. You'll see." We laughed and tried this trick—and what do you know? She gave us a saucy retort in Russian, even though she was supposedly tackling our language now for the very first time.

At that moment I was up to my ears in detective stories and mysteries; rather than stick with ballet, I had developed the ambition to become a novelist. My classmate and friend Marina Tcherinichenko and I collaborated on a detective yarn. We used "TcherKit" as a pseudonym. Now we began to turn our sleuthing to practical use, tailing our Cuban guest, day and night, discovering her fulfilling assignations that seemed to indicate she had no qualms about going all the way. We were agog. (After Menia returned to Cuba, we heard she became Castro's secretary and his mistress.) Eventually we stopped worrying about her morals and didn't give them a second thought. What Russians cannot do foreigners can!

In the fall of 1957, Konstantin Sergeyev was choreographing *The Path of Thunder*, based on Peter Abrahams's novel about an interracial romance under Apartheid. Sergeyev asked our Cuban visitor to assist him, to demonstrate some authentic tropical movement. He didn't want anyone to know that he'd had help, however. They closed the doors and covered the studio windows; she assisted so well he let her choreograph the one piece herself, a dance for six couples with guitar. Several years later, after I had entered the Kirov, I was cast in this dance, which was of course Cuban, not South African at all. We couldn't have cared less: swinging our hips and slinking around, it was the high point of the ballet for us.

Menia stayed in Leningrad three or four years. She slimmed way down, she was able to speak Russian proficiently. And her dancing improved dramatically. "You see how professional a spy she is," Evgeny pronounced. "She's even learned how to dance!"

It was in a Russian history class taught by Evgeny Statskevich that I first saw Rudolf Nureyev's reckless, gleaming eyes on the first day of fall term, 1955. Evgeny was explaining that we would be studying the Tatar dynasty, the Mongolian conquerors who had ruled for hundreds of years. We opened our textbooks; there we found pictured Genghis Khan's cruel high cheekbones and sensuous mouth. Suddenly the door was opened by Zoya Strakhova. Although we had graduated from her literature section, she was the tutor for our grade, responsible for remedial work with any student who needed it. Strakhova pushed a boy in front of her. This could only be the new student we'd been told about, but for me, here he was: Genghis Khan in the flesh.

Rudi's shock of hair hung lower on his forehead than any other guy's in the room, giving the impression that his dark-brown eyes, glittering and defiant, were peering up at you from beneath hooded eyebrows. As the days went on, we ogled this feral-looking creature who evidenced no desire to try to make friends or indeed communicate at all with the rest of us. Rudi was a loner, an alien, who had not only the looks but the manners of his Tatar ancestor. He was billeted in the Mongolian dorm, sharing a room with boys much younger than he. Once I passed a knot of boys outside Rudi's room. I asked them what was going on; no one answered me. But I heard Bach's music coming from inside. I crept to the door and opened it a crack. Nureyev was sitting on his bed, listening to music on an old-fashioned record player, his brow furrowed. A boot came flying, thudding against the door as I pulled it shut. No one was allowed back in until Rudi was done.

Rudi's only real friends were his teacher, Alexander Pushkin, and Pushkin's wife, Xenia. One day I decided to watch Rudi in Pushkin's class. Rudi's hips were looser than most boys', and so his extension was huge, higher than some girls'. His arch was beautiful, but his turns weren't too good and he didn't have much of a jump. He wasn't like any other boy at the school; he didn't fit any of the Vaganova clichés.

Across the studio from me, Pushkin said something to him, and I heard Rudi snap back a rude word, a word we couldn't say to each other, let alone to a teacher! But after class Rudi jumped on Pushkin like a monkey and kissed him, pleading, "Don't be angry with me! Thank you, thank you." What a strange relationship, I thought to myself, but obviously it worked, because as weeks and months went by, Rudi improved rapidly.

By now my class had been together six years, since age nine or ten. Very few students joined any older than that. But the birth rate had been so low during the war that exceptions were sometimes made, especially for boys. Rudi was joining not at twelve, however, but at seventeen, yet he was still so new to ballet that he was thrown in with our class of fifteen- and sixteen-year-olds. So he practiced fanatically, missing classes, literature, mathematics. "I don't need to count!" he insisted. "I came here to learn ballet." He was possessed.

Yet Rudi was often to be seen in the corridor alone with a book, trying to glean as much education on his own as he could. He probably learned, or at least retained, more than the rest of our class steeped in our academic program. One time I saw him reading in the hall, tears in his eyes. I peeked: the book was Saint-Exupery's *The Little Prince*. I'd already read it and I had cried, too. I was both bewildered and impressed: this impudent creature, so tough and brash, and inside sensitive enough to cry over a book? I started to like him.

Twice weekly we had pas de deux class, and everyone made it a point to arrive ten minutes ahead of Pushkin, who taught our advanced division. Those were ten minutes to be boisterous, unsupervised, to practice lifts we weren't supposed to try on our own. We were puppies off our leashes, exploring every step from every ballet. Then by the time we started, we'd be exhausted . . . but by the time we graduated, we'd taught ourselves the entire repertoire.

Before class Rudi liked to measure his extension against the girls'. One day it was my turn. I was tall and my extension high: if he beat me, he was champ for sure. We competed leaning against an old tin stove in the middle of the studio. Up went our legs in a 180-degree split. Rudi called my name. I turned and my leg slammed to the ground. "Oh, I win! I win!" Rudi crowed.

One horrifying afternoon, Rudi decided to try a lift from the *Bayadère* Shades that is one of the riskiest in the repertory. If the man or woman is shaky, the woman can plunge easily. Rudi's partner was a girl, very beautiful and talented, and also very high-strung. Her mother showed clear signs of mental disturbance, and she, too, was later to spend years in and out of mental institutions.

Halfway up, Rudi realized he wasn't going to be up to it. His would-be ballerina hit the ground in a heap and was carried sobbing to the infirmary. An ugly bruise lingered on her hip for weeks. It was all her fault, Rudi claimed. "She has to help me and she didn't. I'm not going to drag her up."

"Dance me" later became a catchphrase said by ballerinas to their partners at New York City Ballet. The men were there to adore the women and to keep them upright virtually at any cost to themselves. That was Petipa's belief—the woman's primary position in the ballet cosmology—of course, just as much. But traditional ballet ideology was not Rudi's then, or ever. Technically, he eventually learned to be a superb partner, but he always refused to put himself out for any ballerina who wouldn't or couldn't do what he considered her fair share.

Dancers in the Kirov were wizards at makeup. They applied a different design for each role, putting their character in sharp focus, adjusting their face's thermostat. No matter what their naked face was like, the princes and the ballerinas looked wonderful and they all *felt* beautiful, too, which of course was just as important. And it was thrilling for us as students in our early teens to start emulating them, especially because we girls would never have gotten away with wearing makeup on the street.

But at the school, makeup class was given in a special room with mirrors and tables that was a facsimile of a Kirov dressing room. We were taught by an actor; his last name escapes me, but I clearly recall that his first name was Alexei. He was in his forties and was a leading member of the Leninsky Komsomol, one of the city's eminent drama theaters. He explained to us that we needed a technique to mobilize our faces the same way we toned and trained our bodies. It wouldn't then matter if one night we felt sick or low; our facial muscles would fall into place automatically. Makeup could help. First we needed to discover which muscles were activated by a clown's leer or a witch's grimace. Then we would paint these muscles to highlight them. Then our deeper artistry needed to take over, and our impact would depend on how much emotion we had to share, how much light and energy and expression our eyes could emanate.

Alexei's own face was like Silly Putty. That first day he mesmerized us with a tour de force: he started with his face completely relaxed and then slowly broadened a smile into an ear-splitting grin, a Grecian mask of comedy. Then he backed into a grimace, a stricken gash, puckering his face, squeezing it dry, so slowly, so subtly, that the transition was invisible. How long had it taken? One minute . . . three? Time stopped while we stared down an eternity of joy and suffering. We all thought he was a genius from that point on, and we came to love him.

He taught us how to isolate first one side of our faces and then the opposite. In front of the mirror we fumbled through the beginner's steps. At first my entire face jerked up or down clumsily. I worked and worked all term, but the facility I wanted always seemed to just elude me.

Once Alexei told us to study our faces in the mirror for ten or fifteen minutes. "What would you like to change?" The usual teenage complaints came from each of us: someone felt her nose was too long, another one worried about the roundness of her face, or the smallness of her eyes, or the thinness of his lips. "Okay," he told us, "we will work on all of that." Anything could be enhanced; he promised that we could work miracles. Drawing thumbnail sketches, diagramming effects, he helped us chart the significant planes and crevices in our faces. We went to work remaking ourselves.

"There's no such thing as ugly," he said. "It doesn't exist. The greatest artists know their physicality. They turn problems into specialties." His words were a balm for our adolescent complexes, an assurance that each of us could develop our own beauty.

A Moldavian boy we called Yavetsa was a member of our makeup class. He was three years older than me. Yavetsa took me aside one day after class. He couldn't go to the movies that night as we had planned, for other adventures were pressing. "Tonight we're going to beat the blue people."

"Who are they?" I asked.

"You mean you don't know? They're men who hate women," he said.

"How is it possible?" I asked. "Why do they hate women?"

"They just do, that's all."

"And do you catch them at night?"

"No, we're going to beat them up."

"Why? Do they kill women? Did they eat them?"

"Oh, you don't understand," he scoffed.

His words chilled me. I started asking around: Who were "the blue people," the blue men who hated women? Were they some type of monster? Was their skin blue? If my friends knew, they weren't saying anything.

Behind the school was the Ekaterininsky Garden, named in tribute to Catherine the Great, whose son Peter commissioned an imposing monument to her in the center of the grounds. Catherine is in the center, bewigged, encased in crinolines. Under her feet circles a frieze, a band of statesmen striking attitudes of noblesse oblige. It was common knowledge that these worthies had all been Catherine's lovers, favorites on whom she had bestowed aristocratic entitlements. Two hundred years later, their marble effigies watched the carousing continue, for the garden was the gay center of Leningrad, notorious for late-night trysts.

Yavetsa and his friends would go to the public men's room in the garden, flirt with gay men cruising there, and then beat them when their advances were returned. Yavetsa himself was actually a sensitive soul who composed poetry and grew up to be a writer and movie director. But back in school I think he had no choice: he could either join the aggressors or turn into a sitting duck.

One morning at the end of winter we were told that our beloved makeup teacher was ill. Yavetsa pulled me aside in the hallway. "Did you hear what happened? We went out last night to catch the blue people. We grabbed one man. We started beating him and he turned to look at us." It was our teacher. The boys ran out of the bathroom, terrified he'd recognize them and turn them in to Shelkov.

A few days later, Alexei returned to class. He seemed ashamed to look directly at anyone, for his dark glasses shielded a bruised face. Not long after, he submitted his resignation, although he never reported on Yavetsa and his pack. After he was gone my classmates and I never discussed him. Having been branded a blue person, he was to us a pariah, for homosexuality was considered in Soviet society one of the foulest perversities and crimes. It was embarrassing even to mention you knew somebody "like that."

And no one was immune from persecution and incarceration. Nikolai Pechkovsky, who was the Kirov Opera's greatest tenor when I was born, was among those imprisoned for six or seven years on morals violation charges. But nevertheless I couldn't help longing to see Alexei again, despite the stigma now attached to him. A few years later, I went to his theater, hoping to buy a ticket for a performance. At least I could see him on stage, then maybe somehow get a chance to talk to him. But when I asked after him, they said that he'd left, collected his pension, and they didn't know his address. I was very disappointed, but also relieved that he was alive and presumably well. I never saw him again, but I never got over him and I never will.

i start to teach

Igor adored his father, Alexander Tchernichov, who was a prominent tenor at the Maly Opera. Years earlier, his mother Eleanora had danced with the Maly ballet troupe. One day Igor had to pick up something from home and wanted me to come with him. I didn't want to. I was shy about meeting new people, and I knew that his father was a great opera star. I was sure that they lived in a lavish apartment like the Vecheslovas. But we arrived at a ramshackle old apartment building, leaking poverty. In a first-floor apartment, I saw an elderly man, obviously unwell, sitting in a rocking chair, warming himself with a pot of hot water.

It was impossible to believe, but this was the same man who had sung the Spirit of the Woods in my *Snow Maiden* fiasco six years earlier. His costume included tights, and his legs were so svelte that he hadn't looked like my stereotype of an opera singer at all. The role isn't long; his voice was already weakening. But his aria had been a terrific success. "You and I made the biggest hits tonight!" he had told me after the performance. But he didn't connect me with the girl of six years ago, and I didn't remind him.

A king-sized wooden bed dominated the room. There were no pictures on the wall; it was really like a bunker, the only reminder of his or Eleanora's professions a Renaissance clavichord that Alexander himself had restored. His voice failing, he now eked out extra money tuning pianos.

Together with his family, Alexander had been evacuated out of Leningrad during the siege, along with the entire Maly troupe. In order to earn extra money, he worked unloading trucks at night after his performances or rehearsals. Freezing and sweating, he eventually contracted severe pneumonia. Since then he had suffered chronic problems with his lungs. Igor had told me that his mother had eventually decided after they returned to Leningrad that Alexander was a lost cause and sold his things. He and Igor now shared one winter coat and one pair of high sheepskin boots. Eleanora had even sold Alexander's tuxedo, thus relinquishing what could have been a lifeline for the family: if he lacked the stamina for opera, he could still—with a tuxedo—have made money contributing an aria to galas the government sponsored throughout the year.

Igor was disappointed to find his father home, for sometimes Alexander ventured out even without his coat. Igor tried to steer him out the door, telling him that he needed some fresh air. Alexander protested that he couldn't move; he felt too sick. "Oh you're lazy, come on," Igor scolded him, "just go for a walk!"

"Don't push him," I whispered, "Can't you see he can't even walk?" Igor asked where his mother was because he needed some money. The cupboard was bare, devoid of even tea or coffee. It was his parents' payday— Eleanora collected a minute pension—and they were cleaned out.

Finally Eleanora appeared, an aging soubrette, still beautiful. "Here I am!" she trilled, a faded but beloved star returning to a loyal public . . . and a new admirer. She rested two big boxes on the table as gingerly as if they were jewel cases and then she registered my presence. "Oh, hello!" Igor introduced us. She had heard about me. "Oh, she's very beautiful. She has beautiful eyes!" It was a ringing accolade that didn't feel like a compliment. "Laura," as friends and family called her, was always so loud that her words were like the audio equivalent of a searchlight trained on you. I felt naked.

"Wonderful, we'll have tea now," Laura announced, "with *everybody*!"

"No, we're too late now," Igor said. "We have to go; we're rushing. We waited too long." He was going to take me home, way across town.

"What do you mean?" Laura bristled. "We have to have tea with the food I brought." They opened one box: there were twenty-five cream-filled éclairs. They opened the other: twenty-five more.

"Mother, where is the food?" Igor yelled. "This is dessert."

"What? It's not good enough for you?" Laura cried.

"Mother we have nothing here, not even bread!" Laura started wailing that she always tried to do good things for people . . . she tried to make a surprise for them, but they didn't understand her . . . they were so cruel! She turned on her heels and walked out the door before Igor or Alexander could ask her for any money.

The bakery was the Elyseyevsky on the Nevsky Prospect, a remnant of the autumnal days of the Romanovs, still clad in vintage marble and chandeliers. It was Laura's haven; probably she had been frequenting it since girlhood. It was one of the few stores in Leningrad that continued after the Revolution to stock baked and canned goods as well as fresh meats and fish, all under one roof. Usually each customer was allowed only five or so pastries. Laura probably had been forced to make a double circuit on line, and weave a yarn: her husband—the *great* tenor, Sashinka Tchernichov, was singing that night and she had to entertain after the performance. The fact was that Laura lived only for the moment and she could sell her soul for sweets.

I never saw Alexander Tchernichov again. His condition worsened and Laura sent him to Saratov, near the Volga River, where his three sisters lived: "If something happens, at least not here." He spent two days alone and ill on the train, arrived in Saratov in extremis, and went directly into the hospital. Only fifty-six, he died there two weeks before Igor's graduation. Igor was forced to miss class and rehearsals to go to Saratov to bury him there. The Maly contributed a fund to pay for the funeral, but Laura pocketed some of the money and went to a spa reserved for performers. Few could afford a week there; however, she managed to stay for an entire month, calling frequently to invite us to come out for a day.

Igor had no food, no father, no mother. He'd come home with me after his rehearsals and we'd talk late into the night, until it was too late for him to catch the last bus. He certainly didn't have enough money for a taxi. My grandmother would put a mattress down on the floor and let him stay over. I think Igor felt more at home with us than at his own house.

§ §

One morning Tyuntina called in sick to the school and told them to let me teach class for her. Perhaps she could see that I had a potential aptitude for teaching. Maybe she wanted to keep me in class because she knew otherwise I'd skip out immediately once I learned she wasn't coming. Sometimes she asked one of her students to come up with a combination to give the class. That was a way of prodding us to think logically as well as ensuring that we paid attention. Stepping in for her that morning wasn't hard for me. I had inherited my father's prodigious memory and could repeat automatically a standard class of hers.

Extracurricular movement classes were often offered to students in many Soviet schools. An elementary school in Leningrad telephoned Nicholas Ter-Stepanov at the Vaganova Institute. Ter-Stepanov taught character dance, and was superintendent for every performance where Vaganova children performed. The kindergarten had already fired two dance teachers and now was requesting that Vaganova send one of its own teachers. Ter-Stepanov called me into his office and told me that instead of going himself he was going to assign me.

I was terrified at the prospect of trying to corral a bunch of small children. Besides, I had reached my final year at Vaganova, and my life was now booby-trapped with final exams. There were eleven in all. During our last two years at the school, we were given a small stipend if we received no grade lower than four out of five. Ter-Stepanov reminded me that if I taught, my stipend would be raised a little bit. "You will be able to help your grandmother . . . It will be a great experience for you," he promised. I really could not say no. I asked Ter-Stepanov what exactly I was supposed to do with the children. "You'll find out yourself," he told me.

Even for professional teachers, beginners are the most difficult students to teach. The onus of responsibility is a heavy one. It is, naturally, much more complicated to explain any theoretical principles to young children, but it's also essential they begin with a correct foundation. Their brains and bodies retain forever what they have absorbed in their elementary classes. If their foundation isn't sound, the students will suffer for the rest of their lives.

To prepare, I thought back to the first-year classes that Tyuntina had given me, but these children were a couple of years younger than first-grade ballet students, and so even elementary ballet was going to be too advanced for their age. I realized how difficult it is for children to maintain their concentration over a long time. How could I make the class interesting for them? They had to enjoy themselves, leave happier than they came in. Adults lap up information voraciously, but children can't swallow too much—they will gag on boredom. I needed to alternate between them standing still for a little piece of training or information and rewarding them with a piece of fun—the freedom to jump and run and work off their energy.

Into the lion's den I went, trying not to show these forty—several classes combined—little bandits that I was trembling. I set them walking then running in circles to the accompaniment of changing rhythms on the piano. Gradually I started to teach them balancé—the waltz preparation—and chassé—a sliding step. They moved slowly in a circle, then faster and faster and faster, until they were laughing, squealing, falling to the ground in heaps. Afterward I immediately put them into a sitting position on the floor to rest, breathe rhythmically, and gently try some basic, proto-balletic arm movements. Then I stood them on their feet again and had them do little jumps without pointing their feet, letting them be just as relaxed as if they were playing in a garden, until they subsided into giggles.

Whenever I felt that their concentration was waning, I'd do something different, ignite an explosion, so that we were switching all the time between release and discipline. Spooning study through fun, work had a good taste, and they could retain what I taught.

For their end-of-term recital I choreographed simple dances to Tchaikovsky's Garland Waltz and a Shostakovich polka. I was told by our own teachers at Vaganova that the polka was the most difficult dance to teach children, but for these kids it worked. A polka uses double chassé on each leg, with tricky changes of arm positions accomplished while clasping a partner; it was a few notches more complicated than the simple chassés that I had already taught them. Their families were happy about the recital, and the children were happy. I, too, was happy that it had turned out well but relieved that it was over. "Why don't you want to do it again?" Ter-Stepanov asked me. But I insisted that I had too much studying to do.

The education we received at Vaganova was superlative, covering every possible base. But I think that a nine-year course of study is too long: it saps your concentration and desire. For years I had assumed that there was so much time ahead that I could miss, skip, put things off. The second half of my final year, however, I worked like a dog. We prepared for our final exams. All of my classes now finally pointed toward a culmination. I finally understood that if my academic or dance grades were bad, I could be posted to the ballet company of some provincial backwater.

In our school theater, Mikhail Mikhailov taught us acting during our final two years at the school. Mikhailov had graduated in 1922; by now he performed mime roles onstage at the Kirov. He had written a classic textbook on acting in ballet. His methods were inherited from Stanislavsky, and he gave us exercises working with imaginary objects. Once he assigned me an incident from Pushkin's *The Queen of Spades*: I would be Lisa running impatiently for an assignation with Gherman. The wings were very shallow, and though I ran onto the stage I was hardly panting. "Breathe, breathe, heavily," he insisted, until finally he told me to run around the circumference of the stage five times so that I would be sufficiently winded.

In the spring of 1958, Mikhailov choreographed a special duet for me and my classmate Nikolai Boyarchikov. It began with him sitting and reading a letter. I appeared, a phantom from his memory. We danced our last dance, we embraced, but soon I slipped out of his arms, leaving him only a sarcastic smile. He returned to reality and burnt the letter.

Mikhailov rehearsed Nikolai and me alone, and he liked acting out Nikolai's part with me. Down to his knees Mikhailov dropped. "Be soft, be more feminine," he coaxed me. "Touch my hair very gently." I stood and looked down at his bald head. "Come on, come on, I don't feel anything! Touch me!" Somehow I did something.

Afterward in the dressing room the girls plied me with questions. "And how was it? What happened?"

"We worked with imaginary objects," I told them, "he kept asking me to touch his hair."

In the pas de deux I was to finally leave Nikolai desolate, despairing on his knees. In my final exit, I was supposed to revel in my victory. "Don't laugh as if you're happy," Mikhailov kept imploring. "Smile like the Mona Lisa." He was a great teacher, but I felt that this schmaltzy piece he had concocted was absurdly out-of-date. Everything was so adamantly realistic. He insisted we burn an actual letter, but our fireman insisted that we couldn't. Mikhailov compromised. "Okay, in rehearsal we won't burn it, but in performance we must!" And so we did.

For my graduation project, Mikhailov assigned me one of Cinderella's mime scenes from Konstantin Sergeyev's 1946 production for the Kirov. I didn't see any histrionic potential in the simpering Cinderella, and I asked if I could instead work on the juicier role of Cinderella's stepmother. He was a little surprised, but he agreed, and picked Yuri Soloviev to play opposite me as Cinderella's henpecked father. Soloviev was my neighbor on

Fontanka Street. I was often at their apartment. Yuri, his younger brother Igor, and their parents lived in one room with an adored German shepherd that looked to me as big as a cow. Yuri and I had played in the courtyard even before we entered the school together. Yuri was always very quiet; his younger brother was more streetwise and outgoing.

For *Cinderella*, we were allowed to create our own costumes. I stacked a tutu under an everyday wool skirt. I wound my hair in a long braid tied with wire and ribbon, extended my nose with Silly Putty, and turned up the makeup volume to drag-queen decibel. Yuri didn't wear a comic makeup; he didn't need to. "Just be yourself," I told him, for he always seemed so very much inside himself. His own forlorn expression was perfect. Our interaction followed the outline of Sergeyev's choreography, but I devised some additional mime to emphasize my stridency and his depression. We played cards: he dealt the deck, we fought, and I threw my cards on the floor. Together with my two daughters, we advanced on him, arms akimbo. The class laughed themselves silly and complimented our creativity.

Since I was tall among my classmates, Pushkin sometimes invited dancers from the Kirov to partner me in his pas de deux class. It was thrilling to work with them. For the pas de deux exam, my partner was Yuri Korneev, a Kirov principal, tall and beautiful. But I also rehearsed with Igor, because he could give me extra help with the double fish dives, where I would plunge almost headlong to the ground into his waiting arms, as well as some of the high lifts that scared me. Sometimes Igor and I would keep practicing until nearly midnight. A couple of days before the exam, Tyuntina peeked into the studio where we worked.

"Wait a minute," Igor said. "We'll do the double fish for you."

Tyuntina said, "Forget it, she can't do a double fish. She's afraid and she's too loose." We did two-and-one-half dives and I finished on his back. "I can't believe it!" Tyuntina said. "Does this mean she's actually taking the exam?"

On the way into the exam itself, I ran into her in the corridor. "And will you dance on pointe?" she asked dubiously. There is no way possible to dance a classical pas de deux on half pointe! But she was sure I would manage somehow to wear ballet slippers rather than pointe, the way I did so often in her class.

I was going to perform the act 3 grand pas de deux from both *Sleeping Beauty* and *Don Quixote*, the White Swan adagio from *Swan Lake*, as well as the bravura Soviet showpiece duet that Vasily Vainonen choreographed to Moritz Mashkovsky's Waltz. We didn't perform the variations and coda, only the entrees and adagios of each pas de deux. There was a lot of tricky partnering involved, but everything went well.

Korneev and I began the exam with *Sleeping Beauty*. The entire class was in the studio, warming up, preoccupied with themselves yet keeping a peripheral eye on their classmates' performance. The jury consisted of every important teacher at the school. Ex-Kirov ballerina Feya Balabina had succeeded Vecheslova as director of the school by now, and she was there, as were Dudinskaya, Sergeyev, Tyuntina, Pushkin, as well as some principal dancers from the Kirov. I was watching Pushkin's reactions as much as I could. It was most important for me to know what he thought. As I danced with Korneev, I saw Pushkin smiling and talking to Tyuntina. When Korneev and I danced close to them, I heard him saying, "She has very beautiful style. But I guess you know that. You've worked with her for nine years."

"No," Tyuntina deadpanned, "she's just a guest in my class."

Our graduation performance took place on the Kirov stage. Pushkin coached Komkova's students for the performance. From Tyuntina's class, he took only me, and selected the *Raymonda* dream pas de deux for me to dance. He gave me compliments that made me feel better and better about myself. During our orchestra rehearsal he sat with Tyuntina on the side of the stage. Pavel Feldt led the orchestra. He was the preeminent conductor at the Kirov, noted as well for his jokes about how unmusical ballet dancers were. Everyone was excited that he would conduct for us.

In *Raymonda* I was to perform a series of jumps diagonally across the stage. Feldt played this passage fast to make it easier for me. But I jumped full out—for maybe the third time in my entire life—and as a result, I finished after the music. Feldt stopped the orchestra: "Let's do it again." He looked up at Tyuntina and Pushkin. "She can jump!" He slowed down the tempo.

For the performance my partner was a classmate named Yasha Batvinik. During the *Raymonda* pas de deux, he was supposed to promenade me twice. The rest we did nicely, but this we fumbled, fumbled, fumbled during the orchestra rehearsal. I kept falling over my leg. Pushkin told me to keep my opposite side steady as I turned. Finally it worked. We finished, and Feldt came up to the stage. "Well, you're very good!" he told me.

But I lacked a true performer's mentality and concentration. Dancing in the studio was for myself and I could enjoy it sometimes. But dancing on stage was living up to my responsibility to others. I was afraid to disappoint the people who put me there, who trusted I could do it.

Nevertheless, our *Raymonda* pas de deux was a success, and I received a good review from one of the city's newspapers. Tyuntina was thrilled; she never thought I'd pull myself together. After the performance, she gave each girl a bouquet tied with a ribbon and a silver-plated spoon hanging from it. In Russia it was a tradition to give children silver spoons when they grew their milk teeth. We were her first graduating class, sprouting milk teeth with our graduation performances.

Yasha and I were scheduled to dance the *Raymonda* pas de deux at each of three graduation performances. Most students were ready to fight for the possibility of dancing even one extra performance on the Kirov stage. But I preferred to observe. I didn't want to be nervous and I didn't want to be up there on stage at all. I thought I had done my job already. Why suffer through two more *Raymonda*s when I could be watching and enjoying? I said my foot hurt, and instead of dancing, I settled into a seat and watched the proceedings. Danced that year by the likes of Sizova, Soloviev, Nureyev, Natalia Makarova, and Nikita Dolgushin, they were spectacular indeed.

A few days later we were going to receive our diplomas. Shelkov came to our class and lectured us about proper dress and decorum. Instead of their gray cadet-like uniform, the boys were going to be allowed to suit up. Not allowed, *ordered*; it was mandatory, like everything else at the school.

"Nureyev!" Shelkov snarled. "Cut your hair and dress nicely! Don't forget, or you won't get your diploma."

However, Rudi showed up for graduation in velvet pants and a black shirt. No jacket. He hadn't cut his hair. There were snickers and nervous giggles from the students, for Rudi looked just like a beatnik, one of those "ugly freaks," the latest perverse offering of Western culture. I was sitting next to him for our class picture. The rest of us struggled to sit erect; Rudi slouched in his chair. "You won't get your diploma," I whispered. "You remember what he told you?"

"We'll see," Rudi murmured. His name was called. He went up and accepted his due. "You see?" he said, settling back into his seat. "Don't ever show you're afraid of them, and then they'll become afraid of *you*."

It was such a relief to finally graduate. No getting up at the crack of dawn, no eleven hours spent every day at Vaganova, no plague of examinations we never had enough time to study for. For years to come, I would dream that an exam was imminent and I wasn't ready. The prison gates were open. I was free . . . or so I thought.

For three years, Igor and I had been a romantic but unconsummated couple. Everybody at the school expected us to marry. They assumed we were only waiting until I had graduated. "When you will be married?" Shelkov asked.

"I am already," I said poker-faced.

"What do you mean, you are? You didn't get your diploma yet!" Staying within the bounds of the permissible was like sidling across a tightrope.

All of Igor's friends, all of my friends pressured me. Tyuntina told me, "You have to get married; it's beautiful; it's wonderful." Even Igor's father, on his deathbed in Saratov, had said to his sisters, "Send hello to that girl with the big blue eyes, *Lucy*, and tell my son I want him to marry her."

In my heart I had already committed myself to Igor. But I wasn't ready to officially marry; instead I wanted to live with him. When I told my grandmother that she was beside herself. I had seen her so upset only once before, when I slept over at a girlfriend's and didn't call because the girl had no phone. Babooliah's parents had selected a husband for her when she was fifteen; my mother married at eighteen. This was thus now the perfect time. I insisted that I wanted to be free. "What do you mean— to be free? Do you want people to think you're 'a woman on the loose'?"

"Living with the same man, like a family, but without this piece of paper—that means I'm a tramp?"

"Absolutely!" I would be a second-class woman all my life, she insisted; the stigma would haunt me forever.

Perhaps she was right. An unwed mother, an unmarried sexually active woman, was shunned throughout the republics. In Georgia on the wedding night the men still paraded in the street with bloodied sheets. When

I was an adult I had a friend, a gynecologist who made a fortune going down to Georgia to sew up soon-to-be married girls who had strayed.

In Russia we had a story: a little boy asks his mother where children come from. "Sometimes the bird brings them, sometimes parents find them sitting in the middle of the flowers, all different ways. Sometimes you buy them in the store."

"Well," the boy says, "you mean in this big building with all these people, nobody's screwing?" At least not so that anyone should know! Nobody was allowed to talk about sex and nobody was prepared. When I was around five, my mother said, "I was in the country and one morning I came out into the kitchen garden. I saw a huge cabbage. Right in the middle sat a beautiful girl with huge eyes. I knew I had to have her." A cabbage? I couldn't relate. Why, I asked her, had I heard about this tall bird with long legs, who made a nest on the roof?

But now as a teenager, I was reading Hemingway's *The Sun Also Rises* and was full of Lady Brett Ashley, a woman who called her own shots, whereas to Russian girls marriage meant being dominated. In peasant and blue-collar families, women still repeated the old cliché that if your husband didn't beat you, he didn't love you. Well, no husband was going to beat *me*! But still I knew I'd be hamstrung by this marriage business.

Igor didn't want us just to live together; he wanted his stamp on my passport. One day in June he suggested that we just go and check how this marriage process worked. "Somehow I don't even want to go inside this building," I said, but I went with him to the registry housed in an old mansion at the intersection of Nevsky Prospect and my own Fontanka Street, near the famous Anitchkev Bridge, guarded by four equestrian statues. Igor, in fact, all but forced me to come along. We opened the doors and I was shocked to see all of his friends laden with flowers and champagne.

Papers were brought to us. "Just sit here and sign," I was instructed. You had to sign an application stipulating the day that you wanted to marry. I signed, since I didn't want to spoil everyone's fun, but I thought it wouldn't *really* mean that I was married. Igor's friends uncorked champagne and we both imbibed and laughed at the corniness. The registry worker asked me which name I wanted to sign, and I started to write my own name. It actually wasn't uncommon for Russian women to retain their maiden names.

"Oh, no, no, you have to change your name," Igor said. I told him that I would prefer to keep my own. But he was vehement. "You don't want to have a German name in Russia! It will spoil your career!"

It turned out that I had indeed just signed my marriage certificate. We came back to my home and more friends of ours were waiting with food and presents.

Tyuntina arrived with a beautiful silk nightgown for me. It was very pale pink, as decorative as an evening gown. In those years in northern Russia it was very difficult to buy fruit out of season and strawberries at any time. You were forced to pay through the nose, and even then the only way to get them at all was to stand on line at the open-air farmer's market. But Tyuntina arrived with a huge crystal tray piled high with strawberries, covered with cellophane, garnished with ribbons. Everybody oohed and aahed, and I went to open the tray and put it out on the table. But Tyuntina wouldn't hear of it. "Absolutely not!" she insisted. "You'll eat them tomorrow morning, in bed, by yourselves."

~ 8 ~

newlywed

We moved with my grandmother into what Russians call a three-room apartment: two bedrooms, a living room, and kitchen, in a modern building, a "Kruschevka" that was a twenty-minute walk to the theater. My grandmother had her own room and no longer had to work. I was pleased that in her final few years, I was finally able to help make her life easier.

She never quite shook the habits of the ancien regime. Under Communism, "servant" was stricken from our vocabulary, but I was one of the fortunate few in Russia who had a cleaning woman and a nurse. They lived in outlying cities and could get permission to relocate in Leningrad if an employer would vouch for them. "Gala is coming today" was how I put it, but somehow "servant" kept escaping from my grandmother. "Babooliah, you know we don't use that word anymore; it's not nice," I would say.

"Okay," she'd reply, until the next time the taboo tumbled out.

I was accepted into the Kirov after my graduation performance. I didn't want to dance professionally, but I thought I would resign myself to it for a while and the find a way to escape to college. But I was already coaching Igor informally, and for me that was much more interesting than thinking about dancing myself. Igor had perfect physical proportions. His torso, his arms, his legs were beautiful and expressive. His jump wasn't exceptional, but by the standard of the time Igor's technique was very strong. He had one of the best grande pirouettes I've seen: he could reel off thirty-two flawless, rapid revolutions, and then finish with a cyclone of pirouettes—seven, or sometimes as many as nine, which is still impressive today. But above all he was a great artist on stage, the centrifugal force holding the stage action together. The emotional contact he made with his fellow dancers on stage was extraordinary.

Igor danced two, three, sometimes four full-length performances a month. It was a lot, but because the ballet shared each performance week with the opera, and because we had so many principal dancers in the two-hundred-member company, it could be months before he danced a particular ballet again. And so if Igor wasn't really catching fire in the first act of a full-length ballet, I would worry that it was going to be a lost performance. Once I went seething into the wings at intermission and started an argument with him about nothing at all, although the performance he'd given really had made me angry.

"Let's go to my dressing room," Igor said.

"No, I'm not going with you!" I hissed. Shocked murmurs from the dancers standing nearby registered my audacity in disrupting a principal dancer's mood during a performance. I walked back to the audience shaking. The second act started and Igor appeared on stage like a tempest. And from that time on, after a great performance by Igor, dancers would ask me, "Did you have a scandal with him tonight?"

After Igor's graduation performance in 1956, Galina Ulanova had come backstage to congratulate him. She told him that she wanted him to partner her, and soon after he received an official invitation from the Bolshoi. He was thrilled, and people around the Kirov told him that he'd be crazy not to accept. Ulanova was then the most powerful figure in Soviet ballet. Igor would have become a bigger star at the Bolshoi, but even so his career at the Kirov progressed rapidly because every ballerina adored dancing with him. The Kirov had always been and would remain a matriarchy, and Igor was one of the greatest partners in the history of the company. Already at age fourteen he could do the trickiest lift. He was perfectly built to partner a ballerina. Men with a long upper body tend to rely too much on their torso to lift a ballerina, with the result that each time they lift, their upper bodies turn wooden. But Igor had a short, powerful back; he used his back's latissimi muscles and his thighs, and as a result his torso and arms stayed free. He was able to keep dancing in the lift, to incorporate the partnering as part of the movement flow. You would not see the gears turning—"the kitchen," as it's called in Russia.

His partnering abilities were put to the test when he began dancing with Alla Shelest. The dancers always said that her partner was not a partner but a victim. In school, we were taught to plié before a lift and let our own resistance stabilize the lift as we went into the air. Shelest didn't signal her partner with a plié and she didn't offer him resistance. She vaulted into his arms looking spontaneous, impassioned, uncontained. But her unbroken stream of movement from ground to air made it difficult for the man to hold her in a beautiful position that was comfortable for her and for him. Igor could handle any weight, however, no matter how it was distributed. He knew every trick to make a lift look effortless. He and Shelest were extremely musical; a shared sensitivity to rhythm and melodic timing helped them to synchronize.

Shelest was probably the only Russian ballerina who never looked directly into her partner's eyes. Eye contact must have allowed unprofessional reality to intrude in the temple of art that she created on stage. A partner as involved and connected as Igor found it disturbing. Yet to the audience, she could send a much stronger message of love, of unity, than some other ballerinas who looked for a personal rapport onstage. Even if she looked *through* him, Igor felt touched by the power emanating from her. They completed each other. He had the shapely legs Shelest didn't have. He gave her security; she gave him rationality. He was a very good natural actor; she was unnatural, aesthetic. He made her a little warmer; sometimes he even succeeded in meeting her eyes. He was twenty years younger, and with him she felt fresh.

Once, Shelest and Igor went to Hungary for a concert tour. They were booked for thirty performances. "She will never make it," Igor said to me. "I don't know what we're going to do." A small suitcase packed entirely with medications went with Shelest. Miraculously, she didn't miss one performance, largely, I think, because of Igor's emotional support. He was one of the few to whom Shelest extended the luxury or the burden of sharing her struggles. One could see her hypochondria as a capricious demand for attention, but even when ill or injured, she never acted like a victim. I never thought of her as a victim, despite what she was forced to endure. Her queenly pose may have been just that—a pose—but her self-respect was genuine.

During these years Shelest invited us for dinner a number of times. She lived in Petrogradskaya, a neighborhood overlooking the Neva, across the river from the Hermitage. The apartment was about four rooms, which was spacious by our standards at the time. The ceilings were high and windows looked out on the river. Shelest was very much mistress of her own home; even with Grigorovich she seemed a little distant and controlling.

Over dinner, dipping bread into a glass of vodka, she asked my opinions on art, architecture, sculpture—but never asked me any personal questions. The apartment was filled with books. One night Shelest showed me the medal she had won for academic scholarship, a citation unheard of at the Vaganova Institute, at least in my time. She told us about what it was like to dance with the Kirov when they were evacuated to Perm during World War II. The theater was heated badly, if at all. In the wings the ballerinas piled fur coats over their tutus and winter boots over their pointe shoes, shedding their insulation only seconds before their entrance. The audience watched in their hats and coats. Onstage the ballerinas' shoulders turned blue as they watched the audience exhaling clouds of vapor.

As I came of age, the Kirov aesthetic was also evolving, due in part to the fact that in 1955, Fyodor Lopukhov became our artistic director for the third time in his long career. Decades earlier, Lopukhov had been instrumental in introducing sportive movements into ballet. In 1927, he had choreographed *The Maiden* for Olga Mungalova, who was called upon to arch her back and curl her leg behind her ear like a cat. It was then that Russian ballet training began to incorporate gymnastics. In our class, Tyuntina told us that we should work to improve our flexibility by stretching after class, doing splits on the floor—all this had been heresy when she had started her own training before the Revolution. During the 1920s, costumes had also begun moving closer to the body, scaling down to tights. Elaborate costumes had symbolized everything the Revolution was against; in its aftermath, the aesthetic would favor simplicity.

During the 1930s and 1940s, Vaganova's teaching invariably worked to highlight the physical and interpretative individuality of her students. She wasn't concerned with ideal bodies; she looked above all for strong, distinctive personalities. But in 1957, Yuri Grigorovich, a reverent student of Lopukhov and his work, choreographed Prokofiev's *The Stone Flower* for the Kirov. As the Mistress of the Copper Mountain, chatelaine of a mythical kingdom to which she spirits the sculptor Danila, Alla Osipenko appeared in her unitard like a celestial sculpture. Osipenko's figure was a dream; in Russia I never saw a body quite like hers. And once more the pendulum was swinging back to Lopokhov's aesthetic.

I watched many *Stone Flower* rehearsals because Grigorovich worked out much of the role of the young hero Danila on Igor, although Alexander

Gribov danced the opening night. Grigorovich began creating the role of Katerina, Danila's peasant sweetheart, on Shelest, after which Irina Kolpakova joined rehearsals and danced the premiere. Even when Grigorovich was not choreographing on Shelest, she was frequently at the rehearsals. As he had during *Valse Fantasie*, he consulted her continuously. She was not a choreographer, but to my mind she was as creative as one. To Grigorovich she provided a crucial resource for information, ideas, and an exchange of thoughts.

Following the premiere, Shelest gave alternating performances of the two leads—she remains the sole Kirov ballerina to dance both Kolpakova's and Osipenko's roles. Sheathed in the Mistress's unitard, Shelest could not embody Osipenko's physical splendor, but her movement was an uncanny illustration of the sinewy musculature visible through the sleek skin of a reptile. As Katerina she was tragic and tender, yet fierce when she had to protect herself and her love from an evil bailiff. She showed the will as well as the innocence of this peasant maiden.

The first time Igor danced *Stone Flower* with Shelest as Katerina I went to wish him luck shortly before the curtain. When I walked into the wings I could not believe my eyes. Shelest was shaking, pale, clutching Igor's arm to steady herself. That was why Igor both did and did not like dancing with her. She was always so nervous, sometimes even when they were onstage, that he often felt he had to protect her rather than engage her as an equal.

Igor and she were often paired in Leonid Jacobson's choreography. Jacobson was the rare example of a choreographer whose new work could actually find a foothold in the Kirov repertory, but his career was continuously kept in check by the authorities.

In 1958, Jacobson unveiled *Triptych on Themes of Rodin*, set to Debussy, which was pure aestheticism of a kind that seemed radical in the climate of the day. The curtain rose on three couples, each one more gorgeous than the last, each frozen in the poses of Rodin's sculptures. Ninel Petrova and Anatoly Nisnevich were "Eternal Spring," Osipenko and Vsevold Oukhov "The Kiss," and Igor and Shelest "The Eternal Idol." The three spotlights dimmed to one and "Eternal Spring" came to life, dancing love's awakening. Then we saw "The Kiss," two lovers under moonlight. "The Eternal Idol" was the culmination of mature, monumental love, employing a plastique derived from Rodin and reminiscent of Isadora Duncan. Igor was a slave of love, but sometimes Shelest became his subject, before they fused back into their opening pose. "The Eternal Idol" was quintessential Shelest, decidedly erotic but always impeccably aesthetic.

In 1958, Boris Fenster replaced Lopukhov as artistic director of the Kirov. Fenster was a good choreographer in the *dramballet* vein who had choreographed extensively for both the Kirov and the Maly. He was married to Galina Shena, a beautiful ballerina in the Maly. Fenster was then forty-two. He brought to the Kirov a kindly and avuncular temperament as well as a forward-looking aesthetic vision. He started taking more tall girls into the company, beginning to change the company's look so that it more closely resembled the long-stemmed one that Balanchine was cultivating at New York City Ballet.

Fenster staged several of his own ballets for the Kirov, and he somehow persuaded the powers-that-be to allow Kasyan Goleizovsky back into the mainstream, after virtually decades filled largely with provincial exile provoked by his aestheticism, his refusal to espouse programmatic content. Goleizovsky began work on *Amour and Terpsichore*, a duet for Igor and Osipenko. The great choreographer whose recital piece for my class had been so memorable was back in the studio creating a very intricate, very beautiful pas de deux. And then suddenly he wasn't. The duet was aborted; he was not allowed to finish choreographing, obviously because objections had come from up high. During the 1960s, Goleizovsky's *Joseph the Beautiful* was revived at the Bolshoi for Vladimir Vasiliev. When I saw it on tape some years later, I thought it doubly unjust that his work wasn't represented in the Kirov repertory.

Fenster was a nurturing authority figure for both Igor and me. He invited us to dinner several times. "Go into my bedroom," he said once, "and take some money from the dresser."

"*No*, we can't," we protested.

"Yes, don't worry about it," he insisted, "I have more than enough, and you need it right now. If you earn a lot, you can pay me back." We tiptoed in and borrowed two hundred rubles: that would have been at the time two hundred dollars. We did need it badly. I can't remember if we tried to pay him back, but I'm sure that if we had, he would never have accepted it. Truly I had never met anyone like Boris Fenster.

my son

In adulthood, Rudi Nureyev was fond of recalling how, soon after graduating from Vaganova, he had found someone to teach him English. He made rapid progress, and so he decided to try French as well. He located an old lady who agreed to instruct him on a quid pro quo basis in which he would clean her room in a rambling communal apartment. She didn't have a bathroom in her own small room, and one of his duties would have been emptying her chamber pot. "I was already a ballerina," Rudi recalled, "and I thought, No way do I pick up somebody else's shit! And you know what?" he said to me, decades later, in his Paris apartment, overlooking the Louvre, "I still don't know French. If you want to learn something, you have to eat shit."

But back in those early days at the Kirov, Rudi wasn't reflecting; he was too busy making his own rules, outraging his elders. He told us that he wasn't going to join the Kirov as a member of the corps de ballet, the way the rest of us had. "You will see, you will see," he promised his classmates.

Rudi and Alla Sizova had scored a triumph at our graduation performance, dancing the *Corsaire* pas de deux. Alla looked like Ingrid Bergman and danced with a pure young fervor. She had a warmth and honesty onstage that reminded me of the Kirov's Lubov Voichnis, whose *Beauty* had so enchanted me as a girl. Sizova jumped like a bullet whistling into the air: she was high above the ground without letting you see how she'd gotten there (with minimal plié, à la Balanchine). Rudi swarmed around her like a panther, and his still very raw technique didn't detract at all from the impact he made.

And then, just as Rudi had promised, Fenster produced a soloist contract for Rudi. It was a rare, almost unheard of event. Fenster began giving Rudi principal roles as well as a full complement of solo places. Most of the dancers and staff carped, saying Rudi lacked the classical purity the Kirov was noted for. Next to the poised correctness of Konstantin Chati-

lov or Vladilen Semyonov, Rudi was wild and wooly, and at the same time
decried by many for being too feminine.

Just a year after graduating, Rudi was already slated to do the full-length
Don Quixote. Igor had danced the act 3 grand pas de deux at his graduation
but hadn't yet been given a shot at the complete ballet. Igor complained to
Fenster, who loved Igor but told him he had to wait. Fenster didn't come
out and tell Igor this, but nonetheless, compared to Rudi, Igor bore the
stamp of the old school. Igor was elegant, his positions were precise. He
blazed with temperament and sex appeal, but his energy was more conventional than Rudi's. For Igor was a man onstage and Rudi was amphibi-
ous. We were entering a new era, and Nureyev was a beacon of the future.

Igor and I sat in the company box to watch Rudi's debut. He appeared
in the traditional black wig and short pants, like medieval trunk hose,
with naked legs stained brown by makeup, and black shoes. None of it
was very flattering. He danced the first little duet with his Kitri, Ninel
Kurgapkina, and they made their exit. A brief pantomime passage was
due to follow soon after. Kurgapkina arrived back onstage on cue. Rudi
didn't. "Where is Nureyev?" the box sputtered: "Did he forget?" Kurgapkina carried on by herself, improvising some stage business and making
a quick exit.

When the first act ended, everyone in the box ran on stage and I followed. "I'm a dancer. I'm not a mime," Rudi was telling the theater command as I arrived. "The mime's not important, anyway. I just don't care
about it." He strutted off to his dressing room, leaving them speechless.

The second act went without further transgression. Rudi didn't dance
cleanly, not at all; instead the audience was pleasurably on tenterhooks,
holding its breath every time he leapt or turned. But each time he managed to land on both feet and the audience cheered.

The last intermission stretched from twenty minutes into eternity. Nobody understood what was happening. Finally, I hurried back to the wings
once again. "They're all talking to Nureyev," someone said. "He doesn't
want to go onstage."

I walked across to the opposite side of the stage. His dressing room
door was open; I eavesdropped from the corridor. Surrounded by flowers,
Rudi slumped in his chair, his legs propped with lordly nonchalance on
the dressing table. Fenster was ill, but Sergeyev was there, and Mikhail

Mikhailov, who coached this ballet. Rudi's dresser was standing by patiently, Rudi's short pants in his hands. Rudi was being told that he had to wear them or he wasn't going back on stage. But Rudi was blasé. "Replace me with anyone you want. I'm not going onstage in them. They're ugly. I'm doing a classical variation and they make my legs look short."

The administration dithered awhile looking for a replacement before circling back once more to Rudi, who absolutely refused to budge. "Only without pants." Rudi was told that he was going to be punished but still the performance had to go on. I ran back to the box. Already it seemed someone had leaked the news among the audience. There was a knowing rustle in the audience and then rhythmic, impatient applause.

The theater *cabine* filed back into the box. The act began. Rudi sprung onstage to a chorus of gasps. He looked naked. The company box erupted with oaths of revenge; he was going to be fired immediately! But at the final curtain, the applause was oceanic.

Rudi's legs were naturally extremely turned out, and he worked to maximize his turnout even at the expense of his partnering. You can't really be a good partner and stand turned out behind the ballerina; it doesn't give the man as much support as when his legs are planted in a position closer to parallel. Men at the Kirov were supposed to care more about the ballerina than about showing themselves off to maximum advantage. To carry the ballerina, they needed the big muscles that the slow, heavy men's classes developed. But after Rudi's success, the Kirov's male dancers started to stretch themselves more to raise their extensions and began concentrating more on improving their turnout.

Nureyev was both always himself and true to the roles he danced. It was in the West that he began to try to go deeper into ballet, but already in Russia he had genius intuition and powers of observation. Even at the Kirov, I think he did understand the difference between Siegfried in *Swan Lake*, a creature of German Gothic; Prince Desiré in *Sleeping Beauty*, an incarnation of the Sun King; and Albrecht in *Giselle*, who is a German Romantic as conceived by the French and then transposed into Russian Biedermeier time. His carriage, his gestures, his walk were subtly different when he danced each prince.

After I'd been hired by the Kirov in 1958, I learned that Valentin Shelkov had continued paying my Komsomol dues for me, despite the fact that I'd never rejoined after my one-year suspension. No dancer who was not a Komsomol member could join the company. "What do you think," Shelkov said to me, "I wanted to destroy your entire life?"

But after Fenster's kindness to Igor and me, I had to tell him when I found out that I was pregnant. I hadn't yet signed my contract. He explained that Kirov regulations would not permit him to hire me knowing that I was going to be out of shape almost immediately.

Our son Alexei was born in December 1959. At age twenty I knew nothing about how to be a mother. I had no model to emulate. And so I was forced to improvise, as much as when I'd first gone to teach children several years earlier.

I wanted him to love to read as much as I did. I saw that when families forced their child to learn, the child often became resistant, until sometimes their appetite for reading was ruined altogether. And so I tried to be very careful with Alyosha. The first book I read to him was Jack London's *Smoke Bellew*, which I had loved when I was a child. Then I started Oscar Wilde's "The Nightingale and the Rose." He laughed and cried, until I snapped the book shut in the most interesting clinch. "Well, I don't have time now; read it yourself." Then he'd continue on his own.

From the time he was very little, I took him to museums frequently. At five, Alyosha's favorite painter was Bosch. His canvases swarmed with so many images that it was possible for a child to watch one for any length of time and still discover something new—it was like suddenly finding the right puzzle piece. Igor and I had a friend, Marc Jebijian, a French citizen whose parents were French and Armenian. He studied at the Vaganova Institute for four years. Whenever he went home to France he returned to Russia laden with records and art books that we couldn't get in Leningrad. Marc brought us a Bosch album, and if I needed to keep Alyosha occupied I would give him Bosch and he might spend hours turning the pages.

Alyosha's appetite was very poor. It was torturous to try to get him to eat. He didn't like sweets, he didn't like even mashed potatoes with caviar. My mother-in-law would spoon-feed him, saying the way one does to children, "Eat one spoon for mother, and another for father, and for grandmother." But Laura's most fervent coaching, I discovered one day, was reserved for the memory of a man she regarded as nearly divine.

Alyosha was sitting with a bowl of soup. He didn't want any of it.

"Alyosha," she coaxed. "Who told you that you have to eat soup? Alyosha, who told you?" Laura tried to please me when I was in her presence. I think that what she was trying to coax out of Alyosha this day was a "Mama." But what came out of Alyosha's mouth instead was something else altogether, a weary "You mean—Lenin?"

cultural exchange

In the fall of 1960, Boris Fenster had been choreographing *Masquerade*, a new ballet for the Kirov based on Lermontov's play. Shortly before the premiere, however, he suffered a heart attack. He was convalescing in Kamorova, in the countryside near the Gulf of Finland, at the same artist's spa that Igor's mother Laura had visited after his father died. Igor and I went to spend a couple of days with him there. "What do you think?" he asked us when we visited him at Kamorova in December. Should he come to the premiere of his ballet, *Masquerade*?

"No, of course not," we told him. "You'll be too nervous, stay here, we'll let you know how it goes." His wife was also trying to persuade him not to go, but he wanted to very much.

Dudinskaya was cast as Baroness Stralle, dancing the premiere opposite Sergeyev and Ninel Petrova. In Russia, when a new ballet was premiered, bows were taken after the second act. Fenster appeared in the wings toward the end of the act, and a chair was brought for him. He sat down and a few minutes later he was dead of another heart attack—at the age of only forty-four. Dudinskaya wanted the performance to continue. "We have to be professional!" she insisted. The performance did go on. His death was announced only after act 3.

At a later performance of *Masquerade*, the conductor Evgeny Dubovskoi died during the first act, also of a heart attack. This time, Seva Oukhov was dancing Sergeyev's role. The orchestra ground to a halt and Oukhov finished his scene to silence and then the curtain was lowered. After that, everyone dancing *Masquerade* became apprehensive that they were tempting a third death, because God was believed to be partial to threes. The ballet didn't last long in the repertory.

After Fenster's death, Yuri Grigorovich was appointed an assistant or deputy artistic director very briefly, and then full authority returned to Konstantin Sergeyev six years after he had relinquished the position to Fyodor Lopukhov. The Kirov's young dancers were disappointed, because we were convinced that the future lay with Grigorovich, who soon after left for Moscow and the Bolshoi. But Sergeyev hated Lopukhov's and Grigorovich's choreography. In Sergeyev's kingdom, only the classics were crowned. He thought Grigorovich's new aesthetic was cold and formalistic, with its indebtedness to sportive and acrobatic movements. But he wanted to show he, too, was on the cutting edge; in 1963 he tried to outdo Grigorovich by making *The Distant Planet*. It was very much under Lopukhov's influence, only it was hysterically awful. The idea, somehow representing cosmonauts as well as avatars of the outer galaxies, together with Boris Miezel's music was abysmal.

In his early fifties, Sergeyev didn't let people get too close to him. His own son Nikolai, offspring of his earlier marriage to Kirov ballerina Feya Balabina, was required to request an audience with him, sometimes two months in advance. Sergeyev would specify the exact day and minute when Kola could come and see his father and talk to him for fifteen minutes.

Sergeyev never showed any agitation, inevitably evincing a lordly calm and detachment. He had a way of talking above you that left an overpowering impression on anyone who dealt with him. He made them feel Lilliputian, and this despite the fact that he wasn't tall at all.

Sergeyev liked Igor very much. Even before Sergeyev had officially retired from performing, he allowed Igor to dance the roles he himself had created in *The Bronze Horseman*, and in Sergeyev's own *The Path of Thunder*. Igor even danced them a few times opposite Dudinskaya, who was by now also at the very end of her long career. Most of the company was so angry at her for clinging to roles that belonged to women half her age that we could no longer appreciate her artistry. But looking back I realize how expertly Dudinskaya plied her stagecraft so that she was still able to give believable performances.

At one point in *The Path of Thunder*, Igor was required by the action to slap Dudinskaya. She was to turn her head away so that her face would only by brushed by his hand. At a certain performance, however, he slapped her a moment too soon so that he clipped the end of her long nose. Her nose was stinging red, and her eyes smarted with tears. Naturally, he apologized profusely afterward, but Dudinskaya was unfazed.

"Oh, no, no, I understand; it's theater." It seemed that the entire company, however, was thrilled, thinking he had done it on purpose. Igor enjoyed a reigning interval as company hero.

§ ℰ

London had always seemed to me like a dream capital. A monarchy remained in place there. I imagined that the city was *Sleeping Beauty* come to life. I was convinced that I would somehow live there one day. I was thrilled that Igor would be dancing on the Kirov's tour to Europe in the spring of 1961. He could see London for me.

Dudinskaya and Sergeyev had originally intended to give themselves the same exposure on the stages of Paris and London as they enjoyed at the Kirov, but both were now fifty and they discovered to their chagrin that the European impresarios did not want them performing. Dudinskaya's prestige had to be maintained; we were told only that the tour had been reconceived and would feature only the company's younger roster. Shelest was only forty-two at the time, but she, too, was scratched from the tour. To Igor she complained bitterly about Dudinskaya's machinations. Both in Paris and London Igor enjoyed an enormous success.

Nureyev's defection in Paris was a revolutionary movement for us. Once again his courage won my admiration. Russians were so used to living in close proximity to their families that Nureyev cleaving himself from the native community could, in most Russian eyes, mean only certain spiritual but also even literal death for him. "You've betrayed the Motherland. You've betrayed our family"—this was the kind of comment that any kind of independent action prompted. And so Rudi's defection was seen as a kind of suicide. But I don't think that Rudi had ever seen himself as inextricably entwined with any family, whether professional, personal, or national. From the moment he arrived in Leningrad, he seemed like he was truly on his own.

Igor and I had been simply too young, too much the product of erratic parenting, to get married; we were frequently demanding and capricious with each other. He was always jealous and I was just as possessive. After returning to Russia from London, the Kirov was scheduled to leave in September for a three-month visit to America, but Igor didn't want to go, afraid to leave me alone for that long, afraid that I would somehow stray the moment that he was out of sight. But I was also longing for all the beautiful clothes Igor was sure to bring me from America. Whenever he went abroad—he had already been with the Kirov to not only London but Egypt and Japan as well—nearly everything he brought back was for me, hardly anything for himself. But the moment I began urging him to go, he believed that his jealousy was entirely justified. "There is absolutely no way I will leave you for three months."

For an entire month, Sergeyev talked to Igor: the country and the party believed in him and trusted him. It was his duty to prove that we were the world's outstanding ballet company. But Igor remained obstinate, and the Kirov left for America without him.

The American tour was also a great success; however, after Europe, the dancers were dazzled by America but many did not find it all that congenial. When they came back to Leningrad they complained that New York was so dirty that while crossing the street swirling newspapers stuck to their legs. Both on this tour and again when they returned to the United States in 1964, they were traumatized by the cement stages of theaters across the United States, so much less yielding and resilient than the wood floors of Russian opera houses. The company believed it was these hard stages that led to the back injury that plagued Alla Sizova for the remainder of her career.

A year after the Kirov made its New York debut, in October 1962, New York came to us when New York City Ballet made its first visit to Russia. Over the years, Laura Tchernichova had on occasion chattered about a "Choura . . . Chouritchka . . . Choura Danilova"—she was referring, I eventually learned, to Alexandra Danilova, who had left Russia in 1924 and became prima ballerina in Europe and America with the emigré Ballets Russes companies. Laura and Danilova had been in the same class at the school and had been good friends, immediately before, during, and after the Revolution. Fooling around before ballet class they would dance their pas de deux together, Laura always partnering Choura, for Laura's angel face belied the strength of a bull. Laura enjoyed Choura and her sarcastic tongue, but didn't have much time for their classmate—later Choura's common-law husband—George Balanchine. (I wonder if Balanchine was recalling Laura's and Choura's pranks when he made *Symphonie Concertante* in 1945 and included a similar passage for the two ballerinas!) Laura was baffled when Balanchine returned triumphant to Russia with his company. A great choreographer? A genius? And so many Western wives? But he always chased the most beautiful girls in the school, she told us, and they didn't want him. He'd come to class early and play piano, and for her he was too much the egghead poseur. (Laura loved reading Fitzgerald and Hemingway, but she was no intellectual.) Balanchine wasn't a great classical dancer, Laura said; once she had offered him half an apple if he could do a double tour. He tried and failed and received no apple. Besides, his face was covered with pimples, she recalled. Someone so gauche, so afflicted couldn't possibly have become famous!

Laura's biases notwithstanding, Balanchine was now the world's most influential choreographer. Yet because he had left Russia, he was a nonperson in the Soviet Union. At school we barely heard his name, only briefly from Marietta Frangopolo, who had also been his classmate. For a long time we actually thought that he was dead, because we associated him so closely with Diaghilev and the Ballets Russes of the 1920s. Diaghilev's emigré company was attractive and mysterious for us, because it was taboo. We looked at the old pictures in Marietta's museum and plied her with questions.

I imagined that Balanchine himself would look like these old photos of Diaghilev, that he would arrive swathed in fur and jewels, a cowering entourage in tow. But when I slipped into the wings to watch him rehearse his company onstage before their opening, was I ever surprised! Balanchine was dressed humbly, casually, with a little scarf tied around his neck. He didn't look magisterial; he looked shy and a little bit lost. I bumped into him on the stairs and gaped, trying to somehow absorb from him something of the flavor of Western life.

Many of the older teachers and dancers were skeptical about the visitors from New York. To them, everything Balanchine was doing was incorrect. They thought he was unmusical because he began one dance phrase in the middle of the parallel musical one, letting that same dance phrase cut into the next musical figure. They thought the prancy little walks on pointe that the girls did were circusy. They thought his pas de chat was wrong because his dancers didn't sit in the air the way we did, both legs bent; instead they extended the front leg straight.

But the students and the Kirov's younger dancers were skylarking with joy. Georgi Balanchivadze, who had been trained at our own school, brought us *this*—a new concept, a new language of classical ballet: no mime, pure dancing, a meld of classical and jazz and modern dance on pointe. There were steps we'd never seen before, a freedom from the classical positions that we'd never dreamed of. I was ready to follow him to New York to watch more performances and see the city.

Dressing room debates were frequent and continued well after the company's return to New York. "But what is correct?" I asked the elder skeptics. "What do you think is correct? Only *Sleeping Beauty*?"

Detractors would say, "You just can't put this step together with that one; it's illogical."

"He doesn't have your logic; he has his own," was my retort. During their season I went to a press conference where he talked a little bit about how he choreographed and ran his school. People asked silly questions, but I didn't listen very much; I just watched him, how he talked, how he moved. It was all a riveting dumb show for me until I saw choreographer Leonid Jacobson, who was Balanchine's exact contemporary, raise his hand and ask, "Please, can you tell me from where you get your choreographic inspiration—these amazing ideas?"

Jacobson was arrogant and never free with compliments. But that day, he met his match. Balanchine looked at him sarcastically. He already knew Jacobson was a choreographer, but he hadn't seen any of his work and he didn't care about his compliments. "Well, it all comes from God," Balanchine said, in a tone that implied, "How can you ask a question like that? How can I tell you from where I take my inspiration? If *you're* a choreographer and you don't know, neither do I."

Balanchine's answer was startling because at this time the government wasn't letting us give any credit to God. Jacobson sat right down again. But it wasn't over yet: someone asked Balanchine who were his favorite choreographers. "Petipa and Goleizovsky." Jacobson undoubtedly felt humiliated. But Petipa's vocabulary was, of course, the wellspring for Balanchine's neoclassicism, while he had seen Goleizovsky's work in the early twenties and always said how much it had influenced him. Studying Balanchine's work during their season, I could see myself the traces of Goleizovsky's handwriting all over Balanchine's asymmetric counterpoint in the corps.

A couple of days later, I heard that Balanchine's wife was very sick, was in fact dying, and he had to fly back to New York immediately. That's why he looked so sad, I thought to myself. I was heartbroken for him. His then-wife, ex-ballerina Tanaquil Le Clercq, had indeed been tragically stricken with polio—but six years earlier. What really happened, I learned only years later, reading his biographies, was that Balanchine was so spooked by midnight phone calls and bugging courtesy of the KGB, and so overcome by encounters with his past, that he fled back to the United States, rejoining his company's Russian tour after about a week's rest in New York.

For me, the highlight of the entire NYCB season was Allegra Kent as Balanchine's *La Sonnambula*: a moonstruck maiden blind to a poet's overtures, his confusion, his desperation that she will not respond. Kent summoned a spirituality so poignant, so fragile, that it was as if it could gutter like the candle she held to light her path. Every movement seemed unrepeatable. I saw every performance she gave; I wanted to somehow impress irrevocably upon my brain every single step of hers. Leningrad presented her with the greatest triumph of any ballerina on that tour.

It was as though a dim image somewhere in the back of my mind finally came clearly into focus. Kent revealed a quality I'd seen flashes of in Russian ballerinas, in Ulanova, in Shelest, as well as in performances by the Kirov's Emma Menchyonok. Allegra was a spirit descending from another plane, a musical essence, not a character, and that was a revelation, having been raised in a repertory that was top-heavy with story ballets. And Russian ballerinas were usually very much palpable in *Giselle*. We had all seen the famous nineteenth-century lithographs, where Carlotta Grisi looked as if she had barely touched the floor. But that quality had become lost. In our day, ballerinas who danced Giselle were told that they were spirits, but coached to do everything very concretely. They tried to convey an impression of weightlessness, but what they did felt so confined to me. Often the second act seemed like a static recreation of the airborne poses of those famous old lithographs.

Something quite different, however, had been seen on the Kirov stage in 1958, when the Paris Opera's Liane Daydé made a guest appearance as Giselle, partnered by Sergeyev himself. The Khrushchev thaw allowed a steady stream of ballet visitors from abroad. Each and every one was something novel for me and I loved them all. No one was more enchanting than Daydé, however. She was twenty-six and looked like a true incarnation of this young, innocent heroine. Her arms and legs were as delicate and perfect as a figurine. I remember how prodigious her balance was, as well as her jump, how lovely her arms were as they suggested bonelessness amid the spectral landscape of act 2.

On the Kirov roster, Natalia Makarova's Giselle was my favorite. She danced act 2 at her graduation in 1959. Six months later, Fenster's interest in promoting young dancers allowed Makarova to dance the full ballet on the stage of the Kirov. Stylistically she did what she was taught, but her kineticism gave a whole new twist to Kirov orthodoxy. No other Russian ballerina's body or style was so unpredictable. She left afterimages trailing behind her. She was here, now there . . . where indeed was she?

Makarova was already nearly thirteen when she entered the Vaganova Institute, joining a specially abbreviated experimental class. Therefore, she had studied for only five years before joining the company, and her first years onstage were a trial by fire. Her technique lagged well behind her emotion and her interpretative depth. Yet for me it was always ten times more interesting to watch Makarova fall off her pirouettes than to see some other ballerinas execute every step perfectly.

Although her teachers and ballet masters weren't pleased by the fact that her academic positions weren't always cleanly finished, that made her ideal for *Giselle*. The great technique she didn't get in school, the perfectly finished positions that didn't come naturally ultimately worked to the benefit of her career, because as her technique strengthened it didn't crowd out this impulsive, unfinished style that became her trademark.

⸹ ⸹

I had thought I would never return to dancing after Alyosha was born. I decided to apply to Leningrad's Theater Institute to study performing arts criticism and began working on the application essay. But Igor told me that my plan was crazy. If I was in school, we would never be together. The only time we would see each other was on the nights when he wasn't at the theater. And so I dropped my plan. Igor impressed upon me that I had taken enough time off, and it was time to finally join the company. After weeks of work in class, I auditioned and, in the spring of 1961, was given an interim contract to dance in the Kirov's corps during the months the company toured Europe. Reinforcements at home were needed. That fall I was given a full corps contract.

Working with a classical corps de ballet, coaxing thirty people to dance in unison, is more difficult than coaching the most problematic dancer one-on-one. The Kirov's Naima Baldachieva was a great ballet mistress for the corps. She had been trained by Vaganova and danced as a soloist in the Kirov. As a ballet mistress, she felt the needs of the ensemble perfectly, and she could use the beautiful style of her own port de bras to demonstrate for us. My first corps de ballet rehearsal at the Kirov was the *Raymonda* dream adagio. Baldachieva placed me in the first line and made a point, at the end of the rehearsal, of saying, "I am very happy that a new generation of good dancers have come to this particular piece."

Outside the theater, Igor pushed me to dance the *Sleeping Beauty* pas de deux with him at concerts around Leningrad. We would often fight during rehearsals, but I was more angry with myself than with him, angry that I didn't have the physical tenacity to live up to my own standards. Once I was sent to an army base to dance, but this time with Yuri Korneev, a principal dancer at the Kirov, who'd partnered me in my school exam. I set off reluctantly on the ten-hour bus ride. We arrived at a small island, carpeted with pine trees, girded with a tall electrified fence. A checkpoint patrolled by armed soldiers waved us through. Where in the world had I arrived, and would I ever return?

We stayed in the officers' barracks. A guard was stationed at every door. The performance was in the soldiers' little theater. Afterward we were taken to the mess hall. Only high-level officers ate there. Soldiers served us, but stayed absolutely mute. All were very excited to be hosting artists. "Ah, she's such a talent," one of them said about me. "When it's real talent; it's real talent. You can't hide it." I thought, if this rank-conscious organization man knew that I was first-year corps de ballet he'd be singing a different tune. The table groaned with tubs of black caviar and salmon, champagne and rounds of toast. No matter how straitened the rest of the country was, the Soviet military lived almost like the old aristocracy.

Still stuffed to the gills, we were awakened at six the next morning so that we could go fishing. We were given a boat and a crew of soldiers. "It's impossible," Korneev laughed, "you just throw out your line and a fish sits on your hook. There must be soldiers underwater hooking on our lines!" When we got back to the base, soldiers built a fire and baked our catch, and also prepared fish soup, served with tons of vodka, champagne, and chocolate. They loaded us up with more food, more champagne, delicious fruit to take with us when we left. But only once our car had passed through those electrified gates did we begin to entirely relax.

It was soon after that Alla Shelest retired and began teaching at the Kirov. Her class was earmarked for "young talented dancers," about twenty-five company members. Igor was determined that I join, but Shelest was skeptical. She may have seen in me class sometime, but she did not know my history. I think she liked me, but she did not relax her standards for anyone. She didn't trust Igor's judgment about his own wife's talent, but he begged and begged until she relented. There were conditions. I would be on probation the first few days. I was to stay in the back of class, and not expect her to give me any corrections. I should listen to every correction she gave to anyone else as intently as if it had been directed to me.

I was very angry at Igor. I had heard that her class was very demanding. Even if she never paid any attention to me, I couldn't insult her and embarrass myself by just slogging through it. In the middle of barre a couple of days later I saw her looking at me curiously. She came over and started correcting my positions with her hands. She held up my leg. "Look at how beautiful her ecarté is," she announced to the class. And from then on, she never walked past me without giving me some correction. She pushed me to work harder than I ever had. "She's lost so many years," Shelest told Igor, about the time I'd spent at home with Alyosha. "It's such a pity." She made me feel wonderful about myself.

Shelest's philosophy of movement was very close to what I teach now. The dancer has to imagine that her body's muscles are coordinated by intersecting diagonals. The working side is always controlled by the supporting axis. I took class with several of Vaganova's ballerinas and strangely enough Shelest was the only one who emphasized this concept. By the 1980s, it seemed to vanish from Russian teaching. In those years when I watched Russians dance, their supporting side often seemed slightly askew, because the counterforce was missing. Shelest opened the door to a logical and easy way to energize the body, to enhance its expressive potential. Everyone in her class improved dramatically.

Dudinskaya had inherited Vaganova's company class after Vaganova died in 1951. (Kirov dancers often began teaching before they were finished performing.) She gave a good, strong, methodical class, based closely on Vaganova's own method. She steamrolled her students into shape and developed great stamina in them. But one by one, even top ballerinas who loved Dudinskaya's class migrated to Shelest to show their opposition to Dudinskaya as well as Sergeyev. The animosity that Sergeyev and Dudinskaya aroused endangered his directorship. It really was war, and Sergeyev needed young, prominent dancers like Igor on his side.

Extracurricular work by Igor—concerts at all sorts of venues around the city—enabled us to rent a dacha in the woods near the artist's retreat at Kamorova. To our dismay, however, we soon discovered that our house was no more than twenty paces from Dudinskaya and Sergeyev's. They maintained separate apartments in Leningrad but shared a driver, a big car, and their dacha. Often they would drive us to the country and invite us to their home for a delicious dinner. At home, Dudinskaya was just as charming as she was onstage. She plied an uncanny enchantment. Her eyes were warm and luminous; you felt yourself being hypnotized, going under their spell. Compared to the way he ruled the theater, Sergeyev was much warmer and more easygoing in his own home, though still rather remote. "You see, Kosik was always this way," Dudinskaya told us. "When he was five years old"—that would have been 1915—"he had a birthday party. The guests asked him, 'Kosinka, who do you want to be when you grow up?' He said, 'The czar.'"

Yet living so close to them was very difficult for us, because we never felt we could invite anyone to our house who was an opponent of theirs— and many of our friends were. In fact, both Igor and I wanted them out. Sometimes when we drove on our own to the dacha, my first impulse would be to draw down the shades on every window. It was no use: we would hear footsteps in the snow, then a knock at the door followed by Dudinskaya's face evincing her most coquettish surprise. "Oh, you're here?!" We kept the house for a number of years, but often we resorted to dropping off Igor's mother there with Alyosha, and letting them stay there while we went back to the city.

I was studying with Shelest when Dudinskaya made a special point of inviting me to join her class. I was panicked. Shelest had done me such a favor, but if I told Dudinskaya no, I was sure there would be repercussions. Fortunately for me, Shelest came down with something; I took Dudinskaya's class for one week, and then crept back to Shelest when she returned to work.

Shelest was a philosopher of movement, taking time to explain the logic behind each movement and the musculature at work. But for many dancers her class was too intellectual. They were used to taking class by rote. They just wanted to warm up and then go to rehearsal. And in class, Shelest had no sense of time. She would have been better working like a research scientist with just a few dancers. For if one dancer's particular problem or attribute preoccupied her, she would concentrate on her throughout the class. The greatest ballerinas might find themselves idling, their muscles getting stiff, while Shelest explained why a corps girl's hip or lower back was or was not working efficiently. We were never able to jump because there wasn't any time—in one and a half hours we barely finished barre.

I didn't have any major professional responsibilities and I would have been happy to listen to Shelest all day. But ballerinas who had important performances to give couldn't afford to let their wheels spin. That was why some said that Shelest was a bad teacher, and some dancers began drifting away. Nonetheless, the exodus from Dudinskaya could not really be staunched, and as a result, Shelest was eventually dismissed. But over the years she would return to coaching and teaching in the company, particularly after Sergeyev was fired in 1970, following Makarova's defection in London.

§ ʔ

Igor's father had three sisters, Antonina, whom we called Tonia, Anna, and Irina, all of whom lived in Saratov, on the Volga River. Igor and I often spent time with them before going south to swim in the Black Sea. Saratov was a cultured region, with several universities, very good opera and ballet companies, as well as a great dramatic theater. Tonia's husband Misha directed a successful collective farm. Stalin's extermination during the 1930s of the kulaks, the land-owning peasant class, meant that Soviet agriculture was run by neophytes who were often inept. Misha's *kolkhoz*, however, was an outstanding success. Cheese, eggs, and sausages were produced there for export to East Germany. Misha was rewarded hand-somely for building an efficient business in the middle of what had been an agricultural wilderness. He and Tonia lived in a spacious five-room ranch house: this was remuneration almost on a capitalistic scale, except that as soon as his pension began, he was required to surrender the house. Khrushchev once came to see for himself how Misha conducted business. In a place of honor in his home, Misha hung a blown-up photo of himself with the premier. He wept when Khrushchev was ejected in 1964.

Every morning at five o'clock, Misha rose to begin his long, sweaty day. Several hours later, Tonia would come downstairs wrapped in a lace peignoir. She'd been a schoolteacher, but after an early retirement her life was spent moving languidly from bathtub to keyboard. "Tonia, your slaves are here," I would call, and she would appear to greet workers laden with baskets of fresh raspberries, staggering under wheels of cheese and ropes of sausage. Misha and Tonia were very honest: he skimmed off whatever of his own produce he wanted for himself, but always reimbursed the government. Their basement was crammed with an embarrassment of smoked meats and fish.

Tonia would inspect that day's bounty and issue instructions about what to bring the next day. The workers bowed themselves out the door. Then she would sit down at the piano to play Schubert or Chopin. After that she took a long bath and then reappeared in time for a very late breakfast.

Tonia and her two sisters looked like characters from Chekhov, their hair plumped up into huge topknots. Anna was married to an army man, while Irina's husband was an alcoholic who was constantly in prison. Every time he was released he'd sell whatever he could find in their home to buy more liquor, or if he couldn't, he would steal something and soon find himself back in prison. He was more pitiful than malicious, but he was completely out of control. Anxious every minute, Irina had no appetite; next to her sisters, she was as thin as a rail.

"Aunt Ira, divorce him," I told her. "Why are you destroying your life? You're such a beautiful woman."

"How can I?" she asked. "He will die without me." She sacrificed herself to stay with him and still he died young.

Igor's father remained an idol to the three sisters; they cherished his records and pictures. They told stories about how even when he was a noted tenor he had never become a snob, had always sent them money when they needed it. Each sister had a singing voice as exquisite as her brother's. Sometimes in the evening Irina and Anna visited Tonia, and after a sumptuous dinner the three sisters harmonized over Russian songs or arias, while Tonia played the piano. They were magnificent.

The house was surrounded by an enormous orchard stocked with scores of different species of apple trees. Some of the apples were transparent: you could almost see clear through to the other side. An enormous pond had been dug near the garden so that the flowers could be watered. The garden was so green and fresh it was almost tropical. Behind it was something like a small oasis, with another pond, this one filled with ducks. I usually enjoyed my morning tea outside near this pond, throwing apples to feed the ducks that lumbered across the pond, as big as pigs. But not a single tree was visible outside this oasis. You could see clear to the horizon.

Fishing was Uncle Misha's favorite recreation, and sprinkled across the desert there were many lakes of all sizes. Since the Koran restricted the eating of fish, the lakes in this heavily Muslim region were teeming. Igor was just as avid an angler as Misha. One time Misha decided to take three days off and lead us on a fishing excursion. We packed a truck with provisions: we took bread, a huge carton of apples, and tomatoes. No meat because it would spoil in the heat, but a large barrel of water so that we could bring back fresh the fish that we caught. We had a local driver who could speak the language. We left Alyosha with Aunt Tonia, who was occupied teaching him to play piano.

After driving all day we approached a yurta made of leather, the windows fabricated from animal intestine. We decided to stop there for the night and bed down in our truck. A woman appeared, her face veiled, body obscured by a gray robe, her face scored by wrinkles and caked with dust. "Daddy Misha," I asked, "she lives alone here, this old lady?"

"What do you mean, old lady?" He pointed out an infant wrapped in camel feces for insulation. Igor and Misha asked her which lake would be the best to visit, which way it was, how we should drive there. She told them something. It was supposed to be very close and we thought we would sleep there.

We stepped inside the yurt, where she kept her own camel on a leash.

I'd never seen one before in my life. I took a step toward it and in a flash the woman was screaming, warding me off as if I was evil. I jumped back. "No, no, you can't touch it!" Misha cried. Camels were the native population's support system. They slept near camels for warmth when it was cold; they needed them for conveyance; they made bricks out of their feces; they drank their milk.

On the wall was a faded picture on which was visible the vague imprint of a man's face. It could have been a newspaper clipping. I asked our driver to ask the woman what the picture was. She said she didn't know, but it was some relative. I came closer. I couldn't believe my eyes—it looked like our very own Vladimir Ilyich Lenin. "Misha? Is it possible?"

He put on his glasses to get a better look. "Yeah, it is Lenin."

We asked the driver again to translate and he told her, "That's not your grandfather. This is Lenin, the leader of our revolution." She didn't know anything about a revolution. Lenin's name meant nothing to her. Yet she hovered near this faded clipping and was anxious about us getting too close to it, too. It turned out that her grandfather had told her that it was very dear to him; it was the portrait of a saint. Lenin had studied at the famous university there, and a relative of hers had probably brought it home at the time of the Civil War right after the Revolution.

We started to organize sleeping arrangements in the truck. The tomatoes we'd brought had been crushed. I thought we should toss them away because otherwise there would be juice all over the floor. But the Kazakh woman saw us about to empty the sack and flew over to us with a shriek, begging us to give them to her. "Of course," Igor and I said, "take them."

But Misha was the complete entrepreneur. "Well now, I will sell her these tomatoes."

"Okay," he told her, "but the price is a picture of your camel." Reluctantly she led the beast outside, Igor perched on top of the camel buffoonishly, and I snapped the shutter.

a masterpiece

Igor and I had become quite close to Leonid Jacobson. Igor danced both the male leads in Jacobson's *Spartacus*: he was Spartacus himself, leading the rebellion, and alternately he was Harmodious defending the status quo. He danced the hero in the full-length *Shuraleh*, a fairy tale that children flocked to. He danced opposite the Kirov's glorious Lubov Voichnis in the one-act *The Bedbug* and opposite Shelest in Jacobson's duets *The Blind Girl* as well as "Eternal Idol" in *Rodin*. And when I danced one of the foxtrot soloists in *The Bedbug*, he signed a program to me, something he rarely did. "You were great," he wrote, "I was very pleased."

We had Jacobson over for dinner one night and he began telling us about a new ballet he was planning. Like his *Bedbug*, inspired by Maya-kovsky, this was also going to be based on a great work of Silver Age lit-erature, Alexander Blok's 1918 poem "The Twelve." He had already begun working with the composer, Boris Tishinko, but Jacobson himself was notoriously slow; he had famously worked on the three-act *Spartacus* for several years before it was finally premiered in 1956.

The Kirov couldn't afford to take that long this time. Sergeyev had told him that only if he finished in three months would he include *The Twelve* in the repertoire. "It's impossible," Jacobson told us. "I could never do it that fast. They're trying to destroy me and destroy this ballet."

"Of course you can do it if you're organized," I said. "Don't call everyone all day and then decide in rehearsal what you're going to do with them." During *Spartacus*, for example, that's what had happened: Jacobson had monopolized the company. "Instead, each night we'll make up a schedule for the next day. It can work." I thought that even if he couldn't finish in three months, at least enough could be accomplished by the deadline that it would be incumbent upon the Kirov to allow him to continue to work.

In the Kirov we had at least twenty ballet masters on the staff, and natu-rally each one was looking for work. Yuri Druginin was Jacobson's customary assistant. He had an incredible memory. Takhir Baldachiev, whose sister Naima rehearsed the women of the corps de ballet so well, was also invaluable to Jacobson. They were shocked when Jacobson chose me not only to coordinate the production but also to rehearse the principal dancers. Sergeyev was equally surprised, each of them no doubt convinced that Jacobson was interested in me only because I was young and attractive.

But it was strictly work that Jacobson was concerned with. We sat until four or five a.m. nearly every night, working on the schedule. I parceled out every minute so that he couldn't waste any time. Once Jacobson had choreographed a section, he would give it to Baldachiev, Druginin, or me to rehearse. In one bar of music, Jacobson might choreograph eight distinct movements, so it was very difficult for the dancers and even for him to remember what he had shown the day before. But thanks to inheriting my father's gift of exact recall, I was able to keep track of Jacobson's work from day to day. He didn't even want me leaving his rehearsals to go to any of my own corps de ballet rehearsals. I tried to explain that I was still working in the company as a dancer. "No, they have to take you out and you will be my assistant." I didn't relish the prospect of more scandal, but he went to Sergeyev and insisted, and he did get his way.

Jacobson let me cast most of the small roles myself. He was envisioning a dark and unsavory ensemble peopled by the suicidal, the sycophantic, and the profiteering. Not without some secret amusement, I looked for an almost perfect match between the dancers' own personalities and their roles.

Before the Revolution, Blok had been the favored poet of a sensitive and philosophical readership. His romanticism made him popular with young girls of the aristocracy; his tone was too rarified, however, for the masses. Blok was one of the intelligentsia who supported the Revolution because they recognized the corruption and impotence of the monarchy. He believed in the cause until he saw how bloody the Revolution was turning out to be. When he wrote "The Twelve" in 1918, the Russian population was divided for and against: everyone's interests were at stake and no one could afford to sit on the fence. "The Twelve" was the first time he chose not to write about love, mysticism, sentiment, internal reflection. Some didn't even believe it was really the product of Blok's own hand; the poem was so atypical.

Throughout "The Twelve," twelve Red soldiers bring about the new system via rape and pillage and murder. But as he was writing the poem, Blok became stumped about how it should end. Who would be the new prophets? It wasn't clear, as Blok was writing, who would lead the Revolution. Lenin was simply one candidate—there was still the possibility of Kerensky returning, there was Tsavinkov, and Trotsky. The prophet Blok finally chose to install, however, was none other than Jesus Christ. "In a wreath of white roses Jesus Christ stood in front of everyone." Blok himself was devout, and in appointing Jesus leader of the Soviets he was blaspheming his own beliefs. Blok confessed in his diary that he didn't know how it came to his head to write those final words. Immediately with this poem he was confirmed against the revolutionaries as well against his own people, the White Russians who were fighting the Bolsheviks. He contradicted himself, parting company with every ideological rank.

When set designer Anar Steinberg showed us his maquette, a futuristic utopia was envisioned, with electrical antennae next to sculptures by Jacobson's beloved Rodin on the street corners. I thought that Steinberg's concept was wrong. How could anyone predict what the art of the future would look like? Steinberg's future was instead envisioned in terms of the past and the present. I gave Steinberg an edition of Blok's poem that was accompanied by Cubist illustrations drawn by Yuri Aninkov. Steinberg screamed that I was destroying his beautiful scenery. Jacobson walked out of our meeting, telling Steinberg that he was to work it out with me. "Why?" Steinberg continued screaming. "Why do I have to talk to some ballet girl? What does she know?" Finally I told Steinberg that I was going to leave and I did. The next day he approached me. "What are you talking about? Where is this book?" When he looked at it himself, he liked it, too. He designed a copy of a city, not abstract—St. Petersburg's Vasilyevsky Cathedral was recognizable—but with all proportions collapsed, askew. It rendered the mood of the city at the time of the Revolution. It was exactly right for the choreography. It looked just fantastic.

I had chills as I watched Jacobson devise the ballet's ending in rehearsal, seemingly on the spur of the movement. Blok had written that the Twelve "with bloodied hands rested and started to think." To illustrate those lines, Jacobson created a visual quotation from da Vinci's *The Last Supper*, in which Igor, who danced the antihero Johnnie, was surrounded by the Bolshevik thugs who march relentlessly through the poem. In four counts the tableau dissolved, the men thinking, beating their foreheads. Then Igor moved his hand and cocked a Lenin salute. His comrade disciples looked at him and everybody started to follow suit. The next eight counts established a transition from Christianity to Communism. Igor began walking slowly upstage toward the backdrop. All the apostles started to follow him in slow motion to quasi-liturgical organ strains, as though all Russia were now aligning itself behind Lenin. In the performance, golden light shone so brightly that the audience turned away. With their backs to the public, the dancers peered into the future, seeing what we in the audience could not.

Destroying everyone and everything in his path, Igor's Johnnie may have been his finest role. Nona Usvanianova and Irina Gensler alternated in the role of his girlfriend Katska, killed by a stray bullet, one of many everywoman victims in Jacobson's work.

I also danced in *The Twelve*. I was one of five whores. Throughout most of the ballet we were on stage as a chorus, a commentary, a persistent reminder. For the first and only time in my life I was excited to go on stage. Steinberg's costumes were also influenced by Aninkov's illustrations. We whores wore what we called a NEP skirt, after the New Economic Policy years of the 1920s: short with asymmetrical hems, here made out of a gaudy patchwork of lace and silk, and trompe l'oeil insertions. As the ballet progressed, the twelve revolutionaries shed parts of their costume until they had stripped down entirely to unitards—red, of course—by curtain fall.

The strong anti-Soviet statement imbedded in the ballet was hardly lost on the politicos who came to vet the dress rehearsal in December 1964. (Khrushchev had just been ousted, and the Soviet "thaw" was soon going to turn into Brezhnev's stagnation.) Representatives from the Kirov's Art Soviet committee, from the Ministry of Culture in Moscow, party officials, bureaucrats from the Leningrad City Hall. The theater was so jammed that not one member of the Kirov itself could find a seat.

Jacobson's position in the Kirov and in Soviet society meant that dancers closely associated with him had a rather dubious reputation. Many chosen for the production were really in it against their wills, and some found ways to sneak out. But many of them were totally committed to the ballet. "Dancers, don't worry," he told us on stage before the curtain rose, "just perform as you have to. If anybody will go to prison, it will be me and not you." Everybody started quaking in fear at the police dogs in the audience, but we were really more frightened for him than for ourselves. The ballet opened with the entire forty-member cast onstage huddling before a storm. It buffeted each group in turn. No one was spared the cataclysms of 1917. Jacobson's words emboldened us, and we dancers went on stage with the zeal of freedom fighters.

"No, it's all wrong; it's wrong, it's wrong," the functionaries in the audience cried when we met after the run-through. They particularly hated the ending. "How is it possible that the Red Army would crawl like ladybugs? They must walk like soldiers into the future. They have to know where they're going and what they want."

"You can't walk like a soldier to the future," I said. It was extraordinary, miraculous what they were privileged to witness. Walking slowly on half pointe, peering through a hole in the door, they were trying not to disturb that miracle.

To conflate Jesus with Lenin as graphically as Jacobson did was certainly asking for trouble. But I remembered what Lenin's minister of culture, Anatoly Lunarcharsky, had written about Blok's poem in his autobiography. He claimed that it demonstrated Blok's belief that Jesus blessed the Revolution. I had a copy of Lunarcharsky's book at home and I gave it to Jacobson: "Show them *this*."

The apparatchiks forced Tishinko to substitute marching music for the organ strains in the final measures. But the ballet was allowed to proceed to its opening night. Nevertheless it was pulled from the repertory after two or maybe three performances. I still felt we had won. We had ensured that Jacobson's work would be seen by at least some. And it had been cheered. I knew it would not be forgotten, and time has proven me right. It was never performed again—writing on water in extremis—but to this day I consider the ballet a masterpiece, and I know that for many others as well it was indelible.

~ 12 ~

seeing the world

The party influence in the company had become stronger following Nureyev's defection in 1961. Previously, ballet dancers had usually been able to get away with non-involvement because they were presumed to spend their time in the clouds, dreaming of sugarplums. No one at the Kirov during the 1960s was forced to join the party, and many dancers who never became members still had good careers. But recommendations were issued, and there were any number of dancers who advanced their careers largely due to party involvement. I'm afraid, too, that sometimes their political activities were all but visible on stage. As one character dancer's party involvement became deeper, her presence became brusquer, the noblesse chipped away. Performing the Queen in *The Sleeping Beauty*, she *commanded* Aurora to dance, her arm rending the air—for a moment she looked like she was exhorting a commission of party delegates.

After Nureyev's defection, Pyotr Rachinsky had been installed as director of the entire Kirov organization, overseeing both opera and ballet. He had been a fireman and amateur musician before he came to the theater, and we in the ballet joked that our best way to gain any understanding from him would be to don fire helmets. What he was really looking for in ballet was a peek under a tutu to discern the best candidates for his bed.

He found what he was looking for in Kaleria Fedicheva, an exciting ballerina who was good in everything she danced, and was sensational in *Laurencia*, a Spanish-flavored ballet created for Dudinskaya in 1939. Once Fedicheva began a long love affair with Rachinsky, she began influencing every aspect of company policy. She stopped watching her weight and all but broke the back of more than one partner. Igor danced with her often. As great a partner as he was, they still had trouble when they danced *Stone Flower* together, and came to a perilous lift we called "roimops," named after a small, sardine-like fish. In this same *Stone Flower* lift, Inna

Zubkovskaya had once spilled out of Askold Makarov's arms, breaking her fall with her hands, while her legs remained straddled around his back. A similar mishap happened with Fedicheva and Igor. The extra weight she carried meant that Igor thought that she'd bring them both crashing to the ground. Had she not been so insolent and been more careful about her weight, she could have been a much greater ballerina. In the White Swan pas de deux, I remember her convincing tenderness that was contradicted by her not very streamlined shape.

One New Year's Day, Fedicheva invited Igor and me to dinner at her apartment. It was a family celebration, and we brought Alyosha, but almost everyone present drank like the proverbial Russian mujik. Raucous, vulgar screaming bounced off the ceiling. Yuri Soloviev, however, sat quietly. He was scheduled to dance the Black Swan pas de deux with Fedicheva at some event that night. She decided to change into her costume before leaving for her performance. We all piled into her car. Half-drunk, Fedicheva plunked down in the driver's seat, her black tutu swimming across the seat, her black feather headpiece scraping the car ceiling. She was speeding down the wrong lane, reserved for government cars on holidays. A policeman stopped her. She rolled down the window. "Can I help you?" Fedicheva asked, insolent as always. The cop peered into the car and was struck dumb by this apparition. "I am running to my concert!" she exclaimed. He gave her an admonition and waved us on our way. She and Yuri danced and then we came back to her house and caroused for the rest of the night.

Igor danced many similar concerts with Ninel Kurgapkina, who was smart and funny. She had graduated from Vaganova's class in 1947, and was a particular favorite of hers. During my very first years in the school, I often saw her eat with Vaganova in the cafeteria. Vaganova wouldn't pull rank by jumping the line; but Ninel—we called her "Nelli"—wouldn't let her wait. Vaganova sat at a table while Nelli snaked through the line, sneaking ahead of us and joking all the way. Nelli had gorgeous teeth; in Russia at this time they were all but unbelievable. "And they're all mine!" she would laugh, flashing her blinding smile and scooping up lunch for her teacher.

Once Igor and Nelli were booked for no less than seven May Day concerts. A car took them from theater to theater. Time was at a premium, and they were driven from one concert to the next in full costume and makeup. They performed Vassily Vainonen's short but very difficult Mashkovsky Waltz duet, where Igor did more partnering than solo dancing, supporting her in a double fish and many other tricky lifts. About the fifth concert he groaned, "I can't move anymore."

"Come on!" Nelli cried. "What do you mean? *I* can still move. Just think about how much money we're making!" The day was indeed as lucrative as it was brutally taxing.

One night Igor had spent time at a sauna and had probably done some drinking as well. The next morning, I came to the studio where he was taking Pushkin's company class. I saw that his muscles were a little weak and I urged him not to finish the class. Instead he went back to try a double cabriole, but he stayed in the air too long trying to fit in the second beat. He crashed to the floor with the entire burden of his weight crumpled between two legs, rather than planted securely on the back leg. I heard his knee crack and rushed home in hysterics, while Igor was taken to the hospital. Hours later the doorbell rang. I opened the door and saw Igor leaning on two crutches, his entire left leg encased in a cast. I fainted dead away.

Igor resisted an operation while he worked on his own to strengthen his leg. At home he was incessantly monitoring his knee, worrying about taking a single step on stage because it might mean it would be traumatized all over again. I began to realize that either he had to agree to the operation or forget about dancing altogether and start performing only mime roles. There he could utilize his marvelous temperament and acting skills. Finally he did submit to the operation, but it wasn't very successful. I recall that it was either the first time doctors had done this type of operation or it was the first time it had been tried on a dancer. They removed most of the knee cartilage, the meniscus itself, but left a stub, which they said would regenerate. But it never did. He had the same problem as before the operation, only perhaps the knee didn't swell as much as it had. He was still afraid of big jumps and technical tricks. The doctors tried a second operation, but by now too much time had elapsed. He stopped performing classical leads and restricted himself to roles such as Jacobson's Spartacus, where he jumped with legs turned in, which was easier on his knee. He had started drinking in his school days, but his drinking now got worse and his character deteriorated. Some nights I would duck out of our apartment and go to a girlfriend's, or just walk through the city by myself.

A friend was married to a doctor. She was charming, intelligent, beautiful—and crazy about sex. She could tryst with not one but two lovers (sequentially) during the day, and that night fall into bed with her husband, still fresh as a daisy. Her mother was a film producer, a progressive, an intellectual. She accepted Natasha's behavior. One time Natasha was very worried that she might be pregnant, but not by her husband. "Don't worry," her mother said, "grass doesn't grow on a busy road." (In this case, she was right.) Sometimes I was jealous. How can she be so free? I thought. How can she not be worried about her husband? And often I was judgmental. She was betraying him. Like my mother and my grandmother, I stayed puritanical at heart.

So when men found me attractive, I was tempted, but I thought instead about what I could do to fix my marriage. There were of course no marriage counselors in the Soviet Union. I needed to do something on my own. I decided to enroll in a two-year program offered by the University of Marxism-Leninism. Classes met once or twice a week. The curriculum included an intensive study of all Western philosophies preceding Marx, dating back to the Greeks. Luckily, the Kirov was forced to allow students at the institute to skip any rehearsal that conflicted with class or research! It was perfect for me.

I also thought that perhaps Igor could try his hand at choreography. He started his first piece, a duet to Albinoni's adagio. He worked with several different couples but was creatively stymied for several weeks. One night we went with Vadim Gulyaev, a student of Pushkin who had just joined the Kirov, to celebrate White Nights—a traditional festival to mark the solstice—on the small Vasilyevsky island in the Neva, facing both the Peter and Paul Fortress and the Admiralty, an ideal lookout from which to view the most beautiful parts of the city. We took drinks and sandwiches, and Igor horsed around. At 5 a.m. I told him I wanted to go home. He threw himself against the wall in a crucifix pose and yelled, "I will start my piece like this." From that point on, work on the duet went smoothly. Igor finished the duet on Gulyaev and the Kirov's Elena Evteyeva. He began making more pieces, performed by Kirov dancers at galas and other special occasions.

In the summer of 1966, Igor remained on the performing roster of the Kirov. The company was going on a tour of Europe, and both he and I were included. Before we left, a company meeting was held. We were told all the things we were forbidden to buy, told not to walk in groups of less than five, not to visit private houses, nor to accept any invitations from Italians. I'm embarrassed to admit that I really did begin to imagine that the moment we arrived we would be beset with every kind of lure to persuade us to betray Russia by defecting. But when we arrived in Italy, we found to our disappointment that no one was chasing us—no one at all. And once we even did go to a private house, after securing an elaborate permission from our authorities. Our Italian hosts wanted to know about our lives in Russia. Was it really like prison? They did ask us playfully if we wanted to remain in Italy, but nobody had the slightest interest in pressuring us to betray our country.

In Verona, we danced our production of *Sleeping Beauty* as well as Sergeyev's choreography for *Aida* in the huge ancient arena. The opening night of *Aida* was celebrated by a long-standing arena tradition. The overture began and the audience lit candles. I thought I was in heaven. My eyes were full of tears.

Verona is not a very large city, and all the local merchants knew who we were the moment they spotted us. One day Igor and I stopped in front of a shop window displaying fur coats. I'd never seen anything like them. The proprietor heard us speaking Russian and started chatting with us in Italian. I asked how much a certain coat was. "Well, it's too expensive," he said.

"No, write it down."

He put down a one and after that a set of zeroes—as many as he could fit. "There's not enough space," he claimed. And so I contented myself with buying a raincoat.

A restaurateur asked us where we were eating. "We all want to know because not one of you is in any restaurant in Verona." To save money, virtually every member of the Kirov had taken food with them from Russia. After each performance, everybody started cooking in their rooms. A strict timetable worked out among the company members couldn't prevail over the dancers' hunger. Sometimes the fuses would short circuit, and dancers poured into the corridors yelling, "We already made a schedule!"

When we moved on to Venice, a group of us toured the Biennale with a translator. My head was spinning in front of Roy Lichtenstein's canvases. I'd never seen any American comic strips. We had our own comic books, featuring entirely different characters. I asked Igor to take a picture of me standing right in front of them.

Later in the sixties, we performed at a festival in Vienna. José Limon was also appearing there with his company. "We will be an oasis in this desert of modern dance," Sergeyev told us. At the festival, Irina Kolpakova was given an award, and we in the corps de ballet also received a special citation. There was also a short season in Salzburg. After one performance, Igor and I walked through the streets with Kirov character dancer Alexander Minz. It was a warm night and the city was gorgeous. To inhibit independent excursions, we had been told that we were only feet away from a particular checkpoint, and it would be very easy to wander into West Germany by accident. We wouldn't be stopped as we crossed the border but we would be barred, so we had been told, from ever returning to Russia.

"Freedom is only fifty feet away," I reminded Igor and Alexander. "Do you want to go?" I asked.

"Absolutely not," Igor said. By now Igor had become the chief of the Kirov Komsomol, which was strictly for teenagers and young adults no older than twenty-seven, although if you had a leadership position, you could stay later. Igor himself was now in his late twenties. His Communist career began as a means to gain clout in the campaigns against Sergeyev and Dudinskaya. Prior to this tour, he had signed a paper recommending that Alexander be allowed to go on this tour. The authorities were suspicious because he knew Westerners and his mind was open. And in addition they knew that he was gay.

"Don't you want to stay here?" I asked Igor on that beautiful night in Salzburg.

"If we didn't have Alyosha, we would," he said.

On this tour we had brought Igor Belsky's *Leningrad Symphony*, much to the annoyance of the German-speaking critics, who claimed that flaunting the ballet's marauding Nazis was a breach of good manners. Nor did they approve of our repertory as a whole. While America loved the Kirov for exposing them to a different, aristocratic culture, to the German critics our classical repertory was antiquated. One hilarious review has stayed in my mind. It went something like this: "When the curtain rose on *Sleeping Beauty* and the great Kirov company appeared on stage, we all turned our heads anticipating the reappearance of the Czar. For everything was exactly the same as in his time: the costumes, the style. We started to hear very weak applause. We couldn't understand it. Then we realized that audience members were trying to crush moths that had flown off the production."

And I have to say that I agreed. In my twenties I hated the classics. I wanted to smudge the marble face of classicism, to stir its placid waters. So many dancers in the company felt just as I did. We had been weaned on the classics; we spent our entire careers dancing the same ballets over and over again. Since I was ten, nothing had changed, not the ballet, not the steps, not the style. It all was fossilized because of the proscriptions against anything that looked Western.

But when I went to the Bolshoi in Moscow to see Maya Plisetskaya dance *Swan Lake*, she made the ballet live again freshly for me. Like Alla Shelest, Plisetskaya championed a new physicality, a new expression on-stage. At the Kirov, there was a cliché about her that she had no real emotion, but that was simply because she didn't twist, bend, or crumple her facial features. Only her eyes were mobile. But in her movement itself there was so much emotion, so much of interest that she seemed to send a seismic jolt through the theater.

Even in the White Act of *Swan Lake*, she was very sexy, a woman more than a bird, but still mythic. I didn't pity her. She would die for her desire, her belief, and her martyrdom would be a victory. None of her positions were academically correct: in Odette's signature attitude Plisetskaya's leg was bent back very high, her arms thrust behind her, uninhibited, unstinting.

Fokine's *Dying Swan* solo provides space for each ballerina to improvise. Fokine supplies the bones and the ballerina fleshes them out. He made the solo in 1907 for Anna Pavlova after he saw Isadora Duncan dance in St. Petersburg. She was a revelation for him. It was an inflammatory time in Russia, the aftermath of the 1905 insurrection. Fokine wanted to remove Petipa's corsets from the ballerina's body, to give it space to scream and breathe and cry. *The Dying Swan* wasn't just a touching cameo of a crippled bird; it was a manifesto asserting the death of Petipa's classical aesthetic and Fokine's inauguration of a new era. The new waged war against the old.

Galina Ulanova came to Leningrad many times during the 1950s to dance *The Dying Swan* at holiday galas. Dancing it, she seemed to be fighting death not by struggle but rather by the power of her own spiritual purity and innocence. Ulanova cloaked herself in tradition. She wasn't fighting to join the future. Watching her, I felt that she was tendering her respect for her time, her art. If she was meant to die, she would; she'd surrender willingly, knowing that her time was over.

Ulanova virtually owned the *Dying Swan* until she retired in 1962, but afterward, Plisetskaya remade it in her own image. More than a half century after it was created, the solo again resounded in her interpretation with its original revolutionary birth pangs. They were especially meaningful for so many of us in the Kirov just then. We continued to fight to overthrow Sergeyev.

Everything about Plisetskaya was unconventional, and everything about our lives was bound by convention and regulation. When we heard about the Western hippies, we were so jealous! We couldn't have an epoch like the West's 1960s because the power of the Soviet state was too strong. But we tried to make our own statements. One of mine was to cut my hair very short and start to wear pants on the street. Pedestrians were outraged, all but hissing at me as they passed.

Igor had begun teaching a pas de deux class at the school. Among the students in Igor's pas de deux class was an exceptionally talented teenager, Valentina Simukova, who was also a member of Dudinskaya's graduating class. Simukova graduated into the company in the fall of 1965, where she danced in the corps but was also given solo parts immediately. By now, Dudinskaya no longer danced with the Kirov, but she continued to star in gala performances that she organized at the philharmonic. Simukova was scheduled to dance the *Sleeping Beauty* grand pas de deux in a Dudinskaya gala. She lived very far out in the city. Rehearsals on the philharmonic stage didn't begin until the evening. Sometimes she was driven back home, but sometimes she had to wait for the last bus at midnight. She developed a very bad cold. Sergei Vikulov was partnering her; he along with Igor described to me how Valya sat hungry, cold, and feverish waiting to rehearse her pas de deux over and over again. For Dudinskaya showed her no mercy. "I *never* cancel any performances!" Dudinskaya insisted, and that was true. "Even if I have a fever, I always go on stage! That's the kind of discipline you have to have." She impressed that credo on all of her students.

One day I stopped Dudinskaya on the stairs of the school, where I was rehearsing with the Kirov. "Natalia Mikhailovna, Valya is very sick. She's running a high fever."

"Well, she's young," Dudinskaya replied. "When I was young, I could dance with a high fever. It's good for her. I love this girl. She is my favorite; I can't do the performance without her."

Dudinskaya spoke with such warmth in her brown eyes, such a pained expression, and so much passion in the grip of her hand on my arm that I told myself either her ability to dissemble must border on the pathological or perhaps she really did believe what she said, which was an equally unsettling proposition.

I remember seeing Valya dance the pas de deux, but I can't remember if she danced one performance of the two or three that were scheduled or whether I only saw her rehearse. But it was obvious that she was alarmingly skinny and shaky, and within a day or so after the opening she checked into a hospital. She was diagnosed with measles that turned into encephalitis and she was paralyzed very soon thereafter. Three weeks later the company lost its golden girl.

Both teachers and students were in paroxysms of grief. The anti-Sergeyev faction seized its chance. Anonymous letters were posted on the bulletin board—bold-type indictments of the "KILLERS." A damaging article even surfaced in a newspaper. But Sergeyev and Dudinskaya were like stone. They took charge of Valya's funeral, dressing her in a *Giselle* costume and pointe shoes. Sergeyev recited one of the sanctimonious orations that were a specialty of his. "Because she was so beautiful, God took her for Himself. She will dance for Him now . . ." He droned on and on.

Yuri Soloviev stood behind me. "Look at that," he whispered. "It's not enough that they tortured her. They're making her spend eternity in pain." It was *The Red Shoes* come to life. All my struggles with pointe shoes came flooding back. My skin crawled, thinking of Valya imprisoned forever.

The next day Dudinskaya stopped me on the stairs and asked if we were going to the country . . . did we need a ride? We decided instead to go on our own the next morning. We came to their cottage and found Sergeyev sobbing, his nose red. Dudinskaya's face was also stricken.

"My God, what a tragedy," I said.

"Oh, absolutely. How did you know?" My blank face prompted from them the news that Timosha, Sergeyev's favorite cat, had just died.

I was stupefied. "What about Valya?"

"Oh, yes," Dudinskaya said, "poor girl."

igor's choreography

Igor Belsky had been one of the Kirov's greatest character dancers. He was in his mid-thirties when he started to choreograph in the late 1950s. In 1961, his ballet to Shostakovich's *Leningrad Symphony* was a big success, and, unlike so many company premieres, it did remain in the repertory, perhaps because of the patriotic message. Two years later, Belsky became artistic director of the Maly Theater, which was becoming known for a more progressive repertory than what was allowed at the Kirov. He now asked Igor if he would be interested in creating a ballet for the Maly, and he offered us several possible libretti. We chose *Antony and Cleopatra*, for which Belsky had in his hands a musical score. Belsky said he needed to attract attention to the Maly. A scandal on stage would help a great deal. We promised him he would have one.

In the summer of 1967, Belsky gave us the musical score by Edward Lazarov before we went on vacation, warning us that we weren't going to like it. He was right. On our holiday we shuffled a lot of the music around—drastically—to the point where some parts written for Antony we instead shifted to Cleopatra.

Igor's concept in *Antony and Cleopatra* was to make movement that was sharp and hieroglyphic and semiotic, a movement metaphor or counterpart to the communicative units of spoken or written words. But when the Kirov's Alla Osipenko came to Igor and said that she wanted to dance Cleopatra, she hadn't even seen the choreography yet. She loved the character of Cleopatra, however, and Igor had been one of her favorite partners. Belsky adored Alla, and was thrilled that she wanted to dance in his theater.

Osipenko was a rare talent. Her arms were ideally harmonious according to the academic canons of Vaganova's personal training as well as highly expressive and individualistic. Alternately sensuous and graphic, her legs were extraordinarily beautiful. I had been enthralled by her performances ever since I was a girl. I remember watching her dance the adagio solo Shades variation in *La Bayadère* in 1951, shortly after she had joined the company. She picked her leg up from a perfect fifth position, then her working leg caressed her supporting leg, passing through every distinct gradation while maintaining a flowing momentum until her leg was fully extended.

Osipenko was courageous and highly intelligent, with a quick and sardonic wit that she was sometimes needlessly impetuous about dispensing. Thus her constant conflicts with theater and political authorities.

We showed her a principal dancer from the Maly, hoping she would want to dance with him, but she had resolved to dance it with her new husband, John Markovsky. He was a great partner, and he and Alla always looked superb paired together. Yet he was no virtuoso, and he hadn't done a lot of contemporary work. "If you work with him, he will be great," Alla claimed. He worked very hard and wound up being good enough.

The composer was awfully angry at the way we'd cut and shuffled his score. His wife was a choreographer, and he'd originally written the score for her. She had staged it in their native Moldavia. He came all the way to Leningrad for the *Cleopatra* dress rehearsal, having threatened to sue us. He made a scene before the curtain went up, and then wanted to leave immediately, but I convinced him to stay at least for the rehearsal. He refused to go on to the meeting with the political people who'd come to certify the ballet sufficiently pure for the Soviet collective. There we faced the customary accusations: what Igor had choreographed was too Western. We played dumb. "What does it mean? We don't go to the West; we don't know what's going on there." They objected to it on stylistic grounds—there were too many second positions—as well as moral ones. But the theater had chosen Cleopatra, we said. How would it be possible to tell her story without eroticism?

Belsky won, and the ballet went on stage as choreographed. The first performance in July 1968 was danced by Valentina Muhanova, who was twenty-three and a rising star at the Maly. Muhanova had flat hips like Osipenko, but broader shoulders and a huge, forceful jump, giving her more of a martial flavor that was wonderfully appropriate for this queen. At the premiere Muhanova brought Cleopatra's political and military exploits to the fore. At the second performance, Osipenko emphasized the love story. But with both ballerinas, the ballet was a sensational success. Much of the highly intimate choreography was considered the last word in what could be permissible on the Soviet ballet stage. For a couple of years every performance was totally sold out. I remember getting out of the nearest subway, several blocks away, and being asked by people standing in the station itself whether I had an extra ticket to sell.

We allowed Belsky to make a one-act reduction for a tour, which Alla and John then started performing on their own at concerts during the 1970s, always with thunderous success.

"You're very honest people," Belsky told Igor and me. "You promised to give me scandal and you gave me more than I was expecting."

In February 1968, I turned twenty-nine. Drumming in my mind as thirty approached was the conviction that somehow it wouldn't be right for me to live longer than my mother had. And yet after her first attempt at suicide, when I believed that I had saved her, I already somehow felt as though I was really older than my mother, more mature, more responsible.

My family recalled that she was both beautiful and very talented in different ways. In the West, the exceptional individual commands respect, provided that his or her talents can be marketed. Knowing what I do today about the West and the United States, it's clear that she might have been just as suffocated there, but back in the 1960s I was convinced that she would have found a way to realize her potential had she somehow been able to leave the Soviet Union.

Perhaps I was thinking of my mother when I suggested to Igor that in the new *Romeo and Juliet* he was choreographing, the two lovers would die because they were different, and thus symbolize the doomed cause of individuality in the USSR. Symbolism had always been meaningful in Russia and was particularly so in the late 1960s. When Stanley Kramer's *On the Beach* reached Leningrad years after its Hollywood premiere, its use of symbolism created a sensation.

Our French friend Marc Jebijian had brought us an LP of Berlioz's *Romeo and Juliet* symphony. Igor fell in love with it immediately. At first he thought he would choreograph only a duet to the adagio movement. We worked underground for perhaps six months just on this adagio with Makarova and Soloviev. Her legs were much more sensitive than today's dancers; Igor made the adagio into a true conversation between bodies. He was motivated to expand it into a one-act ballet after he saw Mikhail Baryshnikov, just graduated from Vaganova in 1967. This was the Mercutio of his dreams: a symbol of life, a butterfly who lives only one summer, but lives fully, completely, not saving himself, living only for the moment. Every step Baryshnikov took was like champagne popping through the ceiling. Tybalt was naturally as dark as Mercutio was light: Valery Panov danced a solo of frustrated aggression. The twelve-member corps became the Soviet population, destroying anyone who didn't conform, a Greek chorus that framed every solo.

Eventually, Igor was allowed a studio showing where the ballet would be vetted by the Kirov directorate and staff. Kids from the school came as well. Perhaps a hundred people filled the studio since it was an unusual occasion. But that was as far as the ballet could go. The Kirov couldn't do many experimental works without provoking repression by the government. The foundation of the company had to remain the classical repertoire. That's what we were preeminent in, what we were famous around the world for. Sergeyev was best qualified to maintain our classical standard. When he was replaced after Makarova's defection in 1970, the classical standard of the company started to decline.

And yet there were always dancers in the company who wanted to work on something new no matter how dismal the prospect of ever seeing their work come to fruition. It was also around this time that Igor started to choreograph Ravel's *Bolero* as a solo piece for a man. In 1961, Maurice Bejart had choreographed his own famous *Bolero*, also for a male soloist (with corps), but we hadn't yet seen it. Igor's *Bolero* was more abstract, more sensual than Bejart's. Each repetition in Ravel's score became another woman in the man's life, another love affair. At the end he couldn't stand the inexorable recurrences in his love life and he ran to the apron of the stage, calling the entire affair to a halt on Ravel's final notes.

Igor's *Bolero* was created on both Soloviev and Baryshnikov. I couldn't generate any real attachment to this piece: in the first, second, and third place I don't like the music. But working on it with Soloviev was exciting. It fit him better than it did Baryshnikov because he was more mature, seven or eight years older. Soloviev had beautiful, expressive legs, arms, feet, and torso. As muscular as he was, Yuri was also very flexible. His natural extension was as high as Nureyev's, although Yuri didn't flaunt it onstage the way Rudi did.

He was hungry for new work and he worked with full dedication. I remember how beautifully he performed some movements with one knee bent to his chin, his hand cupping his heel, but he was just as completely involved in every movement. He generated much sex appeal as well as a certain philosophical comment. Igor eventually began working only with Yuri, and he finished the piece with him. But this piece never was able to reach the stage.

Watching Yuri rehearse we thought what an enormous talent he had, but it was perhaps above all a modern talent: classical dress was too small for him. For me he was always most free and most convincing in modern and neoclassical choreography. He was fantastic in the *Swan Lake* pas de trois. His *Sleeping Beauty* Bluebird was a masterpiece. He was great in *Spectre de la Rose* and *Les Sylphides*, as well as in the role of the Prince in Sergeyev's *Cinderella*. But for me his performances of the nineteenth-century prince roles were not complete; he often gave me the impression that he was both uncomfortable and rather bored in them. Perhaps he was made to conform to an external standard rather than encouraged to develop his own sense of himself. For some reason the theater gave him awful makeup, pasting a finicky painting on his face, which was much more attractive without this maquillage. He had lovely wavy blond hair, but wigs were the custom at the Kirov when he made his debut. Little by little people tried to look more natural, especially after Balanchine's company visited. We all saw how attractive it was to see a ballerina go on stage with her hair pulled into a chignon. In modern roles, dancers wore their own hair, but when Soloviev danced prince roles he either wore a wig or his hair was sprayed into rigid waves that were too prissy for his features.

He would of course have had many more opportunities to do new work had he worked in the West. I think he must have realized that himself. On Yuri's twenty-eighth birthday—August 10, 1968, he had hosted a tenth-anniversary reunion dinner for the graduating class of 1958. The famous solo dancer Makhmoud Asymbaiev called to wish Yuri happy birthday. We consumed lot of food, remembering every funny incident from our school years. Somehow, of all of us there, Yuri seemed the least satisfied. Late in the evening, he and I sat in the kitchen drinking tea. Yuri had been drinking, but he was not so drunk that he didn't whisper as he told me that several years earlier he had been offered the opportunity to defect. He turned down the offer. "I think I made a mistake . . . I was so stupid."

It was almost a decade later, early in 1977, six months after I arrived in New York, that I received word of Yuri's suicide at his dacha. It shocks me to this day. No matter how depressed and exhausted he may have been, he seemed too gentle a soul to ever perform an act of such violence. Circumstances must have pushed him beyond endurance.

In February 1969, I crossed the threshold of thirty. It still seemed strange to be older than my mother was when she died. But I was newly happy about the fact that I was alive. And life at that moment was full and exciting. I had my son. The dancing I did at the Kirov wasn't difficult. I eagerly read samizdat texts, forbidden books printed in minuscule type, hiding them in our kitchen oven; I could have gone to jail if they'd been discovered. But my life wasn't circumscribed by fear, as were so many Russians. Working with Igor on his choreography was stimulating. He had been approached by the supremo of the Odessa Opera House and asked if he would consider choreographing a new *Nutcracker*. Igor and I were both very intrigued. At the Kirov we danced Vasily Vainonen's 1934 production, which was an adaptation of Lev Ivanov's original production of 1892, to which Petipa had contributed a lot. By 1934, Ivanov's *Nutcracker* had been out of the repertory for a while, but Vainonen had tried to retrieve as much information about the original as possible from surviving Mariinsky veterans.

I thought then, and still do, that for children, Vainonen's is the best *Nutcracker*. I love his dance of the snowflakes in act 1, and his waltz of the flowers in act 2 is also delightful. But the act 2 grand pas de deux between Masha and the Nutcracker Prince was patterned after Petipa's Rose adagio, and that to me was wrong. It ignored the tragedy in the music.

I researched Tchaikovsky and tried to gather as much information as I could about *Nutcracker*. Then I drew up a new libretto, in which Drosselmeyer (as if Hoffmann himself) would appear on stage with dolls from different fairy tales and select the Nutcracker doll: tonight it would be his story. Drosselmeyer functioned as a Svengali, conducting the performance, switching scenery, changing the lights, with the help of an on-stage lighting crew. His age was ambiguous: he was meant to be not too young, but young enough so that we could give him a quasi-variation of his own to dance.

At the party, the guests moved stiffly like mannequins and maliciously broke Drosselmeyer's dolls. During a dream sequence, Masha saw the guests arriving at the party with human bodies and rat's heads. Again they started to break her dolls, and Masha asked Drosselmeyer to take her with him to Komfiturenberg, the Kingdom of Sweets. She didn't want to come back to real life. She didn't believe in herself. She didn't think she was beautiful. She had no place in this distorted world. Drosselmeyer imparted to her the realization that it wasn't necessary to conform to external expectations. The grand pas de deux now became a pas de trois with Masha, Drosselmeyer, and the Nutcracker Prince.

Igor liked the libretto, and he told Odessa that he was accepting its offer. We came there a couple of months later to start work. I had been to Odessa only once before, when I was less than a year old. My mother's father lived there with his second wife and their children. She brought me for a long visit. But when the Germans invaded a year later, my grandfather was hung in the city's square and his family shot. When I finally saw this square for myself I was sickened. How could people have stood at such close proximity and watched? In Leningrad or Moscow, piazzas by contrast were vast. It was mentally so perplexing for me that I had a German father and yet it was the Germans who had killed my Russian grandfather.

That year, Irina Kolpakova was to be given her own "Creative Evening" on the Kirov stage. This was a company tradition wherein a star could pick the program for her own one-night celebration. Kolpakova told Igor that she wanted to include his *Romeo and Juliet*. The ballet had been created especially for Makarova, who was not pleased about losing out on it.

"But Natasha," Igor told her, "this is our only chance to put it on stage." Kolpakova could defy official proscriptions against the work.

Thus Igor and I were shuttling back and forth between Odessa and Leningrad. Rehearsing alone with Kolpakova, I told her to imagine Juliet as a revolutionary, a proto-Soviet. Indeed Juliet *is* a revolutionary, defying society, its mentality, rules, philosophy. But in the adagio her movement was meant to be tender and tentative. I told Kolpakova to begin the adagio by touching the floor as if her feet were hands. Each step had to be utterly sensitive, insecure, sensual. Kolpakova did not have legs and a back as supple as Makarova's, but she tried to do what I told her, to experience the movement through her entire body. The sparkling crystal that she customarily polished in roles such as Aurora and Raymonda now became shadowed with sensuality and eroticism.

I also worked with the corps de ballet and the male leads, while we brought Tatiana Vecheslova on board to continue work with Kolpakova. It had been more than a decade since my adolescent estrangement from her began. Vecheslova had been Kolpakova's coach for a number of years. Herself a great dance actress, Vecheslova could inflame her pupils. But at that particular moment Vecheslova was out of the theater altogether. She wasn't diplomatic or political; she was impulsive, always a little too free with her remarks, and that's why she was never able to hold onto an administrative position. She was well-off from her pension; but living without the theater was painful.

She was open to innovation in the arts and had always liked new choreographers and being involved in new work. In 1957 she had been Grigorovich's assistant on *The Stone Flower*. We invited her to a rehearsal of *Romeo*, and she loved the ballet. Vecheslova was grateful to us for bringing her back to the Kirov and warmer to me than she had been in a long time.

Baryshnikov was again Mercutio, while Kolpakova's Romeo was now Vadim Gulyaev. Being one of Alexander Pushkin's favorite students, Gulyaev had been raised on photos of Nureyev and admired him greatly. Rudi—I don't know when or how—at one point saw Gulyaev, and said he should be on stage in the West. To us, too, he did look very Western, by which I mean that he showed his huge extension, employed less facial acting, used a more stretched musculature, a more pronounced articulation of his arch, a more turned-out fifth position than was traditional in Russian male dancing. Evgeny Scherbakov, a blond Viking with an enormous jump, replaced Panov as Tybalt.

Igor's *Nutcracker* opened in Odessa on December 12, 1969. We invited Elena Evteyeva, one of the Kirov's best young ballerinas, to alternate as Masha with Odessa's own Vera Volkova; both were very good in the role.

Kolpakova's Kirov benefit was on the twenty-eighth. The Paris Opera ballet was performing in Leningrad at this moment. It seemed as though the entire Paris company wanted to come to Kolpakova's benefit, but there were no tickets, no place even to stand. The Kirov administration allowed the Parisians to sit on the floor of the orchestra aisles in one of the Palaces of Culture where the Kirov performed while our beautiful old theater was being renovated and expanded.

After the performance Kolpakova hosted a party in her apartment. I sat between Vecheslova and Misha Baryshnikov. We had all had some wine, but Vecheslova was always blunt anyway. Suddenly she turned to me and said, "You are a very *jestokaya* girl." "Jestokaya" is a terrible epithet, meaning someone who's utterly cold-blooded, a killer. She didn't need to say any more; I knew what she was talking about. Vecheslova's mother had died, and I hadn't come to the funeral. Snetkova had retired from teaching by then, and I didn't even know she'd died—I lived in my own world. When I found out afterward, I went to the cemetery by myself.

I now said to Vecheslova, "I've wanted to talk to you for a long time, about everything. I'm very sorry; I know your mother died." I explained why I stopped calling them fifteen years earlier. She had her own child; I felt that they didn't need me anymore.

"I'm so glad," she said. "When I first met you, I thought you were a kind of very special child, very smart and beautiful with a good soul. Later I thought you were horribly spoiled and a bad person." She kissed me; she understood.

to the black sea

The success of Igor's *Nutcracker* led to him being asked to become artistic director in Odessa. He decided that he didn't want to return to the Kirov. He wanted to continue to choreograph on his own company. We requested and were granted a two-year leave of absence from the Kirov.

We arrived in Odessa in late summer 1970 and immediately began making waves. The company had four ballet masters to lead rehearsals. Igor fought with two of them, because he claimed they were too old-fashioned, but actually they weren't bad at all. One left by herself and Igor fired the second. He found a new one, but I became principal ballet master. Igor taught the principal men and the corps men. I rehearsed everything and staged all the classical ballets. The administration also wanted me to dance, but I told them to forget that idea then and there. They were very upset, because their local dancers were acting like a bunch of hooligans. The girls were lazy and overweight; they approached their job as a hobby. Where they wanted to work was in the open-air market, fishing for Western clothes. One day a week the entire city descended. All transportation stopped. Odessa is a port city through which a constant stream of foreign merchandise passes. The locals boasted that anything on earth could be purchased there—even an atomic bomb.

I started to give company class to the corps de ballet girls. The first month they went to the Opera House supremo and complained about me. He called me to his office. "Maybe you could be a little bit nicer to them, and give an easier class."

"Absolutely not," I told him. "I'm being honest with them. If they don't want to take the information that I'm giving them, without playing any games, too bad, they're stupid. I'm not going to make myself stupid, too." But within two or three months I felt as though I had them in my hands. We all got along very well.

Igor and I staged *Don Quixote* exactly as it had been staged at the Kirov. Igor choreographed his own *Spartacus*. We took Oleg Vinogradov's *Cinderella*, which he had originally staged in Novosibirsk, and we presented as well the Kirov's *Giselle* and *Swan Lake*, making some small revisions of our own. We staged Sergeyev's *Sleeping Beauty*, with new scenery and costumes by Svetlana Dimietriva, and Igor made many additions to the choreography. He brought the Vision scene closer to Petipa's original: the Lilac Fairy again participated in the Vision pas de deux between Aurora and Desiré. The Awakening scene was very effective. Sculptures recalling the Louvre were the frozen remains of the sleep-enveloped court. Carabosse delivered a revenge monologue, sitting on King Florestan's empty throne, making jokes at the nobles' expense. The stage was strewn with little drops and spotlights trained on them ad seriatim made it look as though Prince Desiré was passing through a suite of different rooms and a small garden. The lights went up and now he was in the bedroom.

Every year, Moscow invited different companies from the republics to perform in the capital for a couple of weeks, as if to report to the government how its stipend was being spent. The exposure was as momentous for a regional Soviet company as a Western season was for the Bolshoi or the Kirov. Our Odessa company was invited to Moscow and enjoyed a great success and wonderful newspaper reviews. One performance was telecast.

The director of a Congress Hall in Moscow brought our Soviet Minister of Culture, Ekatcrina Furtseva, to watch a stage rehearsal of *Giselle*. Although the Communist manifesto had officially liberated Soviet women, Furtseva was the only woman ever to attain membership in the Politburo, before she was promoted to minister. Where art was concerned, her Soviet blinders were of course impeccable. A story was told that Furtseva had once visited the Venice Biennale, which was impossible to enter without a pass. First Pablo Picasso showed up and apologized because he'd forgotten his pass.

The guards told him, "Sorry, we can't let you get in."

"But I am Picasso."

"Prove it."

He said, "Okay, give me a piece of paper," and made a thumbnail sketch of his dove of peace.

"Oh, sorry, please Monsieur Picasso, you can go in now." The next was Furtseva, who told them who *she* was, but to no avail. They informed her that Picasso himself had just been almost denied admission. And just whom, Furtseva asked, was this Picasso?

That did the trick. "Ah, Madame Furtseva, please come in . . ."

It so happened that I met Comrad Abukumov, director of the Kremlin Theater, and he agreed to take me to see Furtseva. I begged her to help our theater. Our dancers were underpaid. How could we expect to recruit top-rank Moscow and Leningrad talent unless salaries were commensurate? If a factory worker transferred to Siberia from the major cities, his pay was quadrupled, but we were hoping that Moscow- and Leningrad-trained talent would accept a pay cut for the privilege of uprooting themselves to Odessa. Pavel Famin, a principal dancer living in the company's dormitory, had fainted in class from hunger. He wasn't making enough to feed himself, his wife, and his child.

Furtseva was a hard-liner, but her manner wasn't anything like the *Ninotchka* stereotype. She had amazingly balletic legs for a woman who had never studied dance. She tried to be very feminine, warm; at the same time I felt that she was so far away from anybody's problems. However, she was not averse to helping people who did manage to somehow approach her. We were given a larger allotment and a building adjacent to the company dormitory, which was remodeled to give the dancers additional facilities.

I told Furtseva that any Western tours would be an invaluable aid to the company's morale. She arranged for us to tour to Varna in Bulgaria. It was close to Odessa and not all that Western, but it would be an enormous adventure for the company. Unfortunately, as we settled into our new life, Igor became more and more full of himself and more dictatorial, more high-strung and volatile. It was as though every trait inherited from his mother became stoked to a fever pitch. Increasingly, he drank to excess; he'd been impossible during our tour to Bulgaria. Our relationship became absolutely untenable. I finally felt that I had no choice but to leave him.

For fifteen years I always deferred to his final word. The idea of now being able to make my own decisions was exciting. And yet if it hadn't been for his drinking, we might very well have stayed married. Above all, our work together in the theater was gratifying and stimulating.

But in the fall of 1971 I returned with our son to Leningrad. Pyotr Rachinsky was still general director of the Kirov. In Leningrad, Rachinsky told me I should return to dancing, or, if I didn't want to dance, he would make me a ballet master. Now I could stage Igor's *Romeo and Juliet* for the company if I wanted. He was sympathetic, even paternal with me. Crude and ignorant as he was, I found him by no means the worst of the functionaries who directed cultural activities in Leningrad. I officially re-joined the Kirov.

In 1972 New York City Ballet returned to Russia. Gennady Smakov, a university professor who'd started to write about ballet, spoke English as well as many other languages. He introduced me to NYCB's Robert Weiss and his wife Kathy. It was the first time I'd actually talked with Western people—not that I could converse with them, but Gennady translated some of their sentences for me. Mostly I just listened and smiled, think-ing how beautiful Westerners were. They wore spectacular winter coats; they looked so wealthy, so comfortable with themselves. They were like people from a fairy tale. They told us that the corps de ballet at NYCB was paid a thousand dollars per month. Knowing nothing about the exchange rate, we thought it a czar's ransom, since the Kirov's corps was paid a thousand rubles per year. They were curious about how Russians lived. Ricky Weiss had a camera and filmed everything he could. He promised to send some books to us and later did.

Sometime later they returned on a private vacation. It was probably in large measure because of Balanchine that they were so intrigued with Russia; they wanted to investigate the climate that had produced his ge-nius. Ricky had joked that they would put Alyosha, who was by now a student on Rossi Street, in their suitcase and bring him to Balanchine's school. "In three or four years he will be a great dancer." We talked seri-ously about finding a way for him to leave Russia.

Alyosha was now fourteen. He had spent two years at Vaganova with-out ever beginning to apply himself. He was more like me than Igor: he loved to read and study, to visit museums. He was a dreamer who wanted to watch ballet but not spend his life dedicated to physical work. Alyosha idolized Baryshnikov. I told Misha that I wanted to take Alyosha out of ballet school and put him into a school for the children of French diplo-mats. I asked Misha to come over and told him, "Whatever potential you see in him, still tell him that he will never be a really good dancer—give any reason you want."

"Okay, no problem," Misha said.

Misha arrived with pastry and a bottle of scotch. I told Alyosha to go change into his dance clothes. I planned to give him a little class in front of Misha. Alyosha returned, his eyes full of interest and a little secret mirth; he didn't quite believe in the performance I was orchestrating. No more than two steps into class, Misha blurted out, "Oh, my God! With legs like that, I'd be the biggest star on the earth! You're out of your mind."

Alyosha looked at me with a smile. "Okay, class is over," I said. "Thank you, Misha. Is this what I invited you for?"

~ 15 ~

restless

If I'd always dreamed of living in London, my childhood curiosity about the West had only grown with the years. We were now in the depths of Brezhnev's stagnation. A number of my friends had by now resettled in the West. I was restless by nature. I wanted to see the entire world, and that was virtually impossible to do as a Soviet citizen.

If I hadn't already been thinking about emigration, I probably wouldn't have applied to the choreography program at Moscow's GITIS, the graduate institute for theater studies. I had earned my diploma from the University of Marxism-Leninism, and I wanted to go back to school for graduate work in dance. It would have been a lot less trouble to attend the Rimsky-Korsakov Conservatory in Leningrad, but it was easier, however, to leave the Soviet Union via Moscow.

It was not easy to be admitted to GITIS. Candidates had to have professional experience and a degree of maturity. There were students from the Bolshoi and from some of the other republics. But officially no one from Leningrad was supposed to be admitted, since Leningrad had its own Rimsky-Korsakov Conservatory, and the two cities were in perpetual competition. No fewer than eight entrance exams were administered over the course of a week. The Kirov's Nikita Dolgushin, with whom I'd graduated in 1958, was now dancing with Moscow's Moiseyev Ballet, and I stayed with him and his wife.

Rotislav Zakharov was director of the dance program. He had choreographed a number of the most enduring Soviet plot-and-pantomime-driven *dramballets* in the old Stalinist days for the Kirov as well as the Bolshoi. "Don't worry," he told me. "You have a lot of experience and you're from the Kirov." For him at least, that was an asset.

In any case, I was admitted. We were required to study many disciplines, to acquire complete knowledge of how the theater functions. Choreography was the most important class, but we also studied ballet technique, character dance, acting, performance theory, scenery, music, and lighting design.

Raissa Struchkova taught ballet technique. She had been a major diva at the Bolshoi for decades, and she was in fact still dancing. In class now the goal was not to simply repeat the movements automatically, but to understand what each step was about. In class we would concentrate on one step, how it was supposed to function, how the body produced it. The next day we were expected to arrive with a choreographed combination based on that step.

Struchkova's husband Alexander Lapauri, also a principal dancer at the Bolshoi, taught our choreography class. When he invited the class to their apartment for discussions, she would prepare tea and sandwiches, and she was sweet with us. Nevertheless, she and I disagreed constantly in her technique class. Once we had a big fight about *temps lié*. When I showed it to her, she told me that I was doing it incorrectly: each movement was supposed to be articulated distinctly, and instead I was phrasing them with too much Kirov legato.

"Always in Moscow, it's nothing to do with anything except what they decide," I said.

"All you Kirov people are so arrogant; you think you're always right."

"We don't think we're always right, but when we're right, we're right. A *saut* is a jump. *Frappé* is beats; it's in the translation from French. Why do you think the *temps lié*"—linked movement—"shouldn't convey what the translation is?"

The next time she came to class, she said straight off, "I just want to ask you—is Marina Semyonova enough of an authority for you?"

"Yes, of course."

"She's from Leningrad," Struchkova reminded me. "Let's ask her. "

I talked to the great ex–prima ballerina. She had been, in 1925, Vaganova's first star graduating pupil and had danced with the Kirov before being summoned to the Bolshoi in Moscow in 1930. Semyonova knew me, because when I was working in Odessa she had come there to work on *Giselle* with one of her former students, who was a ballerina in the company. "Of course you are right," Semyonova told me, "don't listen to them."

Unfortunately, however, it was the history of the Communist Party that was treated as the most important subject offered. More than twenty party congresses had been convened, beginning in 1899, and we had to know the purpose and proceedings of each one. Our teacher showed up in class with his government medals spread across his chest to proclaim the profundity of the Soviet regime. In all my other classes—even Struchkova's—I received high grades, but I was failing this class. The transcriptions of each congress included contradictions of what had been established at prior congresses. I couldn't remember facts I didn't have any belief in. "I read one page, I turn to the next one, and everything is the opposite of the page I've just read," I protested.

"Don't get smart," my teacher said.

At each congress it was announced that due to advancements in Soviet agriculture, it had been possible that year to plant wheat earlier than ever before. "I really want to know," I said, "did they discover how to grow grain all year round?" Everyone present thought it was hilarious, except the professor, who threw me out of class that day. But finally he took pity on me. I was six months behind and I wouldn't be able to receive my diploma if I couldn't pass this class. He gave me a passing grade and said, "You owe it to me: you have to study this on your own." But I never did.

My second year at GITIS, I was hired to choreograph a musical in Leningrad. I was spending so much time there rather than in Moscow that I decided to enroll at the Rimsky-Korsakov Conservatory after all. The chief there was Pyotr Gusev, a classmate of Balanchine and a storied veteran of decades of ballet trench battles. I declared a concentration in ballet restoration, but most of the work was independent.

Lapauri and Struchkova were organizing a small tour to Canada in which they would star. He needed additional dancers and couldn't get any from the Bolshoi. "Whom do you think I can invite from the Kirov?" he asked me in Moscow.

"I don't think they will let you take Baryshnikov," I said, "but he would be the best one. But really they'll never let you take him on tour."

"Why?"

"I don't know," I said, which was a lie on my part because I knew very well that since he was now the Kirov's greatest success, the authorities dreaded the thought of him defecting.

"With my connections, I can get him," Lapauri assured me.

At the Kirov, Kolpakova was now Misha's most frequent partner. Lapauri didn't want to take her, however, because Struchkova herself was planning to dance the *Don Quixote* pas de deux with him. (And she made good on her plan.) But I think the fact that Kolpakova was forty-one helped persuade him to invite her; he didn't want young ballerinas near his Raichka.

Early in June, Misha and Kolpakova came to Moscow to dance *Giselle* as guests with the Bolshoi. Irina worried that she looked too old next to him, but actually she never looked old onstage. It turned out to be the best *Giselle* I ever saw her dance: her nerves pulled a soft shyness out of her. And that night she looked especially young because Misha showed a new maturity. Sitting in the director's box, close to the stage, I watched Misha illuminate everything around him. Originally, his Albrecht had been brother to Mercutio, but now tragedy followed him from his first entrance. Usually a cooler ballerina, Kolpakova responded with a new flare of emotion.

Afterward, Misha, Irina, set designer Svetlana Dimietriva, and I went to dinner. On the way, Misha took me aside and said, "How was it?"

I said, "Fantastic."

"No, tell me the truth," he said. "Was it on an international level? What do you think?"

I said, "Yes, absolutely." That phrase, "international level," had an odd sound. As I reassured him, his eyes were X-rays searching for any false flattery. I now was sure that he was making plans.

Svetlana had created scenery for Misha's "Creative Evening" at the Kirov earlier that year. She was a dear friend of mine; I often stayed with her when I was in Leningrad, at her marvelous tower apartment on the Fontana Canal. She lived there with her husband, a military officer. She was a member of the party and on good terms with people in the government. I asked her to help. Kolpakova had already submitted a request that Misha accompany her to Canada, but it had been declined.

Kolpakova and Svetlana were good friends. I asked Svetlana if she could intercede with the party. I knew that I was betraying her, but I was sure that she as well as Kolpakova would be able to ride out the storm.

"Lenchik, you think he will defect?" Svetlana asked.

"Absolutely not."

"Well, if you really think he won't . . ." She petitioned the Ministry of

Culture in Moscow, and they agreed on the condition that she sign a letter pledging her confidence in Misha. Misha had bought a new car; he had started talking to Svetlana about preparing another evening that would include a new *Tyl Eulenspiegel*, a wonderful vehicle for him. Svetlana wanted to believe he would be back, and I pushed her in that direction.

"You see he's already started to work with you . . ."

Two weeks later I sat with Misha in his apartment. He was scheduled to leave for Canada in two days. He squeezed himself into a huge armchair, drinking vodka. He was very silent. I wanted to give him the idea that he shouldn't come back from this tour. I told him that I wanted to leave Russia and was trying to arrange for an invitation from Israel. He didn't say anything, he just looked at me, very somber.

"I wish you would stay there," I said. "But it's your life."

"I will be back," he said.

I told him how quickly Alyosha was shooting up and that he'd outgrown his new tights. Tomorrow I'd go to buy him new ones.

"Don't, I'll give you a pair of mine," he said.

"Oh, really, he will be thrilled." Misha was Alyosha's idol. We used to laugh about this, and Misha had brought out two pairs of tights, monogrammed by the theater, and a pair of ballet shoes as a present for Alyosha. He never wore them; he has saved them all these years. I kissed Misha and he kissed me.

"I will see you soon," he said. It was dark by the time I left Misha's apartment, on the Moika Canal near the Hermitage. The street was empty except for a man walking furtively.

Before leaving, Misha visited all of his friends, which further confirmed my suspicions.

"What a pity he won't defect," Genna Smakov said to me.

"Why don't you think so?"

"Because he just bought a new car and he said as soon as he's back we'll go fishing together." But of course he wasn't going to drop any hints. Misha would have been insane to have told even his own his own shadow anything out of the ordinary.

~ 16 ~

émigré

In those days the bulk of emigration from the Soviet Union was granted to Jews. Since my father's father had been born in Dusseldorf, there was some credibility to claiming that I was Jewish, even though my passport didn't say so. "And what?" an official barked at me. "Your grandmother paid a lot of money to change your Jewish nationality?" No, I wasn't officially listed as Jewish, I told them, because my mother was Russian.

I had started choreographing for television and theater. Moscow theater director Pyotr Fomenko came to Tallinn in Estonia, where I was working on a music hall number. Fomenko was looking for a choreographer for a musical he was directing entitled *Relatives*. Fomenko was and still is an important member of the Russian avant-garde; in Moscow he has his own studio. I worked with him on his musical, and also on a three-hour television show, a fairy tale about a magician collecting watches, each one, sixteen in all, represented by a different dance.

At the same time, I prepared my emigration . . . very quietly. Once it was known that you were intending to leave the Soviet Union, you were instantly a pariah. I'd seen how it happened. After the Kirov's Sasha Minz had submitted his application to emigrate to Israel in 1970, almost everyone in the company stopped talking to him. When I sat with Sasha in the Kirov cafeteria, a cordon sanitaire of empty tables surrounded us.

And so by not saying anything, if I wasn't given permission to leave, I could still continue in Russia. I'd work and wait for another chance.

Genna Smakov had emigrated a year before me. Once he arrived in Israel, he started calling me in Moscow. Then he moved to New York, where he and Sasha Minz, who'd also gone first to Israel, were sharing an apartment on Seventy-sixth Street and Columbus Avenue in Manhattan. Genna and Sasha ran up an enormous bill, telling me how wonderful New York was. "You have to come here as fast as possible!" Sasha insisted. "If you won't, I'll send you a dress like Medea sent Glauce!"

*My grandmother, my uncle Leo, my mother, and my aunt Zoya,
Leningrad, late 1920s.*

*My father (lower right) with comrades on a Soviet delegation
to New York during the 1930s.*

My mother on holiday in Odessa before World War II.

My mother with me, summer 1939.

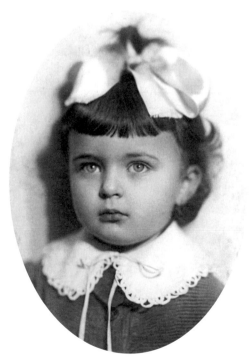

At two, my parents took me to be photographed at a studio on Nevsky Prospect.

*I'm twelve, in my second year
at the Vaganova Institute.*

I'm next to Nureyev (far left) at our graduation in spring 1958.

With my classmate Yasha Batvinik.

At the Kirov, Igor dancing Harmodius in Jacobson's Spartacus *with Kaleria Fedicheva as Aegina. Photo by Nina Alovert*

Together with Alexander Minz in the Kirov's 1963 film The Sleeping Beauty.

Planning Igor's Romeo and Juliet *with our friend Marc Jebijian in 1968.*

*One day I filled in as Romeo for Ivan Nagy when Makarova rehearsed
Igor's ballet in Baltimore in 1977.*

With Mikhail Baryshnikov and Gennady Smakov at the Tatiana and Alexander Libermans in Manhattan, celebrating the publication in 1980 of Natalia Makarova's Dance Autobiography.

With Baryshnikov on stage at the Met, 1983. Photo by Nina Alovert

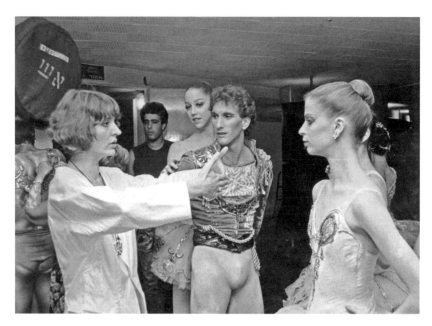

Touring Israel in 1984 with Hilary Ryan, Andrew Levinson, and Elizabeth Carr.

Teaching at Joan Miller's studio in Palm Beach, Florida, 1985.
Susan Jaffe in front.

Celebrating with Smakov and the Libermans at their country house.
Photo by David Moore

With Herbert Ross (far left) and Alessandra Ferri during the filming of Dancers *on location in Italy, 1986.*

Early Glasnost: my aunt Zoya, her daughter Nina,
and Nina's daughter Elena.

Rehearsing Cheryl Yeager and Julio Bocca in ABT's NY studios in 1987.
Photo by Tom Brazil

Rehearsing Giselle *at ABT in 1989 with Andris Liepa and Scott Schlexer.*

Summer 1991 at the Libermans with Joseph Brodsky and Baryshnikov. Photo by Alexander Liberman. Alexander Liberman Photography Archive, The Getty Institute, Los Angeles (2000.R.19).

Rehearsing Brigitte Stadler and Vladimir Malakhov in Giselle in Vienna, 1993.
Photo by Axel Zeininger

Alyosha with Maya Plisetskaya at Helen and Sheldon Atlas's country house in Connecticut. Photo by Helen Atlas

Helen Atlas and I with restaurateur Roman Kaplan.

With Diana Vishneva during Swan Lake stage rehearsal in the formerly Kirov, once-more-Mariinsky, September 2005. Photo by Valentin Baranovsky

Portrait by Marc Hom.

I was convinced that my phone was being bugged, and I screamed at them not to call. But somehow, within two months, which was no time at all for such a process, I was given permission to leave and to take Alyosha with me to Israel. I studied English in a two-week immersion class, in which no one was supposed to pronounce a single Russian word. Diplomats, who already knew some English, were taking the class. I was the only woman in the class. Things routinely got a little raucous. The one English phrase I took away from the class? "Don't touch me!"

Tulips as black as night, daisies like unfurled umbrellas: I was in a weird, resplendent landscape that changed radically with each tier of the mountain I climbed. My last summer in the Soviet Union, I traveled to Sochi, in Central Asia, where I saw spring crocuses blooming while snow capped the mountains peaks on the horizon.

A friend of mine, Kostia, was a brilliant mathematician, highly educated, but eccentric in the extreme. He considered himself a parapsychologist, or indeed he may really have been one. But his biggest satisfaction in life was accomplishing some task that I'd assigned him. Once I told him that a doctor who was treating me for a thyroid condition had prescribed a fruit available only in Georgia. It was impossible to purchase in Moscow. It spoiled within a few hours after picking. The next day, he left and came back in four days, bringing a basket of them to me.

For a year he had been telling me that I had to see a certain witch in the Caucasus who would heal my thyroid. Kostia said that he and the witch had once healed someone with a severed spinal cord. When he began to walk again, the villagers started bowing to them.

I knew it was my last summer in Russia, although I didn't dare tell that to Kostia because in addition to everything else, he was a nationalist, who insisted that everybody who left Russia would wind up in hell or in the Bermuda Triangle. We went together to the remote, mountainous area that I would never have visited alone. We stayed in the witch's house. She worked as a tour guide, taking visitors through the hills, where the blackberry bushes were taller than I, dripping with enormous, delicious berries.

The witch was on an intimate acquaintance with all the flora and fauna in the landscape. There were many different herbs growing wild.

She knew them all; she talked to each species. "They're alive," she told me, "they have feelings . . . you see?" She fingered one; it immediately shriveled from her touch modestly. She removed her hand and the leaves opened once more.

One morning I woke up and went out for a stroll. Sitting in the mailbox was a snake. I am so phobic about snakes that I nearly fainted. I ran to her as she was preparing breakfast. "There's a snake!" I wailed.

"In the mailbox?" she asked.

"Yes!"

"Oh, she's a friend."

"I saw you last night," Kostia told us one morning. "You tried to fly. Both of you."

We looked at each other and I said, "Yes, we did, but you weren't supposed to see."

"But I saw it!" he said with glee.

"You're our treasure," Kostia began telling me. "We have to preserve you."

He had started to think that I was an icon who was supposed to bring to earth a new baby Jesus. In order to preserve me, he had to kill me and then thaw me in fifty years. He and his friends were sure that they could bring me back from the dead. I didn't know whether to take him seriously or not.

What's more, he had decided that he was supposed to be the one who would give me a baby Jesus. He had talked to God and God had given him a message. I was asleep one night when my eyes suddenly popped open to see Kostia standing right by my bed, stark naked. I used every balletically toned muscle in my legs to give him a kick that sent him sprawling across the room. He was whimpering like a puppy while I jumped out of my bed and went in the kitchen. He retreated to his room, but I was so disgusted I didn't want to go back to mine. When our hostess came down for breakfast at six that morning, I told her, "I am in big trouble. Before he does something horrible, I have to leave right now, and you have to help me." Her husband took me to the train station with my bags. In Russia you didn't just a buy a ticket whenever you wanted to, so when the train arrived, I pleaded with the ticket taker. "I'll pay you double! Just give me any seat, or I will stand or sit in the corridor."

The train was scheduled to leave in a couple of minutes. Kostia had found a car and someone had driven him to the station. He ran to the train, saw me on the stairs, and yelled, "You can't go! You have to stay! You have to take me!"

"'Bye, Kostia, I have to leave. I had a telephone call: I have to be back in Moscow immediately."

"No you can't," he kept insisting. Yes, I had to, I kept repeating. The train started to move. I told the ticket taker, who had given me her own seat, she just could not let him on board, because she seemed as though she might be all too willing to take another bribe.

The train started to pull slowly out of the station. "I will stop the train! I will stop the train!" Kostia yelled. The train started slowly chugging down the tracks, then began accelerating before coming to a complete halt. Kostia jumped up and down, "I did it! I did it! I stopped the train! You have to get out!" We were already quite a ways down the tracks. He ran panting behind the train.

"Oh, my God, please God, please train, go, go!" Finally the train left for real. It was dirty and derelict, but for the two-day journey I was oblivious to everything except my relief.

But Kostia was soon back in Moscow and dancing attendance. He brought me a black amber ring. It was all but impossible to find black amber in Russia—only yellow was available. Kostia insisted it would be a protective talisman. Instead that ring almost cost me my life. But I get ahead of myself.

Igor had to give his consent for Alyosha, who had by now transferred to the Bolshoi ballet school, to leave with me. Genna Smakov and I had flown to Kishinev, the capital of Moldova, where Igor was now directing, and asked for his consent. Igor refused categorically. But when he made a brief visit to Moscow, friends of mine came every evening to try to persuade him. One famous Russian writer, director, and critic told Igor that he would never shake his hand again if Igor didn't sign the release. Finally, after a couple of weeks, Igor agreed. I ran to the emigration office. Igor and I went to stage his *Cleopatra* in Estonia, an unpleasant experience I had mistakenly thought would mollify Igor somewhat.

Once we got back, I let Alyosha leave Moscow to visit Igor in Leningrad. There Igor and his relatives started to work on Alyosha's brain. He was literally locked into various apartments and subjected to a barrage of intimidation. They told him that America was a horrible country. "Your mother will never find a job. She's going by herself and she can't even go from Moscow to Leningrad by herself. She always has her entourage. And now for the first time, she's going to travel alone—to America! She won't survive. You don't want to be involved. If she wants to do it, it's her business, but you shouldn't."

They were sincere; they were themselves poisoned by every kind of misinformation. They really did believe that the United States was a horrible place with crime on every corner, where people had to live like gangsters to survive. I wasn't going to able to survive, and if I wanted to do it myself, why did I have to destroy a child's life as well?

Igor retracted his agreement, saying that I had blackmailed him, which was all but true given the pressure my friends had applied. A comrade by the name of Kusheleva was head of the emigration office in Moscow. She called me, gave me the bad news, but advised me to fight for Alyosha—I think she had been offended by Igor's behavior. She helped me by extending my visa for an additional month. I asked her not to tell Igor about it and she didn't.

But Igor called her to check if I'd left because he knew when my original visa had expired. Kusheleva didn't tell him that I was still in Moscow. Igor sent Alyosha to my place and waited in the street, because by this time I had a lot of antique furniture that Igor coveted. Alyosha opened the door. I was there with all of my friends. "How could you do that?" they screamed at him. "How could you betray your mother?" I sobbed that in this case I would cancel my trip and stay in Russia. Everyone told me that I was crazy, that it would be killing myself. Alyosha said that in two years, when he was eighteen and I had my feet on the ground in the United States, he could and would come without Igor's permission. It became an especially traumatic farewell.

It was really due to a copy of Herman Hesse's *Siddhartha* that I was actually able to leave the USSR as planned. At Sheremtyevo Airport in Moscow, every pocket of mine was naturally searched. They confiscated a gold necklace I was wearing, but it was only when they spotted Kostia's ring that things took a dangerous turn. The stone had separated from the backing and a swastika-shaped grid underneath was now visible. It was

February 23, 1976, an army holiday in Russia, which meant that all the airport security officers were drunk. Naturally everyone in the Soviet Union knew that a swastika meant Hitler. "She's a Fascist!" they screeched the moment they spotted it. They had all been drinking to celebrate the 1945 victory against Fascism, and now they thought they had a live Fascist standing before them.

"Oh, my God," I gasped. "I've never seen it before."

"Oh, yeah," they jeered, "tell us this story." They held my plane one hour. They called the airport chief of police. They were so proud of themselves. "It's not enough you betrayed your country, but you're a Fascist."

I was terrified. I could have been put in prison. Everybody who left the Soviet Union was a priori guilty anyway. Thinking quickly I said, "Well, unfortunately you don't know that that is a symbol of Buddhism." I started to explain it to them.

They said, "Yes, tell us, tell us."

I said, "I *am* Buddhist."

They said, "What is that—Buddhist? You're Fascist." But when I pulled out Hesse's book from my handbag, printed on its cover was the very same design. Eventually they were mollified.

A few hours later, I was in Vienna.

2

THE NEW

~ 17 ~

holding pattern

My caseworker at Vienna's Hebrew Immigrant Aid Society treated me with great consideration, but made the mistake of not realizing that the two male émigrés he'd assigned to be my roommates were going to be at each other's throats over who could be more overly friendly toward me. I called my caseworker in desperation and begged him to send me on the set, HIAS-sponsored route to Rome as soon as possible. "There is one train tomorrow," he told me. "But your documents are locked in the safe at the office. I don't know if I can get them and make the necessary arrangements during the night." Yet somehow he did just that, and I took the special train for Soviet refugees. On the platform, a crowd of biblical proportions toted bags, boxes, and sacks sufficient for a wartime evacuation. At each end of every train car a soldier armed with a machine gun was stationed because terrorist groups were making attempts to attack the trains as they reached Italy.

The trip took about twelve hours. The seats weren't numbered; you simply had to look out for yourself. Families clustered together, the cars filled to the ceiling, the corridors crammed. I wedged my suitcase by my feet and could hardly move. I didn't have any food with me. I sat there starving until somebody offered me something. At a station en route where we stopped, I wanted to buy some soda or anything available to drink, but the guards wouldn't allow us to leave the cars. I sat there like a piece of wood, thinking, Whatever will be, will be . . .

For fear of terrorists, they did not take us all the way to Rome. We got off at an obscure little station, about two hours by train from the capital. It was practically an open field. A few buses came to pick us up. The luggage was taken away from the passengers and loaded onto a couple of enormous trucks. Some people screamed in panic, afraid that they would never see their things again. We were still surrounded by Austrian and Italian soldiers, and could not even take a step into the field. At that moment I couldn't have cared less about my suitcase; anything was better than the prospect of having to drag it myself. I held onto my shoulder bag as we walked to the buses. Finally they brought some mineral water and soda for us.

By evening we were brought to Rome and lodged in different pensiones. Mine was somewhere near the central railway station—Stazione Termini. In Moscow a neighbor, the son of a noted professor, a Pushkin specialist, had given me the phone number of his sister, Mila Malach. She had left Russia a little before I had and was staying in Rome, waiting for a visa to get to America. I hoped she hadn't already left. Apart from her, I knew no one there at all.

The elderly couple who owned my pensione spoke only Italian. Still, I tried to explain to them that I needed a telephone and that I wanted to change money. The old woman kept repeating, "Bank, bank." But Italian banks closed at 1 p.m. I tried to explain that I needed change, because all the phones at the pensione had little locks on them. You would give the owner some money, and then she would unlock the phone. Another Russian in the pensione knew two or three Italian words, and finally the couple let me call and pay them back the next day.

By this time it had been a couple of days since I'd had a real conversation with anyone. My suitcase still hadn't arrived. I was getting panicky. "Please come over as soon as you can," I pleaded with Mila. "Take me out of this hotel—anywhere. I am absolutely alone here!"

She showed up about an hour later and invited me out for a coffee. I had been too afraid to go out alone. Street vendors were selling smuggled Marlboro cartons for five thousand lire. I was horrified. Mila calmed me down, explaining that those "thousands" were not worth much. We walked a little, sat down in a cafe, and went back to the pensione. My suitcase had just arrived. Something was banging inside. I thought we should perhaps open it and check. For some reason, my Russian friends had given me a stash of Kuznetsovo plates and *matryoshka* dolls as going-away presents. And for some reason I had packed them all. Mila told me to bring the suitcase to her place and we'd unpack it there. She lived on Via Medaglie d'oro, very close to the Vatican, a lovely area of the city. Mila, her husband, and her son shared a room in a two-room apartment on the second floor of a cottage in a courtyard.

"Oh mamma mia! O mamma mia!" Mila's landlady kept clucking when she saw us open my suitcase in the hall. The dolls were in smithereens. At the Moscow airport, when I went through customs, they had taken everything out of my suitcase, then hastily thrown it all back in. They had opened all the nested *matryoshka* dolls and threw them back into my suitcase one by one, without putting them together. Just one *matryoshka* was somewhat intact. But I wasn't upset at all. Thank God, at least there is less to carry! I thought. We loaded the garbage can with the remnants of the plates and the dolls, as well as the broken spoons and forks that I'd packed. Now the suitcase was nearly empty. Only pink window curtains and a blanket remained.

Mila didn't have an extra bed, but she made up a bed for me right on the floor, and I was so happy. It was like a real home. She told me that their apartment-mate was moving out the next week, and suggested that together we could keep the entire apartment. That was really a stroke of luck! But after my very first day, I couldn't afford to even sit down in a cafe until I could start earning some money. Our refugee agencies paid us a hundred dollars a month, and my room was fifty dollars. As Mila and her husband had their son with them, life was even harder on them.

At the same house there also lived a Professor Vindorchik with his wife and daughter. He was from Leningrad, where he'd known the Malachs, so we formed a little Leningrad circle of our own, each taxiing up for an American or Canadian visa, and flying out one by one. As far as final destination was concerned, Soviet emigrants had little choice: most European countries did not accept immigrants, while Canada and Austria had a strict, selective system. Most people settled in Israel or the United States.

Right away I phoned Sasha Minz and Genna Smakov in New York, and they immediately began calling me regularly. They also told Baryshnikov that I was on my way. He wired me a very welcome five hundred dollars, which would have been all the more welcome if I'd been able to claim it right away. But sandbagged by bureaucracy, I received it only much later, almost on the eve of my departure for New York. Generally, Soviet refugees had no rights in Italy. We all entered on collective cover visas. We were stateless, as we had been forced to renounce our Soviet citizenship before emigration (paying a substantial sum in rubles to the government for that privilege). Naturally we didn't have European work permits, so some tried working "off the books" and usually kept their jobs a secret from the refugee agencies.

Mila took me to the Tolstoy Foundation, which was monitoring my U.S. immigration. I picked up my allowance, signed registration papers, took care of all the formalities. In about a week the foundation called me and said that there were two ballet schools that were interested in a ballet teacher (I guess the Kirov and Odessa theaters on my resume looked impressive). I was naturally thrilled at the idea of working again. One of the schools, owned by the charming Maria-Grazia, was for children aged seven to eleven. The other one was set up in a former apartment of Sophia Loren, in a sixteenth-century building, founded by the very rich Signora Lombardi who had bought this apartment, so I was told, when Loren ran into problems with the Italian tax department.

That was indeed a very unusual ballet school: parquet floors, sculpted ceilings, marble statues—one could hardly jump in the class for fear of bumping into the ornate architecture. This school was for amateur adults. In my class there were usually about a dozen people. Signora Lombardi was over sixty but periodically joined my classes.

I worked every day, alternating between the schools, and was paid a very welcome fifteen dollars per lesson. Since the Tolstoy Foundation had found the jobs for me, I felt a little awkward, so after I received my first paycheck I asked them to remove me from the charity list. "Forget it," they said. "It is not much money and an extra income will not hurt you." Mr. and Mrs. Stuart, my caseworkers at the foundation, were extremely pleasant people. They were not like the seasoned bureaucrats who worked at other agencies. Funded by White Russians who were not very wealthy, the foundation functioned on a small scale, with a modest budget. The Stuarts and the foundation became like a second home where I'd often visit for coffee and a friendly chat.

Jewish emigrants usually rented apartments or small houses in Ostia, a Roman suburb near the sea, about thirty minutes from the city by train. By the time I got to Italy, there was in fact a little Russian-Jewish ghetto in Ostia. Shopkeepers and barmen there had by now learned essential Russian. But apart from our circle of friends, in Rome, I seldom met fellow emigrants except a few times when we went to a huge market in Trastevere. An entire section was occupied by ex-Soviets selling *matryoshkas*,

phonograph records, linens, electrical appliances, caviar, and vodka—
the latter among the very few things that émigrés could take with them.
(Each was allowed two bottles of spirits and one tin of caviar.) It looked a
little like the famous Odessa market, with goods spread out on the ground
and people hawking the merits of their merchandise to puzzled Italians: I
heard that in Ostia there was also a lot of crime. Car theft became a problem; there were even a few murders.

But all this was far away from me. Italy seemed like paradise. I had a
professional job; I earned some money. Soon Mila and her family left for
the United States, and I was able to retain the entire apartment. The landlady raised the rent, and I paid $130 a month. But it was worth it; when
my friend Genya Poliakov finally arrived in Rome, each of us had a room.
Genya had been a teacher at the Bolshoi Ballet School. He and I had actually intended to leave Russia together, but his passport had been stolen in
Moscow two days before he was to leave.

I spent all the money I had. Before I left Moscow, I'd given away all
my clothes to friends. Whenever any Russian dancer went on tour, she
bought as many new clothes abroad as she could; somehow, in one part of
my consciousness, I wasn't leaving forever but just going on a trip! I still
had only the one pair of jeans and a few shirts that I'd left with. I wanted
to send more to my friends in Moscow, and good things were quite expensive: I remember paying thirty-five dollars for a jar of facial cream to send
to Moscow. One of my Moscow friends, Katya, worked in an American
bank; her apartment had been full of canned goods from the States. She
came to Italy to visit me, and I sent back with her a suitcase of presents.

When I took a short vacation in Capri, Genya subbed for me in my ballet classes at Maria-Grazia's. When I returned, he kept on working there,
giving me more time to walk around, visit churches, museums, as well as
read a lot of Russian books Genya had brought, together with some we
bought in the Ostia market.

Genya celebrated his thirty-third birthday one day that spring. In the
morning he left for his class. I spent the day putting things together for a
birthday party—he already knew a lot of people in Rome. In the afternoon
I was in the apartment alone when I looked out the window and saw a
monk passing by. By this time I knew a little Italian, enough to ask him
to bless me with the sign of the cross. Then he asked, "May I come up?"

"Yes," I said. As Genya had now reached the age of Christ, I had decided to give him a cross for his birthday. The monk gave me a blessing. I
told him about Genya's thirty-third birthday and the cross, and asked him
if he could bless it, too. He agreed and said that everything would be fine
with me and Genya. A moment after he left, I looked out the window and
he was nowhere to be seen. I had an almost mystical feeling, and when
Genya came home, I gave him the cross and told him about the mysterious monk.

He was deeply impressed: "This is a sign that I should stay in Italy."
I was angry at him—we were planning to go to America together, and
now it was if he were walking out on me! But from this moment, he had
changed his mind irrevocably.

~ 18 ~

new york

After six months of paper pushing, my U.S. visa came through. I'd loved my stay in Italy but was more curious than ever to finally see America. My last days in Rome I'd tried to spend as many lira as possible, since I was under the misconception that I wouldn't be able to exchange them in New York, just the way we had been forbidden to change foreign currency in Leningrad. I walked out of JFK airport with a hundred dollars exchanged from my remaining notes. Baryshnikov sent a limousine to pick me up at the airport. When I got to their apartment on Seventy-sixth Street, Sasha and Genna grabbed my hundred dollars and went out to buy ice and juice. They had never told me that they were actually penniless, and now their phone had been cut off.

That night, Genna took me to see Baryshnikov and Makarova dance *The Sleeping Beauty* with American Ballet Theatre. It was the closing night of their season at the Metropolitan Opera. I was disappointed by what I saw: neither Misha nor Natasha was great. Natasha was stiffer and skinnier than when I'd last seen her dance six years earlier.

In the hunting scene, Misha wore high boots and an enormous hat; he looked like Puss in Boots, not Prince Desiré. ABT itself looked like an immature company. I had the distinct impression that many of the dancers did not entirely know what they were supposed to be doing. Stylistically they weren't academically clean or refined, and of all classical ballets, this is intended to be the most refined of all. But the audience didn't seem to notice; they were perfectly happy and awarded Natasha and Misha ovations.

Backstage, Natasha opened her dressing room door. She started giggling hysterically and I was laughing to beat the band. Finally she asked, "What are you laughing at?"

"What are *you* laughing at?"

"Oh, *Elenka!*"

"*Natashka!*" We kissed.

"Well, what did you think of me?" she said. I told her a little white lie. We downed fingers of vodka while Natasha shot more questions at me. Since she seemed to really want to know, I did tell her diplomatically that I didn't think her arms were very correct and her extension wasn't as high as before. ABT was reopening across Lincoln Center Plaza in a few days' time for a six-week season at the New York State Theater. Natasha asked me if I had time to give her private classes. I most certainly did! Baryshnikov invited me to go eat with him after the performance. I did go, but by now I was too sleepy to even know where I was.

The next day Genna and Sasha took me to their friends, Helen Atlas and her husband Sheldon, a polymer chemist. Sheldon went off with the guys to pay the phone bill. Helen was Russian and French, had worked for Sol Hurok, and was now editing the monthly *Dance News*. We began a friendship that has continued to this day.

Soviet propaganda told us that there was filth, crime, and bacchanalia on every corner of New York City. Our journalists on occasion visited the city to return with footage documenting the meanest, roughest streets in town. During my first weeks here I was afraid to walk a single block by myself. And there was no question about it, New York was much dirtier than Leningrad or Moscow, where, as in European capitals, the streets were cleaned nightly. Social ills were more visible here. It was terrifying to see homeless on the streets. It was also, that June of 1976, hot as hell.

But I was shocked most of all by people's eyes. Looking at them I understood that yes, they *were* born free here. I know now that Westerners are just as insecure and full of complexes as Russians. But they weren't betrayed by their eyes, which were not afraid to look straight into mine. In Russia people seemed to always be glancing furtively, avoiding direct contact, trying to deflect exposure of their inner feelings.

It took me weeks to get over my fear, but once I had, I found I loved to be in the street constantly, to be part of the crowd. Body language and body mentality was the litmus test: how people moved, how they dressed. Russians were stiff and uptight even when walking. But down New York's streets I saw a choreography performed by relaxed, uninhibited bodies— much more than I'd seen even in Italy. Italian streets were hunting grounds for men, who all seemed to be impersonating macho playboys. They were tough and rough and rowdy. The men were much better dressed than the women, and they were obsessed with sex. If your eyes brushed theirs, even for a moment, you were almost caught, until and unless you made it absolutely, categorically clear that you weren't interested. Here glancing at someone might begin a casual, friendly conversation, without any obligation or expectation. Though I was armed with my "Don't touch me," I never needed to use it.

The 1960s were over, but something of their flavor remained. The spirit of New York seemed to be that you could do whatever your personal etiquette dictated. New Yorkers were almost a different population than anywhere else in the world. Here, for the first time in my life, I saw a woman sit and put her feet on a dinner table as we ate, without any evidence of the slightest complex whatsoever. Russians, like Asians, are reticent about exposing their feet. Walking barefoot for us was almost like going topless.

Professional opportunities came to me immediately. In those days, all Russians had a mysterious allure in the United States. Compared to today, there were so few of us. First, Robert Lindgren, dean of the dance department at the School of the Arts in Winston-Salem, North Carolina, invited me down there to teach for a week. A flattering article was written about me in a local newspaper. My next job was in the summer program of the Baltimore Civic Ballet School. Jeannot Cerrone, an ex-dancer who was now an administrator and all-around *macher*, recommended me to the School of American Ballet in New York, and they sent some of their students to my classes in Baltimore. Cerrone was also friends with Rebekah Harkness, who had recently closed her ballet company but still maintained her school in an old mansion on the Upper East Side.

Jeannot took me to meet Rebekah at her vacation house in the Hamptons. I had never in my life seen such opulence in a private house; it was a virtuoso exercise in kitsch. She pointed out her children among the many pictures spread around the house. She didn't tell me, however, that her son was in prison for second-degree murder, and that Edith, the younger of her two beautiful girls, had spent years in and out of mental institutions and had attempted suicide. Yet while Rebekah was tyrannical and possessive, I sensed a woman who was broken inside.

It developed that Rebekah wanted me not only to teach but to direct her school, but I wasn't ready to take on such responsibility. My English wasn't good enough, anyway. Rebekah was over sixty, but still took Spanish dance classes, with castanets, in a small studio with a private instructor. Sometimes she watched my class, sitting quietly in the corner. She kept asking me to give her a private class. I think I did once, but it was difficult to coordinate our schedules. But my workload was very light: after my morning class, I was free the rest of the day.

Dancers came from New York City Ballet and American Ballet Theatre. Allegra Kent shook my hand and said, "Thank you very much. It's a very beautiful class." As much as I had loved seeing her dance with NYCB in Leningrad, I didn't recognize her without makeup. Anne-Marie D'Angelo from the Joffrey came. Misha sometimes came. He complimented me when he told me that my class was close to Pushkin's, his own teacher. But I still wasn't looking at my own class analytically; I was just teaching what I thought worked. Alexander Filipov also appeared. He and Misha had studied together under Alexander Pushkin in Leningrad. Sometimes when they both took class with me, I'd give them especially difficult jumps and they would compete good-naturedly.

As the summer went on the class continued to fill up. Eva Evdokimova started taking class with me and also asked me to help her with the Black Swan pas de deux. I remembered her from the 1970 Moscow International Ballet Competition. The public was on her side, rooting for her to win a gold medal, after she performed the *Giselle* pas de deux gorgeously. When the gold was awarded to a Soviet dancer instead, even the Russians in the audience screamed and stomped their feet in rage.

People advised me to make my class easier, so that I would attract still more students. I don't blame teachers who do that, because usually it is a question of survival for them. But I was lucky that Rebekah paid me a hundred dollars for each class without counting how many were attending. I never needed to be dishonest about my work.

In Russia Makarova had not been a party member and had been given no opportunity to be a diva; in the West she was now the diva of divas. That's why when I began giving her private classes I gave her only small corrections, very carefully. Then she started asking me to watch her performances. Soon I began rehearsing her as well.

One day Natasha took me to meet ABT matriarch Lucia Chase, the company's co-director, with set designer Oliver Smith. Lucia had been a young society matron who pursued a ballet career in the 1930s after the sudden death of her husband. She had since poured a considerable amount of her personal fortune into ABT.

Natasha warned me to not to wear anything black, because that was Lucia's least favorite color. But I thought, Well, I love black and I'll be at a loss if I don't wear what I feel most comfortable in. And so I dressed in solid black.

"You're crazy!" Natasha scolded me when we met. But at this time I was rather blond, and Lucia did approve of blondes.

In any case, when Natasha took me into Lucia's tiny doghouse of an office at the ABT studios, Lucia was very nice to me. She had a long and deep connection with Russian ballet. She had studied with Pavlova's one-time partner Mikhail Mordkin, who relocated to New York after the Revolution. Lucia had become a ballerina in Mordkin's little company; she was one of a small group of Mordkin students who in 1940 founded Ballet Theater, as it was originally called.

She dropped a few Russian sentences, explaining that she had learned them from Mordkin. When she said she understood Russian "sometimes," I told myself, Be careful. She liked to give the impression that she was scatterbrained—it was easier for her to manipulate that way. But from that first meeting I felt that she knew exactly what she was doing at all times.

I liked her immediately. She did appreciate Russians, and she certainly extended us certain privileges. From that point on, when Natasha and I would arrive at the ABT studios in the morning, Lucia would immediately leave her office and let us use it as our dressing room. Sometimes she watched our class or rehearsals. Eventually she told me, "You have to work with us."

I said, "Well, you go on tour a lot and I already have a job." I lied to her that I'd signed a two-year contract that Rebekah had offered me.

"Rebekah Harkness?" Lucia said. "That's not the right place for you. You have to be here. I will buy you out of the contract."

Oh my God, I thought, what if she finds out that I lied? I had never signed or returned Rebekah's contract. Indeed during my first few years in America I was almost phobic about not wanting to sign any contracts.

It felt like putting myself into a cage, erecting a barrier around possibilities—subconsciously I think I found it too close to the oppression of Soviet life. And so for a while I stalled.

❧ ❧

Makarova's dressing room, five minutes to curtain, her table crawling with icons, candles, and good luck charms. "Dina, go, go, go," Natasha hissed. "I need time, it's late."

Natasha's assistant and right hand, Dina, would leave and I understood that I was supposed to, also. Natasha needed time alone for prayer and reflection before each and every performance.

During the day, Dina would bring holy water from the church. Even if a guest was allowed to visit Natasha's dressing room prior to the curtain, which happened rarely, he or she was never allowed to take a photograph before a performance—even Dina, who was also a photographer. No one was ever permitted to predict that the performance was going to be great.

Earlier we would have gone to the stage for a warm-up. But she was already glazed, too immersed in her role to hear more than the simplest corrections. If she was dancing something modern, I'd concentrate on stretching her and warming up her back. If she was going to do something classical, I'd focus more on tendus and passés to bring her feet alive, to start them thinking. I'd talk to her, pulling her out of her trance. I didn't have a formula pep talk; it depended on the ballet, on how nervous she was, on whether I had to bring her feet on the ground or lift her up a bit *off* the ground.

Whenever Natasha danced, improvisation always co-starred with structure; she invited impulse, the imperative of the moment, to guide her as she lived and breathed her roles. She never felt the same way two nights running and never could repeat herself—for years afterward, every performance of hers remained distinct in my memory. The slate was blank for every performance, and that meant extraordinary excitement for the audience—but torture for some of her partners.

Makarova never compromised with a partner; her personality was too vehement, her artistic impulses too sure. Yet his support, emotionally as well as physically, was crucial. He could inspire her to new heights, but if she sensed indifference, he could ruin her performance. Ivan Nagy supported her beautifully. In *Giselle* she went through his arms like mist. He was very demonstrative, and he helped her to express herself.

No approach, however, could have been farther from Natasha's than Misha's. He was disciplined, programmed. What he rehearsed, learned, and planned in the studio he did on stage. Natasha nettled him because she was so utterly unpredictable. When they danced together, he might feel abused and she might feel thwarted, her fabulous expressiveness a little pinched. Their paths might diverge, and you'd see a moment of clumsiness, although Misha was too professional to refuse to follow her, the way Nureyev did once. Natasha went her way; Nureyev continued on his, and he let her go splat to the ground.

In some ways Natasha and Misha were made for each other onstage. Their training, their bodies, and body language blended perfectly. But there was more rivalry than rapport between them. Sometimes they weren't speaking at all, and when they danced I would have to go back and forth between them with messages. But though they squabbled frequently, I knew that they had great respect for each other as artists. And if they couldn't express their respect, I thought there was nothing wrong with my doing it for them.

"Misha has told me so many compliments about you, Natasha."

"Oh, you're lying."

"No, it's true."

"Really?"

Misha was just as pleased when I started directing some reciprocal good feeling his way. In the middle of this detente during the summer of 1977 they performed a stupendous *Giselle* with ABT at the Mann Music Center in Philadelphia. Whenever Makarova danced a role, she felt as though she were participating in the entire span of her character's life. A few hours became a lifetime, and that night Natasha seemed to have drawn Misha into the telescoped intensity, the felt experience of her onstage world. They were two instruments playing exactly the same notes. The outdoor setting of the Mann Center contributed its own enchantment. The theater was packed, their success unbelievable. I was elated for days afterward.

After a performance like that, words always feel small and false to me.

Yet I came to Misha's dressing room and told him the performance had been incredible. He was startled—maybe because I'd never said that before to him. Maybe he hadn't been satisfied. "What was incredible about it?"

"Everything!" was all I could say at that moment.

It was clear that Misha's reading, his experimenting with modern dance in the West had enriched his performances in the classics. His movement became looser; he acquired that bold swagger which had come so naturally to Nureyev. His maturity gave the mime in *Giselle* a new believability. Some of the emotional honesty of his Russian performances was gone, but his interpretation was deeper.

His technique had likewise become more Western. Russian women, but particularly men, took slower and heavier preparations than dancers here. Their jumps also were slower and heavier. The influence of Western classes and dancing Balanchine's repertory at ABT had already made Misha faster and crisper than he'd been at the Kirov. He had honed his attack; he now pointed his feet extra hard, as if to give his line a Manhattan dynamism.

Natasha was dying to somehow finally perform Igor's *Romeo*, in which she'd been usurped by Kolpakova at the Kirov in 1969. She asked if it would be possible to revive the ballet here. I thought it was anything but possible. "Natasha, it was seven years ago, how I can possibly remember?" Makarova herself had worked six months on the ballet, yet she didn't remember a single step. And it was an entire forty-five-minute ballet, with corps de ballet as well as principal dancers.

Natasha implored me until I began listening to the music—incessantly. I became nearly obsessed; it was hard to eat, to sleep. For two months, I closed my eyes and soaked in the score, until little by little steps reappeared. The ballet was reappearing in my mind just like a film slowly being developed, until I was convinced that I had correctly recalled the entire ballet, except for a few stitches in the corps de ballet material that had to be rewoven entirely.

The Baltimore Civic Ballet, where I'd taught a year earlier, now agreed to produce the revival. In March 1977, Natasha finally performed her Juliet, partnered by Nagy. Then Lucia took the adagio into ABT's repertory. At times, Lucia's erudition could be suspect. "How much do we have to pay him?" she asked about Hector Berlioz.

"Lucia, he is dead."

"Thank God—fantastic news!"

One day that spring in her dressing room, Natasha told me that she was pregnant. She wanted a baby, but she was thirty-six and she saw her career going up in smoke. One year would be lost altogether, and then she couldn't be sure if she'd ever regain her form. She made me promise to help get her back into shape, which I did, and she actually was able to return to the stage in better shape than when she left.

Natasha didn't want me to tell anybody, especially not Misha. But because they were fighting, I was afraid his fingers might dig into her waist just a bit more than was called for. "Can you keep a very big secret?" I asked Misha.

"Of course, you know me."

"Well, Misha, you're dancing with two tonight."

"What do you mean?" His back up immediately, he thought she was going to cancel after the first act.

"Natasha has a baby inside. You have to be very careful."

"Oh my God!" he gasped. "It's not true!" It hadn't seemed as though she were planning to have a child. But Misha was very careful with her, and they gave another great performance.

Sasha, Genna, and I had now moved to another apartment, seven blocks farther south on Columbus Avenue. Soon after, a stroke of luck took me from the near squalor of living with two confirmed bachelors into the lap of the most fantastic luxury. Eugenia Delarova, who had danced in the Ballets Russes and once been married to the choreographer Leonide Massine, now was married to a wealthy French businessman, Henri Doll. Eugenia remained passionate about ballet and never missed a single performance of Makarova's.

Eugenia and Henri lived on Fifth Avenue and Sixty-fourth Street, but they also kept a "spare" house on Seventy-fifth Street between Madison and Fifth Avenues. When Eugenia went to Baltimore to see Natasha dance Igor's *Romeo*, she invited me to stay in this five-story house. I was happy to accept! It was stocked with servants and impeccably maintained. The house was decorated simply, beautifully, comfortably. On the ground floor was Henri's office, a small ballet studio, and a lovely garden. Each floor above that could function as a self-contained apartment. One floor was reserved for Galina Vishnevskaya and Mstislav Rostropovich, but I never saw them there.

For one entire year I had practically no bills to pay, and Eugenia made sure I earned extra money by paying me to give private lessons to her granddaughter. Genna Smakov and Sasha Minz would visit me and Genna would cook for us. I asked Eugenia if it was okay to have people over.

"Oh, *dushka*," she said, "I'm very happy about it, because I was concerned you were completely alone in the house." After a while, I began to think of moving out to someplace that I could furnish myself. Eugenia was shocked: "*Dushka*, rent is very expensive, and you will have to pay for everything: telephone, electricity."

But soon there was another reason that I wanted to move out on my own. I fell in love with a young ballet student, fifteen years younger than me. Charles's life has taken him so far from ballet that he doesn't want his last name mentioned in this book.

Despite the age difference, it was Charles who was focused and mature about practical matters that I was prone to ignore. He was very talented but had started ballet only in college, not because he wanted to but because he actually won a scholarship to the Sorbonne on the strength of his dance potential. But what he was passionate about was literature: I used to say that he ate books.

I told Eugenia that I'd met Charles and asked her permission to let him stay over.

"How wonderful," she said. "I'm very happy about it." But six months later, Charles and I came back to the apartment on Sixty-ninth Street and Columbus Avenue when Genna and Sasha moved out, each having decided he wanted his own place. In the fall of 1977, we were married.

~ 19 ~
kirkland and baryshnikov

A year earlier, in Nureyev's dressing room during his "Nureyev and Friends," season on Broadway, he had asked me to watch his performances from the wings and let him know what I thought.

"Well, I thought it was a little bit boring," I later told him about the program he'd chosen.

He laughed, "Yeah, all you Russians want to have is fun, only fun, always. Everything's boring for you." And with those words, I had suddenly realized that Rudi was not Russian anymore.

Misha, too, was determined to show that he was now an American. In rehearsal Makarova and I spoke in English as best as we were able. But between us, when we were standing and talking, we might launch into Russian, and he would scold us: "Stop speaking Russian! Speak English!"

"Misha, it's ridiculous for me to speak English with you," Natasha protested in Russian. "Really ridiculous."

Backstage at ABT, Sasha Minz, who was now performing character roles with the company, introduced me to Gelsey Kirkland as a new arrival from Russia.

"Oh, God!" she cried, "Again Russians; we won't have any more performances!" Sasha assured her that I was a coach and not a dancer. Kirkland had left New York City Ballet to join ABT and dance with Misha two years earlier; she was now one of ABT's greatest and youngest stars, but already one of its most erratic and volatile.

On stage, her partnership with Baryshnikov was a perfect union in which every line, every sinew, every crook of their bodies complemented the other. Never had a Giselle and Albrecht seemed more destined to be together. But their work together was fraught.

That fall of 1976, Misha asked me if I wanted to watch Gelsey and him rehearse for an upcoming appearance at the White House. Painfully thin, Kirkland teetered on pointe, trying the same preparation over and over again, while Misha warmed up. They said nothing to each other. When they started to rehearse, however, Gelsey asked if they could change some steps in the *Corsaire* pas de deux to make the choreography easier; she was having too much trouble staying centered. Misha was very aggravated, for simplifying steps was anathema to him. He changed them only to make them more difficult. In any case, at one place in the pas de deux, they became stuck when Gelsey obsessively asked him to repeat something again and again. Finally Misha had had it. He stormed out. Gelsey's eyes were full of tears as she stood and watched him leave. I went back the next day. She tried very hard and he was nicer to her, with the result that they were almost able to reach the end of the pas de deux before it started to unravel and he walked out again.

By the following spring, however, Kirkland had made one of her cyclical comebacks, and was now again in near-peak form. For me, her Giselle was a revelation. She had prepared herself for her debut two years earlier by watching tapes of Makarova and working with her own coach, David Howard. What she did was perfect for her; I wouldn't have changed anything.

Kirkland couldn't be a medium for Giselle the way Makarova was; she didn't feel a character so deeply inside. Yet Gelsey's elfin appearance was perfect for this heroine, and whether moving or poised in arabesque, her body was a portrait of infinity. If in *Giselle* her style was Russian-influenced with a British accent, her statement was altogether American. Gelsey's rebel spirit manifested itself in sublime revisionism. I loved the way she broke rules that were inviolate in Russia. Altering the musicality and timing of familiar passages, she produced effects that were startling, freshly expressive. In the spectator they produced the emotion that Gelsey herself did not experience.

Summoned by Myrtha, Giselle emerges from her grave, sinks into a low obeisance before Myrtha, and then from stillness begins her initiation dance with a whirlwind of hops on demi-pointe. The original is very uncomfortable for the ballerina. Resting on the floor behind her, her right leg lifts, and then her left leg has to initiate this vortex without any visible lurch or adjustment. But here Kirkland asserted her maverick daring: Gelsey slid her right leg forward, stepped onto it in plié, whipped it behind her, and used that impetus to then send her left leg spinning. It made it easier to start her turns, and it powered them with delirious momentum. Some would call it cheating, but she was spectacular.

During the vision duet that follows, the ballerina takes the classic *Giselle* arabesque, both arms silhouetted to the front, then steps into another arabesque, this time raising her arms and back leg higher. She performs the two arabesques stage right, then does two more stage left. This brief passage is something that I could spend more time coaching a ballerina on than almost anything else in the entire ballet. These arabesques can suggest a specter ascending higher and higher into the sky, or they can look pretentious or earthbound. The movement's character is determined by the connection of the ballerina's feet to what should no longer seem a flat floor but, rather, clouds shifting with each one of her steps. Every time she takes the arabesque, her back leg should rise so fast the spectator barely notices it ever returned to the floor. Kirkland was stunning here. She took the walk twice as fast as anyone else: for every two arabesques the ballerina usually takes, Gelsey took five, so that the transition from arabesque to arabesque became invisible.

A childhood refugee from Stalin's Soviet Union, Remi Saunder was for a time Misha's unofficial manager, but most important she was nearly a mother surrogate to him. She was interesting and funny, sharp and energetic. She had great connections; she had known many unusual people in all walks of life, from Leonard Bernstein to Albert Einstein. If she needed something, or if Misha needed something, she would wield an irresistible charm and invariably get exactly what she wanted. But if she felt that she or Misha was being put upon, she could be extremely blunt.

Charles France had worked his way up from driver for ABT trustee Justin Colin to head of ABT's press department, and he was a close friend and advisor of Misha's, for whom he wrote the book *Baryshnikov at Work*. If not for Remi and Charles's powers of persuasion, Misha probably never would have had the confidence to choreograph *The Nutcracker* for ABT in 1976. After its success, Remi told Misha that his next staging project should be a full-length *Don Quixote*. Basilio had been Misha's greatest role in Russia, and he was sensational dancing the act 3 grand pas de deux at ABT. At Remi's apartment, he asked me to work with him on the new production. We started during the summer of 1977, a month before ABT returned from vacation. The first thing he did was to choreograph a new

act 2 gypsy dance, using me as raw material. Then ABT's Clark Tippet arrived and he and Misha partnered me. After that, Misha called in some
girls from the company who were willing to give up their vacation time.
Progress was slow because Misha, even after the success of his *Nutcracker*,
felt very tentative about the entire undertaking.

Naturally, Misha was going to dance Basilio at the opening and Kirkland was to be his Kitri. Gelsey made her first appearance when the entire
company reported back to work. I taught her the role and worked a lot
with her alone. I gave her a lot of stylistic corrections about her arms;
after that she took lessons in authentic Spanish dance and worked with
David Howard. Gelsey was still a little weaker than desirable for such an
explosive, bravura role, and she was very insecure about her own performance. But I thought she would be very good.

Petipa's custom had been to bring into his ballets as many principal
dancers as possible, to use them like floats in a parade to enliven the performance. The Street Dancer who cavorts throughout act 1 with the mata-
dor Espada needed a dancer with strong personality, because there was
nothing especially technical for her to do. At the Kirov, the stars never
had enough performances because the company was so huge, and so the
biggest ballerinas, including even Dudinskaya, all performed this role at
one time or another. At ABT, it should have been danced by a ballerina of
the caliber of Cynthia Gregory or Martine van Hamel, but Misha knew
that ABT's stars were overworked as it was and would refuse to take on
something like this. But he combined the Street Dancer's role with act
2's Mercedes and had her lead the act 3 Fandango, in line with his goal to
give individual roles more heft and more continuity across the three acts.

At the Kirov a new ballerina appeared in act 3 after the adagio of Kitri
and Basilio to dance a bravura variation that allowed the principals a little
rest before their variations and coda. Lubov Voichnis had been so chic,
charming, and brilliant in this variation that no matter who the Kitri was,
the Kirov was packed when Voichnis danced the solo. I told Misha that
a corps de ballet girl or even a soloist didn't have enough personality to
perform it; it needed a ballerina. But Misha instead assigned it to one of
the soloist flower girls.

"It's a ballerina's variation," I told ABT's girls. "Whatever your rank in the company, when you dance this variation you have to bring to it a ballerina's presence."

We chose corps members Cynthia Harvey and Julinda Menendez for the first-cast flower girls. Lucia objected to promoting people from the corps.

"But they're good, strong dancers," I argued, "and someday maybe they can be soloists."

"It doesn't matter," she said. As so often, her consideration was budget. "They will get one part, and next day they will be in my office asking for a soloist contract." But Misha and I prevailed.

It was very difficult to train ABT's dancers in the act 1 Seguidilla, where character-dance arms and accents needed to be articulated with swirling, sizzling speed. And it was particularly difficult for the demi-soloist girls dancing before the act 3 grand pas de deux to preserve the Spanish flavor in their arms, while swishing their hips flirtatiously. But in the end everyone was not bad at all.

I was happy when Misha decided to call this a "ballet-vaudeville," since the production as he conceived it had been brought closer to American popular entertainment. But I was disappointed that we had to cut children from the vision scene, the ensemble in which I'd once had my periscopic look at Natalia Dudinskaya. We didn't have children from the ABT school available, and to coach children in every city on tour, or borrow some from the School of American Ballet in New York, was too complicated, too much extra work, and too costly.

Don Quixote was going to premiere during ABT's season at the Kennedy Center in March 1978. Misha was spitting bullets before the opening night. Nobody could keep him calm and I didn't try. "You're fired!" he screamed at anyone who was in the wrong place on stage. Every day the company asked itself who would he fire that day? There wouldn't be anybody left to dance, not that Misha had the authority to do more than take someone out of his own ballet. When he got very wild, I wouldn't even sit with him during the stage rehearsals.

Santo Loquasto's scenery included a canvas floor cloth that was so slippery that dancing across it was like skating on glass. Gelsey was terrified about it—everyone in the cast was. But Misha thought it worked very well with the scenery. Shortly before the opening night, I led a stage rehearsal.

"Do you think I could change some things?" Gelsey asked me timidly. Could she do that or that in her act 3 variation?

"I don't know; you'll have to ask Misha."

Her face clouded. She steeled herself and started again, dancing exactly what Misha had set. Halfway through, she burst. "I have to change it! I just have to!" she cried, and vanished before I could say one word.

Misha knew that I hated appearing on stage, but he told me in no uncertain terms that I was to bow on stage with him, Loquasto, and lighting designer Jennifer Tipton. I went to the Valentino boutique in the Watergate complex and found a red chiffon gown that cost a fortune, but red was perfect for *Don*, and presumably no one in Washington would be wearing the same thing. (In the West I was free to indulge my love of clothes to a financially ruinous degree!) I went to have my hair done because Misha told me that if I wore it up formally he would give me a special present: a Spanish comb. I applied full makeup, which I hadn't done for a long time. I later heard that in her box, Lucia said during the bows, "Who's that? Who did Misha bring on stage? His girlfriend?" Backstage she came up to me: "Who are you?" She was a little tipsy.

"*Lucia*, what's wrong with you?"

"Oh, my," she said. "It's you. Oh, my—you look like a model!"

Later in our Washington run, van Hamel injured her hip in Kitri's act 1 entrance. They closed the curtain and hunted down Gelsey and Misha, who had danced the matinee that same day. They were having drinks in a nearby restaurant. The intermission lasted an entire hour, as Gelsey and Misha were hustled into the theater, into their costumes, and pushed onstage. Gelsey, who usually spent hours on her makeup, made do with a smear of lipstick. In the farcical pantomime Misha was a little overdone, but in general it was their best performance. Gelsey was uninhibited and spontaneous as she so rarely could be onstage. But when I came to Misha's dressing room after the performance, he was gray with exhaustion.

"I have news for you," Misha told me in Washington. "Don't tell anybody. I'm leaving ABT." I was shocked when he told me that he was going to join New York City Ballet, but Misha said that living in the same city with Balanchine and not taking the chance to work with him would be an incalculable loss. And he told me that both Lucia and co-director Oliver Smith wanted me to work full time with ABT. I still wasn't sure that

I wanted to make any binding commitment. However, things had gotten very strange at Harkness House. Ex–Ballets Russes dancer Nikita Talin arrived to direct the school. While he introduced me in front of the staff as the school's principal teacher, it was clear that he wanted me out. Rebekah had now begun complaining that she didn't feel well.

I shudder remembering the last time I saw her, in her suite at the Carlyle Hotel. Nikita and a friend he'd installed at the school were living with her. By now she had been diagnosed with cancer, but Nikita had evicted the resident nurses. Rebekah wore a cast on her arm and leg. A delicious lunch was served on a gilt table and chairs, covered with a fake-looking gold appliqué. I thought that if I had all the money in the world, I would never buy something as ostentatious.

"I fell last night," Rebekah told me. "I fell out of bed. I screamed all night for help and nobody came."

"Oh, she's joking!" Nikita twittered. "We're here all the time." Nikita called the day nurse he had permitted to remain and ordered an immediate injection, which rendered Rebekah so foggy that she could barely speak. Nevertheless, we discussed a television special that Leonard Bernstein's son Alex wanted to film at the Harkness school. I'd been asked to participate.

Rebekah was very enthusiastic. "Oh, you can do it; it will be wonderful. You can do whatever you want," she said. "Use our costumes." The Harkness Ballet's properties were all lying fallow in a warehouse.

"Okay, okay, okay, you have to go," Nikita insisted. "She needs to rest." He took me by my shoulders and steered me out of the apartment. I left feeling that I had been a helpless witness to a terrible crime. I decided that I did not want to be connected in any way with Harkness House anymore. The issue was moot, anyway, because soon after that Nikita fired me.

abt's stars

I didn't want to go on tour with ABT, but Joyce Moffatt, who had recently become general manager, called me to her office in New York and told me that with Misha now at New York City Ballet, I was needed to supervise his *Don Quixote*. Lucia's stars used to change choreography to do whatever was more comfortable, or interject new tricks that they had discovered at will. Baryshnikov was certainly not going to tolerate anything like that in his production, over which he maintained control, as is customary in ballet, despite the fact that he had left the company. Joyce had great powers of persuasion. I signed my contract, and the next day she and I flew to Los Angeles together. I went straight from the airport to a rehearsal at the Shrine Auditorium. That began my twelve years working with ABT full-time.

Now that I'd finally gotten to Hollywood, mecca of my childhood fantasies, I found the tackiness of much of the culture and the landscape disappointing, on this and many subsequent tours. But there was certainly a mutual fascination between their dream factory and ours. A friend brought me to Warren Beatty's home. He was working on *Reds* and was very interested in Russian people, in our characters. Some time later he even came to the Harkness school in New York to look for me, but I had long since left.

Beatty loved ballet and had just had a fling with one of our ballerinas. "She's so simple and so open, without any bullshit," he said. "She just undresses and goes to bed. Are all ballerinas like that?" he asked.

"Well, it's possible to think this way, because they spend their lives undressed, but I don't think all of them go to bed that easily." He tried to pronounce some Russian words that Maya Plisetskaya had taught him—all obscene. "She's just incredible," he said. "I adore her."

Another onetime lover of Julie Christie's was there also. "The hardest years of my life," Beatty sighed about Christie, and both men laughed, but their affection for her was clear.

Baryshnikov and Makarova were always open to learning. They knew that no dancer is perfect—ever—while ABT's native stars, it seemed to me, were much more likely to consider themselves already finished products. Their work ethic seemed much more casual. An ABT star in rehearsal would say to his coach, "Yeah, I have to repeat that . . . I will do that . . . I will do it . . . and thank you!" Nevertheless, the dancers seemed to understand immediately that I had something to offer them, and as with Makarova, I began with gentle corrections before attempting to make more substantive ones.

Marianna Tcherkassky was just making her debut as Giselle. She had a wonderful tenderness and a freedom in the second act that I liked very much. She had the most beautiful hands of any American ballerina at ABT, and we made her port de bras even more expressive by retraining the way she used her lower back. Then as now, Americans generally don't use the lower back to set their upper body, and when arms grow from the shoulders rather than the waist, it makes the shoulders hunched and the arms constricted. Marianna was open to suggestions and she continued to enhance her lovely style over the years.

Cynthia Gregory had been born to be a ballerina. She was never embarrassed to be on stage, never, even when she wasn't right for a role. Anything she did, she believed she could do. Her natural gifts were unsurpassed. She had begun doing pyrotechnics so early that she had never developed any apprehension about them, whereas other dancers, even though they were ready to do certain tricks, could be spooked by them, held back by fear. But a wealth of native ability brought bad habits, too: Cynthia relied too much on her upper back to help her turn and balance, with the result that it became stiff—or perhaps it was naturally rather inflexible and in some way that gave her extra stability. Which was the particular chicken or egg here, nobody could be really certain. Yet she was such a queen onstage that she won over the audience completely, whatever she did. I loved the power of her sleek, beautiful legs. Cynthia did not have the singing body of Natasha or Gelsey, but instead a faultless ear for music, an ability to dance impeccably on the music.

It was always a pleasure to work with Martine van Hamel. It was possible to pull something unexpected out of her. You could give her a selection of ideas about a role and she would always know which were right for her and which were not. She was rich material for choreographers or ballet masters: she had many different lines in her character and you could pursue whichever you wanted.

Nevertheless, I was certainly surprised to see both Cynthia and Martine cast for Aurora in *Sleeping Beauty*. According to Kirov rules, that particular ballerina role required a shorter and slighter ballerina, with a different muscular temperament. In Russia we'd been told that Aurora had to dance like a young deer, light and unpredictable. It was difficult for Martine to make her movement register as impulsively changing direction. But we could make her feel light, and approach movement with a special lightness. With Cynthia I concentrated on making her arms more baroque; throughout *Beauty*, the ballerina's arms and hands need to give us the impression that they are resting on invisible panniers. In Aurora's morning radiance there must be something tentative. Cynthia, however, embodied the full shining refulgence of midday. Yet as with Martine, ultimately the audience believed she was Aurora, and so did I. Perhaps that was the beginning of my reconsideration of some needlessly stringent parameters of Russian casting.

Ever since ABT had brought *Lilac Garden* to Russia in 1960, I'd wanted to meet Antony Tudor. Graham—I'd seen only pictures of her company—Tudor, and Balanchine were the three Western choreographers I wanted to know. So naturally I was excited when Tudor said he wanted to talk to me.

I came to a rehearsal in New York and he was being harsh to the dancers. I was surprised, because I'd pictured him very differently. When he turned to me he was faultlessly polite. But his eyes were full of an inquiring sarcasm. I was afraid that with my still-limited English—every single day I made lists of new words to memorize—I wouldn't be able to make conversation. However, he was full of patience. He offered to order tea; I think he saw it as my security blanket. "I know you Russians drink a lot of tea." And from that moment, I started to feel very comfortable with him.

He explained that he was trying to revise ABT's *Sleeping Beauty*, to make it more stylistically homogenous. He tried to refresh the mime, the fairies' first entrance in the Prologue, and the Polonaise in the wedding scene.

He asked me to show him the Kirov's setting of the act 3 jewels divertisse-ment. "I like it a lot." He asked me to teach it to the company as I'd shown it to him, and they then performed this version.

I was fascinated by the deep emotion in his ballets, and he knew that. Several years later, after Baryshnikov began directing ABT, he begged Tudor to revive *Pillar of Fire*, which had been out of the repertory for sev-eral years. Tudor was for some reason reluctant. "Okay, I will give it to you," Tudor finally said, "if this Russian ballet master will do it." I don't even know if he was serious, but Misha told me that, in that case, I had to take on the role of Tudor's tormented Hagar. But at forty, I was certainly never going to put on pointe shoes ever again. Eventually, Tudor did re-lent, and Hagar was danced powerfully throughout the 1980s by several of our ballerinas.

ABT's backstage atmosphere was much less disciplined than what we'd been used to in Russia. At the Kirov, regisseurs were posted on both sides of the stage to ensure that everybody arrived on time and where they were supposed to be. But here dancers could cheat. Corps de ballet members in a crowd scene could be late for their entrance, or even fail to show up at all without any penalty. From the audience it was almost impossible to count every member of the milling townspeople or nobles, and there was no one stationed in the wings to check. Once I walked into the wings and saw dancers who were supposed to be on stage, drifting in from the cafeteria. "What is the matter with you?" I screamed. The ranks of Ameri-can ballet companies, even the most prominent ones, were shaved to the minimum, and so it was especially important that every crowd member be at his or her post to ensure at least an illusion of fullness.

At the Kirov no one could talk in the wings and nobody except a regis-seur or a dresser stood near a ballerina when she made her entrance. It was a more respectful and more hierarchal environment. Here the wings were always crowded, and in studio or at the theater the atmosphere was egalitarian. Even later, when Baryshnikov was director, a dancer could sit in Misha's customary chair and not get up when he appeared in the studio.

After Misha decamped to New York City Ballet, Lucia hired Anthony Dowell from the Royal Ballet. Dowell was unfailingly cordial and well be-haved, a true English gentleman, as well as a great artist who understood immediately any suggestion about a role, a style, an expression. Only you had to be very clear and sensitive with him because he was trusting and malleable. He could follow bad directions as willingly as good.

Now, Dowell and Makarova consolidated a partnership in which a unique intellectual and spiritual cooperation prevailed. In *Giselle*, Dowell's Albrecht was a Renaissance humanist who was genuinely in love with Giselle and everything she represented. She was an escape from stifling court etiquette, an escape to a world closer to the natural order than he had ever imagined. It was a shocking epiphany, and it was in order to experience that, to enter Giselle's world, that he disguised himself and deceived her.

Anthony could invest so much meaning in a single gesture. When Albrecht is finally unmasked before Giselle and Albrecht's fiancée, Bathilde, Dowell's eyes lingered on Giselle until the last possible moment. With his head still low, he checked her reaction furtively. Then his head bowed to kiss Bathilde's hand as if dropping in defeat.

No less than Makarova, Dowell never subordinated himself. But he adjusted to whatever key she was in on a particular night. At the same time, with him Makarova was less consuming than usual. Dowell knew who he was at every moment in his roles and Makarova collaborated with him. He was gentle and intelligent, and he could influence her. Dowell didn't quite have the muscular strength of Ivan Nagy, but he had intelligence and gallantry in spades, and a sixth sense of movement, so that it was fine with him when Natasha let the feeling of the moment lead her. With Anthony, you never saw infrastructure: he integrated transitions between patterns or combinations into a unified sweep of movement. He carried a ballerina as if in one surging breath, and that is very rare.

Makarova and Dowell were prominently on view during a brief season ABT gave at the Met in September 1978, something of an impromptu pendant to the long spring run there. Also dancing was guest Rudolf Nureyev in Misha's *Don Quixote*. There certainly didn't seem much chance to enforce obedience on Nureyev. In addition, he'd already staged his own production of this same ballet.

"Don't let him change anything," Misha said to me.

"That will be very difficult," I said. "Wouldn't you like to try and talk to him yourself?" I don't think Misha did. In any case, before we began rehearsals, Rudolf pledged that he would stick to Baryshnikov's version entirely.

Just who his ballerina was going to be, however, remained uncertain. Nureyev kept pushing me to ask Makarova, who told me she wasn't planning on *Don Quixote* that year; she wasn't sure about her jump. I told Rudi, who said that in that case they could cut out her jumps, which would have rendered the role of Kitri very flat indeed. Yes, Rudi, I thought, you wouldn't mind if she cut all her variations, too. Instead, he chose Kirkland.

"Just one thing—can we change?" Rudi said soon after we began our first rehearsals. Gelsey frowned, because despite the compromises she'd made to protect herself against Loquasto's floor cloth, she was still loyal to the letter as well as the spirit of Misha's production. She stiffened and began to argue.

"It's very little, Gelsey," I said, "let's do that." My eyes begged her to humor him. Moving right along, Rudi announced that something else was ridiculous, and instead he was going to do it his way. The farther we went, the freer Rudi felt. He started to take over until striking Gelsey's flashpoint.

"Absolutely not!" she said. "I'm not going to do your steps. You're dancing with us. We're supposed to dance Misha's version."

Rudi put up his dukes and spouted he had his own version, his own production, and it was the best one. He stomped out. I went into the corridor.

"I can't! She's a beautiful ballerina; I want to dance *Romeo* with her. I want her to be my partner. But she's impossible."

I asked him to try again and he did.

"I'm sorry," he said to Gelsey. "Let's work." That was *very* rare behavior for Rudi; he must have really admired her. We continued, trying not to let the tension that fogged over the studio cloud visibility altogether. All played their roles, nursing their own agenda. Gelsey felt like she had to try to dance with Rudi because Misha had invited him. She had to do it; she was part of this company. Rudi wanted this performance because he wanted to stay in ABT's good graces. He had staged his *Raymonda* for the company in 1975, and other opportunities might be in the offing. And I was there to step into the breach and forge a DMZ between these two fire-breathers.

But finally Gelsey lost it altogether. "No, I can't. I'm sorry, I'm so sorry," she whispered frantically. Backing out of the studio, she trailed apologies: "Sorry, sorry. No, I can't. I'm so sorry, I'm so sorry." Gelsey all but tripped over her regrets, while Rudi ran behind her. They talked in the corridor, but I understood it was all over. He wound up dancing with ABT's Yoko Ichino. When they got on stage in New York, Rudi interpolated his own choreography only for his act 1 variation, but he was very sneaky about it. Onstage before the performance, he taught four men from the corps de ballet the steps they were supposed to dance behind him.

"What's that?" Misha said when we watched the performance. It was just as much a surprise to me. Misha delegated me to go backstage after the performance.

Rudi defended his intrusion by saying, "It has nothing to do with the production. I'm alone here. How did you like it?"

"Well, it was okay," I said.

"What do you mean it was okay?!" I said nothing rather than run the risk of being slapped.

It was a lot easier working with Cynthia Harvey for her debut in *Don Quixote*, partnered by Dowell. Here I did dare add something of my own to Misha's choreography. I suggested that they incorporate a trick that had been a trademark of the Kirov's Boris Bregvadze and Ninel Kurgapkina. Bregvadze was a great partner, and both he and Kurgapkina were ebulliently comic. In the act 2 tavern scene, Kitri was supposed to come flying at Basilio from way across the stage, landing in his arms in a fish dive. But Bregvadze and Kurgapkina played this moment as if he had been taken completely unawares by her parabola, only staving off disaster when he turned to catch her at the very last possible moment.

Even when the man is staring straight at her, all Kitris are afraid to jump from so far away, but I told Harvey not to be afraid. She had a prodigious jump, and it would get her across the stage in time. She adored and trusted Anthony and was willing to take a chance with him. He stayed with his back to her, fixing his cuffs, and only at the very last second did he turn to catch her. We rehearsed it in the studio and it worked. At the stage rehearsal I told her not to try it, but instead save it for the performance, because that way the dancers on stage would react with authentic shock. And did they ever! They shrieked with terror. But exactly as planned, he caught her just in the nick of time. The public of course burst into applause. ABT talked about it for weeks afterward: nobody believed it had really been planned. I was proud of Cynthia Harvey for being brave enough to do it, despite debut nerves and not as much rehearsal time as would have been ideal.

~ 21 ~

émigrés and defectors

The Russian émigré community in New York was of course much much smaller in the 1970s than it is today. It was perhaps inevitable that I met Joseph Brodsky again here. I'd first met him five or six years earlier, shortly before he was expelled from the Soviet Union in 1972. My friend the set designer Svetlana Dimietriva had invited a few guests to her Leningrad apartment. Brodsky arrived with a girlfriend, Masha. We were eating and drinking when Svetlana's husband, an army officer, let himself into the apartment. The minute Brodsky saw his uniformed host, he stood up. "Let's go, this place is not for us!" he announced, and he and Masha walked out.

I renewed his acquaintance at a birthday party Genna Smakov threw for himself in his walk-up apartment on Central Park West. Brodsky was a deep and philosophical person. He thought ballet was mindless and so were the dancers. His attitude began to lodge into Misha's consciousness, since Misha looked up to him as an intellectual mentor. I wanted to change Joseph's mind.

"You don't know ballet," I scolded, "you don't understand it." It was beautiful, it was highly difficult, it had something to say on different levels. I took him to an ABT performance where Misha danced wonderfully, and to another that included a ballet by Anthony Tudor. Joseph seemed to become a little better disposed toward our art form.

At Alexander and Tatiana Liberman's home, I enjoyed a window into the wider worlds of art, fashion, and the media. Alex was editorial director of Condé Nast as well as a painter and sculptor. Tatiana was a redoubtable hostess who orchestrated almost a salon, and had fostered many careers. She had fled Russia with her family in 1925 at age nineteen. Now, in what was the final decade or so of her life, she developed a renewed passion for Russian culture, literature, and film.

It was in the summer of 1978 that Joseph called to invite me to drive with him to a birthday party for Tatiana that her daughter, the author Francine du Plessix Gray, was hosting at her home in Connecticut. Joseph had gotten his driver's license only a couple of weeks earlier. I've spent half my life on planes, but both flying and driving frighten me. I told him no, I wouldn't go with him this time, but maybe next time (when he'd had a bit more road experience). He was insistent, however, and despite my conviction that this trip would mark my last on earth, we set off together. We both had bad senses of direction: the drive should have taken three hours at the most, but wound up lasting twice as long. On the way we stopped and ate hot dogs and had tea, but we didn't want to eat too much because Francine was serving a full sit-down dinner. While we ate, Brodsky composed a poem saluting Tatiana on her birthday. Finally we arrived. Tatiana adored Joseph and had been trying to keep people from sitting down to dinner. But it was now 7 p.m. and they were beginning to eat.

Joseph had promised that there would be interesting people there, and there certainly were. Arthur Miller told me that he was very interested in the Soviet Union. I think he was a Communist. But I didn't have much to tell him that he didn't already know. I made the mistake of asking him about Marilyn Monroe; it was well known, but not to me, that he didn't like to talk about her. "She was very difficult," was all he would say.

By the time dinner was over it was 10 p.m. We stayed over at Alex and Tatiana's house nearby. In the morning, we embarked on a not-very-restful drive back to the city.

Alex still went to the office every day, but he and Tatiana spent every weekend in the country. She began inviting me to their house parties, where each weekend she entertained herself by inviting a different and motley group of people. She was always elegant, always made-up, and customarily changed clothes for dinner every night. She and Alex both loved glamour and success but also the less tangible rewards of mental exploration. Tatiana set aside a couple of hours every morning to read poetry. She loved to discuss literature, and Genna Smakov's erudition was one of the reasons that he became almost like a son to her.

As a rule, Tatiana was dominating, and she could strike terror into first-time visitors. But with me she was softer and more relaxed. I came to love both her and Alex. I idealized them, their relationship—the way in the evenings, when we watched Russian movies together, he sat holding her hand—their knowledge, experience, background in Russia before the Communists.

By that point, in the late 1970s, it was almost impossible to imagine Russia without the Communists, thus making what little relationship I could still maintain with my son both precious and precarious. His life since my emigration had not been easy. He was dismissed from the Bolshoi Ballet School in Moscow, after he injured himself ten days before end-of-year exams. I think that was really officialdom's retaliation for my emigration. After I left Russia, Igor was given the directorship in the city of Kuybyshev on the Volga River. Now Alyosha was finishing his education in the ballet school Igor had opened, attached to the Kuybyshev company. Igor had remarried no fewer than three times, and so Alyosha had to contend with three different stepmothers.

Alyosha and I talked very infrequently by long-distance telephone. Booking a call to the United States from the Soviet Union required at least a week's advance notice—the tape recorders had to be readied—and a short conversation cost as much as the average monthly salary.

It wasn't all that much easier from my end. I was of course constrained about what I could say to him. I could tell him a ballet that I was rehearsing but could not even mention a defector's name. In letters I sent via friends—some émigrés could even get permission to visit the USSR on vacation—I could be a little bit more forthcoming, but not very much so. There was always the possibility that they would be confiscated.

Arranging a defection was about the last thing I knew how to do or wanted to do, given Alyosha's situation. But in late summer 1979, Alexander Godunov called and asked if he could visit me. He was dancing at the Metropolitan Opera with the Bolshoi Ballet. Also visiting me that day was émigré photographer Vladimir Bliokh, who was at my apartment, I soon realized, not entirely by coincidence. It was very important that I see Godunov, Bliokh told me. We waited several hours, which was very odd since Godunov and the Bolshoi were staying at the Mayflower Hotel, a five-minute walk from me. Bliokh nervously ran down to the street to look for him. Finally the buzzer rang. I opened it and he was standing in the corridor. He was drunk.

"What's the matter with you?" I asked Godunov. Why had he taken so long?

"I was walking around Central Park," he said. "I was afraid that I was being followed and I wanted to lose them."

We sat in my kitchen. He wanted beer, but I didn't have any, so Bliokh ran to the store to buy some. Godunov said he was very hungry, but when I fried some eggs for him he took only a little piece. He said he felt nauseous and asked if he could lie down. I took him to my bedroom, where he fell asleep immediately. He slept for a couple of hours. By now my husband had arrived. We were supposed to go to the country, and Charles was restless. Finally Godunov woke up and walked back into the kitchen. He began questioning me: How much did dancers make in America? How was life here?

"Very difficult," I told him. "It's not as easy as you think, or people in Russia think."

He took in my words. Finally he said, "I don't think I want to go back to Russia. I want to defect." He had been considering it for a year now. I told him that I simply could not help him, but I went into my bedroom and called Brodsky. "Osinksa, I don't know what to do. I have a Russian star here who wants to defect and I'm supposed to go to the country."

"Don't move," Joseph said. "In thirty minutes I will be in your apartment."

When Joseph arrived, he had already called Orville Schell. Schell was a Wall Street lawyer, a human rights advocate, and soon to become chairman of New York City Ballet's board. Orville had told Joseph what steps he needed to take. Joseph left with Godunov; Charles and I went to the country.

In the country the next morning we heard Godunov on the radio announcing that he was defecting. Joseph called me and told me that he was taking him to a safe house. It turned out to be the home of a doctor and his wife who were survivors of Dachau. They lived somewhere in the country. Joseph called me every day, sometimes more than once, to give me bulletins. The moment the Bolshoi season closed, the Soviets made sure that his wife was immediately en route back to Moscow, while the rest of the company went on to fulfill tour engagements around the United States. Godunov, however, insisted that his wife really wanted to remain with him. Once an airport attendant recognized Lyudmilla from a newspaper photo, the state department was called in and the Moscow-bound flight embargoed. Godunov and Brodsky were determined to meet with Lyudmilla. The Soviets refused, claiming that since it was their plane, the dancers were now in Soviet territory. The Americans wouldn't give clearance for the flight to leave. The stalemate went on for three days until Godunov and Lyudmilla did meet. All this time, Brodsky and Godunov spent their days in the minibus parked at the airport, and their nights in a local motel, accompanied by an FBI agent. No one was supposed to know they were there: they had to climb into their rooms by the fire escape. Godunov and the FBI agent were put together in the same room. Once the agent placed his gun under his pillow when he went to the bathroom. When he came out again, Godunov had the gun in his hands and was pointing it directly at him.

"Put your hands up!"

The agent turned white.

"How can you protect me if I can kill you right now!" Godunov taunted him, before handing him back his weapon.

"It was just like in a detective movie!" Godunov told me later. I'm afraid that he tended to treat everything in life as a game. Only when the games blew up in his face did he belatedly struggle to assess relationships and situations. By then it was usually too late.

That fall Sasha Godunov joined ABT. His first appearance in America was at a gala concert filmed especially for television in a studio in Los Angeles, where he danced the *Corsaire* pas de deux opposite Cynthia Gregory. All of ABT's ballerinas were instantly on the hunt the moment that he appeared. Cynthia felt herself very much a woman around him. She was particularly charming and feminine whenever he was near.

When we reported to the TV studio, however, we discovered neither conductor nor orchestra score had been secured. Finally a conductor was brought in who didn't know the correct tempi and couldn't put dancers and musicians together. It became necessary for me to stand alongside him and guide him while Cynthia and Sasha danced. But it did all work out. They danced superbly.

Sasha had a vulnerability inside him that he was afraid to reveal. With ballerinas who were smaller and looked softer, such as Evdokimova or Makarova, he didn't need to be as assertive; he was more natural. Cynthia was too tall, too queenly on stage, to let him relax that way. Next to her he felt he had to be even more macho not to lose himself. He was certainly one of her rare partners who could live up to her height and her presence. But offstage, compared to the peremptory way he treated so many ballerinas, Sasha was quite nice to Cynthia. They felt comfortable with each other, and from that point on always worked well as a partnership.

Perhaps it was rehearsing the corps in the White Swan adagio that really acclimatized me to the challenges of the America ballet world. The adagio is approximately eight minutes long. Dancing in the Kirov corps, posing absolutely still in formation started to feel like standing on knives, as our feet lapsed into a condition of numbness mixed with piercing pain. It was all I could do not to run off stage.

Our nerves shredding, we women in the corps de ballet judged the ballerinas dancing in front of us as we saw fit. Our favorite was Dudinskaya, since she was the fastest, for legato certainly was not her forte. Our nemesis was Makarova—who danced Odette divinely—because she stretched out the adagio longer than anyone.

And now, fifteen years later, rehearsing *Swan Lake* with ABT, I saw that the corps here had worked out its own solution: after thirty-two bars, they switched their legs, shifting one foot in the front of the other. One girl, a deputy for the others, said, "It's too long to stay on one leg. We always do that." At first I thought: How could they dare? Yes, it was a tiny movement, but still it would be visible to the audience. I thought that they were rudely disrupting the mood of the adagio.

It made me furious . . . and I realized they were right. After a while, I thought, why *should* they suffer when instead they opened their arms slightly and switched their legs so it seemed like an integral part of the choreography. It wasn't going to destroy anything. Dancers here performed eight times a week. In Russia there were only three performances a week because we alternated with the opera, and so corps dancers could physically endure those minutes of pain. The Soviet government was paying for everything, and the company's corps de ballet was capacious enough that most corps dancers did only one act. A new group usually came in for the last act White Swan ensemble. In the United States, nobody wanted to pay—not the government, not the rich. At ABT we couldn't afford injuries;

we never had enough dancers. The same girls soldiered on all the way to the fourth act curtain. That's how dare they! The longer I was in America, the more answers I gave myself.

Each wave of Russians who visited New York noted the corps's adjustment immediately, and they were all incensed. I tried to explain, but in the end always had to resort to saying, "You know, you can't understand until you work here with us."

~ 22 ~
makarova's bayadère

Makarova had decided that after Baryshnikov's success with *The Nutcracker* and *Don Quixote*, it was time that she, too, stage a full-length ballet. It was late in 1978 when she told me that Lucia Chase had asked her to stage the complete *La Bayadère* for ABT, to be followed by *Swan Lake*. Natasha asked me to collaborate with her on both ballets. Instead, I suggested to Natasha that we split the credits and the work. She could sign her name to *Bayadère*; I would be her assistant. Then I wanted the chance to do *Swan Lake* alone. That was fine with her and fine with ABT.

Petipa choreographed *Bayadère* for St. Petersburg's Imperial ballet in 1877, and it held the Russian ballet stage ever since, but underwent revisions by many different choreographers. For decades after the full-length *Swan Lake* and *Sleeping Beauty* entered the international repertory, the West saw only glimpses of *Bayadère*: in 1963, Nureyev staged the Shades scene for the Royal Ballet, and ten years later Makarov, with Michael Lland's assistance, brought the Shades to ABT.

Since the 1920s, the final act, the temple apocalypse, had been omitted. When Igor and I were working in Odessa in 1970, I planned a staging of the ballet that would include a reconstruction of Petipa's final act. But the idea didn't go anywhere after Igor and I separated. Now, Genna Smakov was writing a book on Petipa and had collected rare archival material sent to him from friends in Russia. Thanks to Genna, I had access to photocopies of Petipa's own notebooks, pages crammed with diagrams and summaries. I described Petipa's final act to Natasha: at her wedding, Gamzatti the murderess was haunted by a vision of the snake-laden bouquet, after which the gods poured forth their wrath and the temple came crashing down—allowing Nikiya and Solor to be reunited for all time. Natasha agreed it was worth it to try to piece together the act. Following

Petipa's intentions as much as possible, we knew that we ourselves would still have to rechoreograph a great deal.

As Natasha and I worked with Lucia on the *Bayadère* budget, Lucia kept fretting that everything about the production was just too costly. ABT always lurched from money crunch to money crunch, but this season things looked particularly bad. Lucia had sunk millions of her late husband's fortune into the company, but now, after forty years, even her resources were parched. And box-office receipts had gone down in the last year, now that Misha had left ABT.

Herman Krawitz, who had been indispensable to Rudolf Bing at the Metropolitan Opera, was now our executive director. Trying to shore up ABT's finances, Krawitz and our general manager Joyce Moffatt heard the complaints of potential funders that Lucia, now eighty, was simply too old to pilot the company. Nevertheless, Natasha and I argued that *Bayadère* had to be opulent or there was no reason to stage it at all. Perhaps this wasn't the right time; perhaps we should wait another season or two. But Lucia knew more than I thought she did about the writing on the wall. "It has to be now," she said.

In the spring of 1979, Natasha and I went to Paris, where I coached her for her debut with the Paris Opera, dancing Giselle. By the time we came back to New York, the *Bayadère* structure was in place. John Lanchberry composed an entirely new score for the final act; we couldn't get the music from the Russian archives, and besides much of Minkus's last-act score had been rerouted to an earlier place in the ballet, the wedding celebration of Gamzatti and Solor, in the Kirov's 1941 revision by Ponomoarev and Chabukiani. That was the production still danced by the Kirov, and it would serve as the basis of our production. I wasn't very happy about Lanchberry; I thought his style was too sugary. But at this time he was ABT's principal conductor, and Natasha wanted to work with him. She also wanted to keep the original divisions of four acts but cut the divertissements in the betrothal celebration; I preferred to keep more of the divertissements but condense the acts. We compromised on three acts and kept some of the divertissements, but not as many as I would have liked.

During these months, Misha was in my apartment for lunch frequently, looking and acting morose. At New York City Ballet, he'd been assigned a blizzard of new roles, was felled by one injury after another, and his adjustment to the Balanchine style was rocky. It was his first real experience of negative reviews. Balanchine, after open-heart surgery, could not make good his promise to create new ballets for him, although this had been one of the most attractive reasons for Misha to switch companies. His invaluable champion Remi Saunder had always been opposed to his joining NYCB; it was her opinion, expressed openly to Misha, that Balanchine was humiliating him deliberately. I was sure that Misha wanted to return to ABT and the repertory in which he was supreme. But he had talked himself into a corner, vowing in some tactless interviews that he had no intention of ever returning to ABT and its old-fashioned ballets.

Teary eyed, Lucia told me "Misha will be back; I know that. He has to be here." His insults seemed to make no difference. She was too shrewd to take what dancers said personally. Her biggest stars were always throwing tantrums, usually as publicly as possible. I don't think that Lucia cared very much; she insulated herself from caprice. If she needed someone for her company, that was all that mattered. The rest was white noise. But she certainly adored Misha as much as she knew that she needed him.

Florence Pettan had been Lucia's handmaiden for many years. I told Florence that Misha's pride would never allow him to return to ABT simply as a dancer; it would have to be something more. Florence understood what I meant. Alone with Lucia I told her the same thing, hoping that she would understand, too. Lucia parried with a frequent ploy: she pretended she hadn't heard what I'd said. But she saw my point.

A week later, her eyes were again teary as she said, "I know what you meant, but I want to have a couple more years as director. After that, I don't mind; I think Misha will be the best one. Only I want to teach him myself. I want to pass the company from my hands to his."

It was Krawitz who organized and directed the campaign to install Misha. ABT trustee Justin Colin was also a great supporter of Misha; he'd even loaned him an apartment on Park Avenue. Remi, on the other hand, thought that he was too young to direct, but I tried to persuade her, until she offered at least her token support; I think she was simply grateful for any prospective way to get him away from NYCB.

Krawitz told me that I had to talk to the dancers, prepare them. We needed their consensus. It wasn't just a question of filling Lucia's shoes: not only the director would change, but the entire concept of the company.

Lucia had served a smorgasbord of ragtag corps de ballet, hit-and-miss productions fronted by glittering guest stars from anywhere and everywhere. Now Americans were sated. At New York City Ballet, Balanchine's ensemble demonstrated how the company itself, as an integrated entity, should be a star as glittering as any ballerina. That was today's standard; we could not get around it. ABT dancer Victor Barbee spent time convincing many members of the corps de ballet.

After Misha was voted in, both his handlers and ABT's governance decided Lucia must bow out immediately, rather than be given the grace period she wanted. Patrons were complaining they didn't know where the company was going, who was at the wheel. For myself, I had mixed feelings about Lucia guiding Misha's transition. At Lucia's age she couldn't understand that the company's very philosophy had to change. But she could have been a great help about the day-to-day administrative logistics. On the other hand, Herman and Joyce were both expert tacticians; between them I was sure they could fill the breach opened by Misha's youth and inexperience.

Lucia finally agreed to step down: the 1979–80 season would ring down the final curtain on her forty years.

During the summer of 1979, Natasha and I were to look at Jose Varona's scenery designs for La Bayadère with Lucia and Oliver. Natasha ushered us into the living room of the vast apartment she had just bought on Park Avenue. Two magnificent antique bookcases had been a present from Lucia. We settled deep into a Victorian leather couch—lifted from the Pickwick Club, someone quipped.

I'd first met Varona two years earlier, at Misha's, when he was designing a new Theme and Variations for ABT. I thought we had good rapport, but unfortunately his ideas for Bayadère were all wrong. He had conjured temples made from cornhusks, monster faces peeking from magic trees. But Bayadère is not a native fable of genies and goblins; there isn't traffic between supernatural creatures and humans. Varona had looked to authentic Indian art for inspiration, but Bayadère isn't about ethnographic accuracy any more than is Aida.

Oliver and Lucia had recommended Varona to Natasha. They said they liked what he'd done. Then my shoe dropped. "That is not Bayadère. Everything's wrong." I explained why. "It's not your fault," I told Varona, "you were given entirely the wrong orientation." Understandably he was appalled, but everyone stayed calm. Oliver was the most polite gentleman I ever met in ballet, and Lucia always knew how to control her emotions. I never heard her voice raised.

"It's your production, do what you want," I said. "My name's not on it. If you're all happy with these designs, it's your business. I'm only telling you my opinion, otherwise don't ask." I went home very depressed.

"My husband's arriving tomorrow," Natasha said. "I will ask him." Edward Karkar was a businessman and antiquarian. As promised, she ran the designs past him and called me afterward. "Edvard says it's not good. We can't go ahead this way. What are we going to do?" It was hairy because Varona didn't want to revise. He told Lucia he'd done his job, had followed Natasha's rather vague instructions, and now he had to be paid. Once again, Lucia came to the rescue, rustling up the money for a new designer.

My friend and fellow émigré Genya Poliakov was still in Italy, and he recommended Pier Luigi Samaritani, an opera designer, gifted with an Italian sense of color and beauty. I told Samaritani that the scenery couldn't be sketchy or abstract . . . we wanted epic! Operatic ornateness at its best. Only he needed to leave the stage open, to build as little as possible. Too many ballet set designers construct in 3-D: the period may be right, the visions beautiful, but their edifices swallow the dancers' space.

The scenery had to be made in Italy and transported, while Samaritani jetted back and forth: more money, more money, more money. Lucia and Oliver kept balking, but Samaritani rewarded us with ABT's most magnificent production. There was a cross-sectioned palace through which the horizon shimmered gold, an impossibly riotous garden, an underground temple scored with reliefs. Everything was suspended in the light and air of a tropical climate, bathed in "heat bounce," but nothing was real: depth was chimerical, perspective laid down on a flat canvas. Even the temple porch, down which the *bayadère* Nikiya makes her entrance, was an illusion, stairs placed against a door cut into canvas.

The Kingdom of the Shades, the warrior Solor's opium vision, is Petipa's masterpiece. One by one, in Russia no less than thirty-two in all, the women's ensemble appears out of a shadowy grotto, stretching into long, deep arabesques, then arching their backs. They repeat that simple phrase over and over again. Summoned by the warrior's opium high, the Shades gradually fill the stage like languid rings of smoke. A giant might be in the wings, puffing a hookah. The ranks slowly swell until they coalesce, facing the audience, in what is usually now six—but was originally eight—corridors, each one four girls deep.

Nothing in their movement or gestures is literal, so it is timeless. The Shade maidens pulse on pointe, faceted like crystal in one sculpted position after another. Slowly their arms raise, their legs lift, lulling, narcotic, banishing linear time. The girls are one body multiplied into infinity by Solor's hallucination. The Shades act is pure, distilled: the women stand in ecarté, their bodies still, but at the same time movement has to sing inside their bodies. They can't stand like sticks.

When I arrived at ABT, the girls were ramrod straight in their entrance, not arching their backs the way we did at the Kirov. It was more comfortable for them, but not as plush or as beautiful for the audience. It was always easier to make the corps expend extra effort by providing a rationale, a motivation: I told them to stretch as if an invisible force was pulling them back inside the grotto from which they emerge.

Finally Nikiya appears, no longer a temple dancer, now a goddess who must raise Solor high above the ground, from reality to the lofty plane on which she exists. Nikiya divulges her mysteries: what she is, who she became, what she knows. A goddess, a spirit, she walks above kings and queens. A ghost from the netherworld, she greets the man who betrayed her. At ABT I told the ballerinas that when they crossed the stage—the universe separating them—that yearning had to pour from every step, a magnetic pull drawing her to him.

There are reminders of the relationship they once enjoyed: her bourrées are like a call to him, the tilt of her head could suggest a fall back to the grave. I added an accent to flavor their duet: a beckoning with the arms that we hadn't done at the Kirov. They dance with a chiffon scarf, a symbol of his smoky intoxication. It billows, floats, bonds them forever.

The first-cast Gamzatti in our *Bayadère* should have been Cynthia Gregory, and it was going to be at one point. Instead Makarova ultimately chose Cynthia Harvey, who had a strong technique but needed to work at looking and feeling noble onstage, to learn to keep the back of her neck straight and strong. I also told her not to do too much with her arms, to keep her gestures economical, and never to look down at anyone—to always keep her gaze a little bit above people. She developed a very good look for the role. Gregory, who had ensured that her contract guaranteed her the first-night Gamzatti, sued when she was preempted, won her suit and danced the second performance with redoubtable authority.

For the danseur, Solor is an even more difficult role than Nikiya is for the ballerina. Funneled through the refined, florid Indian aesthetic is the power of an indomitable warrior. The dancer has to find the right balance. I worked on making Anthony Dowell's lyrical body and style a little more sinewy, prompting a fiercer charge into his movement. He transformed for the role even more than I thought possible.

"Don't worry; it will be good," I told Natasha boldly at the dress rehearsal. It was the first time in my life I tempted the Fates like that, but I was sure.

She paled and pleaded, "Don't say it; don't jinx it!"

Opening night, May 21, 1980, I felt the Met audience envelop Natasha in waves of love from her first entrance. In the first act her stage fright helped her performance: she was never more vulnerable, more responsive. By the Sacred Flame, she and Anthony shared their secret tryst, and they were sensational. Her nerves underscored illicit passion with desperation. Applause erupted at every scenery change. Steeples of flowers climbed to the ceiling in Natasha's dressing room. Onstage, kisses and thank-yous, backstage the smell of victory, the corridors streaming with well-wishers. *Bayadère* has remained in ABT's repertory; the company still performs it today, thirty years after our production's premiere.

~ 23 ~

baryshnikov takes over

Misha took to directing ABT with an almost childlike glee. He began wearing three-piece suits and smoking cigars. I thought back to my years in Odessa, when I had put on glasses in order to look older and more serious. Charles France had now left the press office and was assistant to the artistic director, and he, too, was filled with enthusiasm. Richard Tanner had left New York City Ballet to become regisseur at ABT. (In Russia, the regisseur is primarily an administrator, drawing up schedules, whereas here it meant something closer to assistant director.) Dick also supervised the Balanchine repertory. He was an excellent ballet master, intelligent, and could be charming. Misha, Charles, Dick, and I each believed that our work would be a new beginning for the company.

Misha had insisted upon a three-month rehearsal period before we began the season's annual four-month national tour in December 1980. During those weeks, he was in the studio rehearsing the dancers every day. Sometimes he also taught class. Together we rehearsed the character dances in a new suite of excerpts from *Raymonda*. Misha rehearsed with great passion. His corrections were good, and the energy and style with which he demonstrated provided an unsurpassable example to the dancers. Misha also hired Diana Joffe, the Latvian dancer who'd first brought him from Riga to the attention of the Vaganova Institute, to continue to maintain the character repertory.

During the summer, eighteen-year-old Susan Jaffe came to audition for us. She was already a member of our junior company, ABT II. She returned after losing weight, and we accepted her into the corps de ballet. I put her in the front line of Wilis during our first rehearsal of *Giselle*, act 2. Often girls in the corps were embarrassed to show their feelings. They just tried to do the steps accurately. But rather than simply doing the correct steps, Susan was *dancing* at that rehearsal. She stretched her leg up to the sky impudently; what she did wasn't right for *Giselle*, but it was a great show of impersonating a ballerina. And at that moment ABT needed ballerinas desperately.

Makarova had left to form her own small company. Kirkland had begun her cocaine binge with ABT's Patrick Bissell. We hired Magali Messac from the Pennsylvania Ballet, who was French-born and -trained and had an old-world elegance that I liked. She was a real ballerina, but she was too tall for Misha, who badly needed a partner, yet was dead set against importing guest ballerinas from other companies. Doing so was a pet policy of Lucia's that Misha felt should be discarded. He thought it was wrong to use guest artists as bait to sell tickets, to prop up the company. ABT needed to become an institution sound enough to depend on its own stars, its own principal dancers. He did import Dominique Khalfouni from the Paris Opera as a guest ballerina for himself—he had danced with her when he was guest in Paris. But like most of the Opera's stars, she did not like to leave Paris for too long.

We scoured the ranks of the company, searching for who could be groomed—quickly—to dance with Misha. Jaffe definitely had something, and she was the right size; she hadn't yet quite grown to her full height. "Let me try," I told Misha and Charles. I rehearsed with her after work was over for most of the company. We tried Odette's act 2 variation. The opening ronds de jambe didn't work, nor the final diagonal of pirouettes. But the middle section, the diagonal of sissonne fermées into arabesques, was good. She had a beautiful arabesque and she was able to respond to my corrections very quickly. She looked really promising.

I had told Misha, Dick, and Charles not to visit until we'd worked at least several more times. I didn't know her, and she had to start to feel comfortable with me. But a half hour into the second evening's rehearsal, the door opened and all three of them walked in.

"What are you doing here?" I said.

"Oh, we want to watch a little bit. We'll wait for you."

They sat down on the floor. Now that we had visitors, I concentrated on the diagonal to show off Susie's strengths. The arabesque can't be frozen; you still want the movement impulse to continue while the ballerina balances on one foot. It's very difficult for even the most experienced ballerina, and we were all impressed by Susie.

Misha jumped up: "Let's try the pirouettes from the second act." He tried several more partnering passages to see how compatible their bodies were.

Jaffe's face was red. "What—I'm on trial?" she asked when the rehearsal finished.

"Kind of, sort of," Dick said.

"And did I pass?" she said. That was something only time would really be able to tell.

In December, we opened our U.S. tour at the Kennedy Center in Washington, D.C. Kirkland had been scheduled to dance "Pas d'Esclave," a pas de deux from Le Corsaire, on opening night. The pas de deux had been assigned to Jaffe as well, but she was third in line and hadn't even begun to rehearse it. But when Gelsey and Patrick didn't show up for a stage rehearsal in Washington, Misha fired them. Gelsey was out of "Pas d'Esclave," and Jaffe was in. Replacing Gelsey with a first-year corps de ballet girl was the harshest slap Misha could deliver.

Susie and I spent the day of the premiere working feverishly. We made her part easier by changing some jumps and pirouettes, adjusting the choreography to give her more of a chance to show off her extension. Godunov was her partner, and he was spectacular in the pas de deux. Susie was young and beautiful, and her dancing was not bad at all.

Misha was hungry for experimental work, eager to lead himself and the company into the future. He planned to spend his first season pulling together the classical repertory before steering ABT toward new choreographic adventures. We made slight changes in Les Sylphides, substituting the man's variation danced at the Kirov for the later solo Fokine had replaced it with in 1940 when he joined ABT. We changed a lot of small things in ABT's Giselle; we staged act 3 of Sleeping Beauty and act 3 of Raymonda, staying more or less faithful to Sergeyev's production at the Kirov.

In Sleeping Beauty, Misha and Charles both wanted me to perform the Lilac Fairy, her role here consisting only of pantomime. Charles had an interest in perpetuating patterns and precedents: at New York City Ballet, Balanchine and Robbins still performed mime roles in old age. I told Charles to instead cast ABT ballet mistress Georgina Parkinson, formerly a principal dancer at the Royal Ballet in London. She wanted to do it; she loved going on stage in these kind of acting roles. But Misha kept talking to me until I agreed. I wore a purple wig and makeup, and Charles himself designed a new purple costume for me. I complained that it was like a cocktail dress—later one of the critics was to say exactly the same thing. But Charles thought that Lilac could affect any type of look. "It looks like you've succeeded there," I told him. I disliked being on stage as much as ever.

In his youth and impatience, Misha had scheduled too much work for one year. The company was just not ready. The new dancers were raw; while many holdovers from Lucia's ensemble could barely do the more difficult steps. I had many conversations with dancers who complained. Frequently it fell to me to mollify them. "You see what he's doing?" I said. "He's trying to use the classical repertory to raise the quality of the company. It's like a senior class in school. Next season he will really implement his plan for the company. There will be a lot of new work by choreographers. If you're right for them, you will be selected. But now is the year when he wants to get the company in shape."

§ ¿

My marriage to Charles broke up after four years, primarily, I think, because the age difference between us made me insecure. After our divorce he earned a master's degree, became an executive in arts administration, and is now an independent financial investor. For years after our divorce we didn't speak; finally, at the beginning of the new century, we became friendly again. Since then he has more than once helped me untangle my financial and administrative affairs.

Following our two-month Met season in the spring of 1981, I was taking a small group of dancers headed by Godunov on a tour of France. I wanted to buy a country house in Connecticut near the Libermans; saving the per diem I collected on tour enabled me to save money for a down payment. Alex put me in touch with a real estate agent in Litchfield County. For three days I stayed with him and Tatiana while he and I went to look at prospective houses. In New Milford, I found a house that needed work but was situated on fifteen acres of magnificent rolling countryside, at the foot of a ridge of hills. I purchased it just before I left for France.

The Libermans were very generous neighbors. Once, when I was having a party in my house, they sent over a truckful of flower arrangements that I spread around my pool. Another time, they sent over, via Genna Smakov, a case of a French red wine they had with their meals. I don't like red wine, but when I served it to Peter Martins, he pronounced it "Fantastic!"

§ ₹

"Aren't you sick and tired of Petipa?" Dick Tanner asked me. He wanted me to work with him on the Balanchine repertory. In the fall of 1981, Dick made me his assistant for ABT's reconstruction of *Bourrée Fantasque*, which Balanchine had created for New York City Ballet in 1949 but which hadn't been performed by his own company for over a decade.

Balanchine himself came in to watch a rehearsal of our revival. We had met a couple of times before, when I'd gone with Misha to see New York City Ballet perform. Now Balanchine asked me if I was related to Lubov Tchernicheva, his ex-colleague in Diaghilev's Ballets Russes a half century earlier. I told him no, and he said, "Oh, God, it's good; she was very beautiful but a bitch." He gave a few corrections to the dancers; he spent some time working with Jaffe on one moment in the second-movement adagio when she wasn't really correctly on pointe.

"What does it remind you of?" he asked Misha and me about this adagio movement.

"It's the *Bayadère* Shades," we said almost in unison.

"Ah, yes, you are right!" Balanchine cried. "Sometimes I think, What will be left if I took all of Petipa out of my choreography?" he asked us.

"Broadway," Misha said. Balanchine laughed. I was totally charmed by him. I thought, When people possess genius, they're never afraid to acknowledge the recipes they've borrowed—their own talent will always make it original.

"You're so lucky you have such a good company," Balanchine told us. "I've never had a company as good." He was a very tricky man, and I'm sure he didn't mean it, since for years every member of his company had been handpicked from his own school. But we took it as a great compliment, since for years he had been dismissive of ABT.

I was afraid that with no company to administer, Lucia Chase would die immediately, but she lived six more years. A titular vice-president and trustee, she still kept an office at our studios. Occasionally she appeared, a ghost. She should have swanned in like the Queen Mother. But to the new dancers Lucia was passé, and they wouldn't even waste a hello on her. My God, I thought, she sacrificed everything for this company, and this was the respect she received. Whenever I saw her I'd go over and say a few words, and her face would beam with gratitude. Once, we chatted in the Met cafeteria before a performance. She was very upset because she wanted to talk to Misha, to pass along her management secrets, but he didn't have much time for her.

~ 24 ~

russian men

Rehearsing any Russian male, I made sure that I took end runs around his ego. If I was rehearsing him with a ballerina and something in the partnering wasn't working, I would act as if the problem was that the ballerina needed to do something differently. She had to stay *this* way, because then he would be able to stay *right* behind her supporting leg and keep both hands right *there*. And I would hope that his ears would pick up those corrections aimed at her—but really meant for him.

Rehearsing Misha should have been exciting for me, but unfortunately it was not. It was just too much pressure. Sometimes he was waiting for corrections, but I wasn't sure if he would accept them, and anyway, I would avoid saying anything in front of the other dancers. Technically he needed very few corrections, but stylistically, comments might sometimes be in order. Once when we were rehearsing *Les Sylphides*, Misha was dancing his soutenu turns off-center, the way he did in Twyla Tharp's choreography. But here in Fokine it was anomalous. I told him and he accepted it. Another time, when we were working on Jerome Robbins's *Other Dances*, Misha was running with very small steps à la Nureyev. "Don't run like Rudolf," I said. After the performance he told me that as he was about to run he heard my voice in his ear and it helped.

Susan Jaffe was the rare dancer who did not want to hear compliments from me. She was suspicious, even hurt when I said "Very good," or "That's enough." To her it meant that I wasn't interested in helping her anymore. She was able to absorb corrections into her body quickest of all our young dancers, and she demonstrated an endless capacity for arduous, repetitive work in the studio with me and on her own.

We changed her arabesque; formerly Balanchinian, it became closer to Vaganova style, the torso less parallel to the audience and positioned at closer to a right angle. We worked a great deal on improving her pirouettes. Each dancer takes a different pirouette preparation, because each body is unique. Jaffe's feet are unusually long. She would begin a preparation on the ground, her center in place, but in the extra millisecond those long feet took to spring on pointe, her center would have shifted. She was banking on her turns, which made it impossible for her partners to support her. Finally she learned how to rise onto pointe without shifting her center.

A year after joining ABT, Susie was making her debut in *Swan Lake* during our 1981–82 cross-country tour. Misha was her partner. We had rehearsed the ballet for only two weeks before the performance, yet backstage before the curtain she seemed like she couldn't wait to go onstage. I was checking her makeup and costume. Misha walked around, white as a sheet.

After a while Jaffe asked me, "Can you please show me my entrance down the corridor?" I thought she was blacking out from nerves, because she had a very good memory, but she told me, "No, we never did it. I just don't know it at all." In our haste we had concentrated in rehearsal on the most important parts of the role.

It was simply a short mime dialogue, but still it would be very difficult to remember onstage without having first tried it in the studio. I was in shock that I had overlooked it. I sang the music and showed her the mime.

Misha ran over from the opposite wing. "Enough! Enough!" he hissed. "Leave her alone." He thought I was still giving her more coaching ideas.

"Misha, she doesn't know the entrance."

"Oh, my God!" he gasped, and then disappeared. He looked like he was going to faint. But she actually performed the entrance without any problem, and her Odette/Odile was a very good beginner's performance. Her technique was already much stronger than it had been only a year earlier. She emitted a real magnetism, acted like a ballerina onstage, and naturally Misha gave an added boost to her success.

It was thanks to Alex Liberman that *Vogue*, in its February 1980 issue, had featured an article about me for which I was photographed by Arthur Elgort. That spread also included a picture of Godunov in the air taken by Richard Avedon. I had accompanied Sasha to Avedon's photography studio. After Avedon photographed him, he took pictures of us together, and gave me one. Many years later I saw Avedon again at a party at the Libermans'.

"You probably don't remember me," I said.

"How could I forget eyes like yours?" he replied. I certainly understood how he and his camera had beguiled the world's fashion models and celebrities.

In the December 1981 issue of Italian *Vogue*, Jaffe, Godunov, and I were photographed by Barry McKinley in the ballet studio. "We thought you'd be an old woman with a stick!" McKinley said when I walked in the door. He took fashion shots of me to go along with the rehearsal ones. I don't think a ballet coach had ever before been featured in a fashion magazine. Challenging stereotypes was a heady index of success, and a boon for my petty ego!

In November 1982, it was an old copy of *Vogue*—no, not one of "my" issues—that I took to give Balanchine in his room at Roosevelt Hospital. I thought it would divert him. A year had passed since his visit to ABT. He had just been admitted due to mysterious problems with his hearing and his balance. I had checked into the hospital with a slipped disc. Balanchine would die the following April, of what was finally diagnosed as Creutzfeldt-Jakob disease. But when I went to his room, he looked very energetic, and his cheeks were pink. He invited me to have breakfast with him every morning. He sent over to my room a bottle of water from his native Georgia that someone had brought him.

Balanchine demonstrated an unabated appreciation of the female form. My hospital gown tied at the waist and the neck, leaving my back bare. When I told him that my doctor wanted to operate, he traced his finger from my neck to my waist: "Oh, you don't let them cut your beautiful back."

For years there had been talk that Balanchine would stage his own production of *The Sleeping Beauty*. As a boy, he had appeared in the lavish, four-hour production at the Imperial Mariinsky in St. Petersburg. Misha had told me that Balanchine had described how he wanted to make it as extravagant as possible. I think he was frustrated that he never did it, and perhaps realized that it was now too late. I told him how interesting it would be to discuss that particular ballet. "Okay," he said, "maybe another day."

I was only in the hospital three or four days, since I decided against surgery and instead went into traction at my apartment. But it seemed clear to me that Balanchine was reverting to his Russian roots. I brought a picture of him, looking like a real Georgian horseman, astride a *djigit*. He inscribed it to "To Lenuchka"—a diminutive that no one had applied since I'd left Russia—"wishing you much good luck." And then he signed it as he would have in Russia, "Georgi Melitonivich."

I'd come to visit one day, and he asked me to sit on his bed. A teacher from his School of American ballet was also there. Balanchine spoke Russian with us. Peter Martins arrived. He was deputizing for Balanchine and the following spring became the company's co-head with Jerome Robbins. Peter began conversing, naturally in English, but Balanchine answered him only in Russian. "Mr. B., it's me: Peter Martins," he finally said. "I don't understand Russian." But Balanchine continued on the same way. He may not have taken in what Peter was saying, but I also think that, intimations of mortality aside, Mr. B. was still out to prove that he remained the one and only czar.

Misha and Charles France whispered together about casting, and I was usually the last to know with whom I was going to work. But once I began rehearsing a dancer, I started to feel that she or he was almost a part of me, and I was willing to fight for the opportunities I felt she or he deserved.

Leslie Browne's career in ABT had started out auspiciously. She joined in 1977, right after she starred opposite Misha in *The Turning Point*. ABT coach Jurgen Schneider wanted to work with her for *Swan Lake*. I thought that she should do *Giselle* first. Then she left to make the movie *Nijinsky* and almost died from appendicitis during its filming. After she returned to ABT a year later, Dick asked me to work with her for the Sleepwalker in Balanchine's *La Sonnambula*. She had an intriguing quality in the role that reminded me of Allegra Kent.

By the time we started rehearsing *Giselle* in 1982, however, Misha and the company's administrators had put a cross on her. She was dancing solos but was no longer being considered for ballerina leads. I knew she had everything a dancer needs for Giselle, but hardships had taken their toll on her body. Ideally each muscle in a dancer's body is taut when it works but relaxed the moment it isn't in action. Hers were becoming clenched all the time. Leslie was filled to the brim with emotions and acutely sensitive, but she had reached a point where she was unable to connect her feelings to her muscles in motion. She told me how frustrating it was to feel her physicality divorced from her soul. She knew how she wanted to look and to dance, but it was as if her body was not listening.

Leslie was just about the only ballerina I worked with who actually identified with Giselle. Yet it was a challenge with her as well as with most ABT dancers to create a characterization that was true to the milieu of the ballet. They found it difficult to fully understand that in the first act Giselle is a three-dimensional girl existing in a specific context, both theatrical and historical. It isn't like *Swan Lake*, where Odette is an image, a creature; a ballerina there can make her character more ambiguous. *Giselle* is a product of Théophile Gautier's poetic fancies, but innocent, pious girls like Giselle certainly existed in the 1840s, and still do even today.

When Giselle and Albrecht sit together on the bench, Giselle listens to him with her ear close to his but her face turned down. *Never* a direct look from her to him as he whispers his endearments. Sometimes Western ballerinas related to Albrecht the way they might to a man they met at a party. Why did Giselle have to be shy, some of them asked. But unless Giselle responds that way, her devastation doesn't make sense: does a coquette go mad when she is betrayed?

Leslie was ready to dance Giselle during our 1982 Met season, but I still could not secure a performance for her. Early in 1983 I took her to Israel for some guest performances of act 2. But Browne did not have Jaffe's single-mindedness; she was in and out of shape, in and out of ABT. She had been pushed into ballet by others; I wanted her to love ballet herself. Since she wasn't sure what she wanted to do and be, at least ballet would give structure and discipline to her life.

Not many ballerinas can visit Giselle's madness at every performance. But all the information the ballerina needs is in the choreography. I never asked anyone to visit an asylum, the way that Dudinskaya and Shelest had reportedly done. But even ballerinas who can't immerse themselves need to somehow shift to a comprehension of Giselle's distress. Otherwise the mad scene can look empty and formalistic, or like a naive period piece.

Yet I thought Cynthia Harvey in her Giselle debut in 1982 *should* look old-fashioned. She had the classic Giselle look: a small head, black hair, a beautiful face that was slightly doll-like, very delicate arms. She was really like one of the old portraits. For her debut we arranged a mad scene that was built more on poses. It worked very well, but little by little she went deeper into the role. I was pleased as she filled up the poses with empathy.

§ §

Misha had never been very happy that Alexander Godunov was at ABT. Sasha's star quality was so mesmerizing that the public couldn't help but love him. Misha resented it, and Sasha made it easy for Misha to dismiss him by acting badly, often under the influence of alcohol. He was consuming a lot of that, and a lot of the company's oxygen as well; it seemed like everybody was complaining. I talked to him, but it was hopeless. He was invariably drunk at night when we could be alone; the next day he wouldn't remember anything I'd said.

Godunov was lost without his wife. An Israeli impresario promised that if he came and danced there with the Paris Opera's Ghislaine Thesmar—for very little money—they would arrange an emigration for her, which was possible because she was Jewish. Like most dancers, Sasha was worried about money all the time, but he was willing to pay any amount to secure her release. I went with him to Israel, but from Moscow his wife made it clear that she didn't want to join him in the West. This was a blow from which he never recovered.

Godunov resisted learning any new choreography, and Misha wanted to do new work. He told Sasha that he didn't have any repertory for him and didn't renew his contract at the end of our 1982 season in New York. Cynthia Gregory, who was not very happy with her life in the new ABT, was now further aggrieved, since Godunov was one of her most frequent partners. Both Gregory and van Hamel resented how much time I was spending on younger dancers who were, compared to these two prima ballerinas, artificial creations to some degree. And while Charles loved Martine very much, he somehow wasn't as concerned with protecting Cynthia.

After Godunov left, Cynthia danced more often with Patrick Bissell. Rehearsing them in *Giselle* in 1983 was a challenge. Cynthia understood and felt the role very well inside. Onstage she would truly involve herself emotionally: sometimes she cried real tears. But her body worked against her. If she could have had a more vulnerable body and a softer line, if her face had been not so strong and striking, she could have been a great Giselle.

Her acting instinct was to play sweetness and innocence in her heroines. Even when she danced Gamzatti, she was reluctant to be really nasty in the confrontation with Nikiya. Applied to Giselle, her instincts could look overdone. But Cynthia had her own vulnerabilities as a woman, and rather than let her try to simulate innocence too strenuously, I tried to bring out her own vulnerability—simply by not editing it out whenever I saw it appear. There remained a very alive and vital statuesque quality to Cynthia's body, but it was still possible to glimpse a fragile soul within. There were interesting moments in the performance when you believed her.

On the one hand, Patrick Bissell was a good choice to partner her in *Giselle* because next to him she looked gentler. But he was on drugs and completely erratic during their rehearsals. Cynthia was visibly apprehensive, afraid that she could get hurt because of some carelessness on his part. Onstage his emotion was fed by artificial stimulation: when Cynthia as Giselle dropped dead at the end of act 1, he fell on her, sobbing hysterically and shaking her frenziedly. He clutched her to his breast, then let her fall to the ground while he held on to her skirt until her costume was torn to shreds. "Never again!" Cynthia screamed once the act 1 curtain fell. She stormed off to her dressing room, where she raged that Patrick's roughness had violated the ballet's style. He had ruined the first act by confusing romantic ballet with Greek tragedy.

~ 25 ~
kirkland cataclysms

Gelsey Kirkland had been rehired by Misha in time for her to dance in ABT's spring 1981 season at the Met. She left the company again after a final disastrous *Don Quixote* with Misha.

"It wasn't as bad as it could have been," I told him in his dressing room.

"I was never so embarrassed in my life," he said. He was such a perfectionist that he couldn't tolerate any laxity on the part of a fellow dancer. She'd not only been a mess technically but had also delayed the start of the third act. Later, in her memoir, *Dancing on My Grave*, Gelsey shocked the ballet world with a nightmarish evocation of her addiction problems—an account that rang true, I think, to all who lived through them.

In the fall of 1982, Misha allowed her to she rejoin ABT, largely, I think, because he knew she was flat broke and needed a job desperately. They were still the most magical couple we had in the company, as well as our biggest box-office attraction.

On tour that season in Los Angeles, their *Giselle* was cheered until the canyons shook. Gelsey and Misha had done everything they could to destroy their partnership, but they simply could not extinguish the enchantment they produced together.

Gelsey sometimes watched my *Giselle* rehearsals on tour, but when she asked me to work with her on the role, I said I couldn't. I didn't have time to nurse her; indeed no American ballet company could afford the time to nurse anyone. Several years earlier, Gelsey had told me about a dog she'd had when she was dancing at the City Ballet. She was never at home, and he missed her badly, so he began urinating in her bed—both to punish her and provoke a punishment from her. When he was punished, Gelsey told me, he felt that she really loved him. And I realized that was the way Gelsey herself operated, too. I had seen it that first day I watched her rehearse with Misha for the White House.

When she felt tired or self-conscious, Gelsey had now taken to asking her coaches to show her how something should look; sometimes, indeed, she demanded from them a full performance. One day I passed a rehearsal studio and saw Georgina Parkinson red-faced, sweating, out of breath. It seemed that at Gelsey's request Georgina had just danced the act 3 *Sleeping Beauty* variation twice, full out, on pointe.

Sometimes I saw Gelsey working by herself in a studio, trying the same preparation over and over again. It seemed like a way to convince herself that she was really working, when she didn't have the strength to practice more difficult steps. I had the feeling that she had to cover a certain amount of working hours so that she could give herself a passing grade. But it wasn't all funny business. She could still improve some quality. She obviously felt that the preparation didn't flow, didn't feel natural. She had always worked on the infrastructure of dance; on what came in between steps. Balanchine had definitely given his dancers the conviction that there should be no such thing as ponderous preparation and then a technical trick. It was all equally important movement, it was all dance.

One day toward the end of our 1983 season at the Met, Gelsey barged into a rehearsal of mine. "I'm sorry, can you help me with *Sonnambula?* It's just one position. I can't find—I don't know how to move here. It's so uncomfortable. I feel so clumsy."

"Maybe after my rehearsal, Gelsey."

"*Please* . . . just five minutes." She had just walked out of her own rehearsal in frustration.

"Okay," I said, "five minutes, everybody." It wasn't really much of a disruption; I was rehearsing three or four dancers on some mime passages. Victor Barbee, who often danced the Poet, was part of my rehearsal. Gelsey asked him to lie down on the floor so that she as the Sonnambula could discover his "dead" body. She danced the moment when the Sonnambula realizes what is blocking her path. Her transition from contracting in apprehension to contracting in grief was troubling her.

"Do it one more time," I said. She did. "Try to relax completely," I told her. "Walk around like a real Sonnambula. The tragedy will be in your body. Be simple, you don't have to do any ballet positions." She asked me to walk around Victor myself. "You really have to trust yourself," I told her, "whichever emotion you feel comfortable with."

"Do it for me," she insisted.

I improvised something; it was most natural to perform the Sonnambula as a high tragedienne. "Let your head fall back completely and be still. Scream like a Greek mask."

"Oh, thank you so much." She left without trying anything, to work by herself yet again.

Her debut was that same night. I always watched when she did something new. In Gelsey's condition, her performance wasn't all it could have been, but still her Sonnambula was spectacular. I waited to see how she'd handle that moment, and she didn't disappoint me. Since that afternoon she had worked out exactly the right solution for herself. Applause shuddered through the theater and I got goose bumps. A few days later, in the *New York Times*, Jennifer Dunning described how "the almost convulsive gesture of her arms and head when she came flush with his suddenly dead body, her white sleeves hanging like sculptured wings, had a look of terrifying, cataclysmic truth."

More than ever before, I saw that within this will-o'-the-wisp body resided the volcanic passion of a Medea, a Phaedra. Had she followed her own instincts more often, rather than trying to remake herself into the image of her many idols—among them Farrell, Makarova, Plisetskaya—Gelsey's interpretations could have been much more special, more interesting and controversial than they were. It was clear that deep inside herself she knew that she could be anything she wanted on stage . . . but she wasn't able to listen to herself. She was at the mercy of things beyond intellect, but still I ask myself: how could a woman of Gelsey's intelligence have been so foolish?

~ 26 ~
abt's problems

The fall of 1982 had brought a strike by ABT's dancers, the second in three years. Our rank and file were paid considerably less than their counterparts at New York City Ballet, although ABT's stars made more than NYCB's principal dancers. Indeed, Lucia Chase's entire economic orientation had been top-down, given her reliance on celebrated guest stars from around the world. When ABT had struck in the fall of 1979, our first-year corps were making a little over eight thousand dollars annually, less, as it was noted in the press, than many dishwashers in Manhattan. Coming from the Kirov this was all baffling to me, because the Soviets had ensured that every dancer was paid a living wage; even corps members were given a comfortable pension. Misha had already worked to make the ABT pay scale more equitable by insisting that principal dancers accept a weekly rather than per-performance contract, and by largely eliminating guest stars. Many of our principal dancers supported the strikes. By the time Misha resigned as director in 1989, the pay disparity between NYCB and ABT's corps had narrowed.

By the time the strike ended at the end of 1982, we had been forced to cancel several weeks of tour performances. To compensate, several additional weeks were added to our Met season, which became a financial disaster for a number of reasons.

Misha and Charles had added many more Balanchine works to the repertory, but audiences could see Balanchine performed with greater authenticity at lower prices by New York City Ballet, rather than taking in what we were offering at the Met. They were dancing simultaneously across Lincoln Center Plaza at the New York State Theater, which was theirs to share with the New York City Opera. (NYCB paid no rent, therefore making lower ticket prices possible.) We no more needed to recreate the Kirov's policies than New York City Ballet's. On tour in Detroit during our spring 1983 season, Charles had programmed the *Bayadère* Shades before the two-act *Giselle*. It was the last week of our four-month tour, and the corps was exhausted. The Shades plus *Giselle* meant a marathon for them as well as for the audience. Charles reminded me angrily that the Kirov had sometimes programmed *Les Sylphides*, another white tulle ballet, as an opening act before *Giselle*. "Not everything the Kirov did was good," I told him. *Giselle*, *Sylphides*, and the Shades were all "white" ballets, constructed around a corps de ballet in tulle skirts, but each one had an utterly different mood and temperament. Running them together would only confuse and bore the audience.

Misha had dropped *Swan Lake* from ABT's repertory. Our production dated from 1967 and was falling apart before our eyes. Nevertheless, people wanted to see *Swan Lake*, be the production good, bad, or indifferent. When Misha first took over, I'd told him that his first projects should be a new *Giselle* and *Swan Lake*. But instead he spent a lot of money commissioning some terrible new ballets.

Inviting different new choreographers supplied the fresh blood the company needed to prevent it from becoming stagnant and stale. And it was easier to raise money from funders for new work. But too often we were hosting choreographers who were not right for ABT but suited instead for regional ballet companies, whose standards do not necessarily need to aspire to world-class. Why invite choreographers whose limitations were already quite evident and expect them to work miracles—when we were footing the bill? Not everything was a waste of time by any means: husband-and-wife team David Gordon and Valda Setterfield, who made two pieces for ABT in the eighties, had taste and standards. They weren't untalented, immature fakes, like some who worked for us.

We also needed to give our dancers a chance to choreograph. Dancers who were interested could be given a showcase performance, and if we saw something valuable in the workshop, we could put it on ABT's stage. It wouldn't have meant any sacrifice on our part. We'd let the aspirants work in our studios for free, but they wouldn't be paid unless their ballet was brought into the repertory.

In addition, the way our rehearsals were scheduled was very bad. We couldn't afford to dedicate a whole day to classical or modern choreography, but the rehearsal agendas weren't planned carefully enough. The classical repertory needed to be rehearsed directly after class. The dancers' bodies were then properly prepared. Instead, the prime early afternoon rehearsal time was always given to commissioned choreography. But this put the company's quality and style at risk. Straight from class, the dancers would go immediately into a modern rehearsal calling upon different muscles and coordination. Then in the evening I would try to put them together again in the classical style. But by that time their feet were sometimes so swollen they couldn't even stay on pointe.

Rather than underwrite the whims of mediocre choreographers, I thought it better to give the dancers a little bit more money or augment the ranks of our roster. ABT's budget was now much larger than it had been under Lucia Chase. Misha's name was magical, and executive director Charles Dillingham, Herman Krawitz's successor, knew how to merchandise it. But we could only afford to have thirty-five girls in the corps de ballet, whereas a company with a repertory the size of ours needed at least twenty more. We still sometimes couldn't put on a full twenty-four-member ensemble into the *Bayadère* Shades or *Swan Lake*. (And twenty-four was already downsized from what was the norm on Russian stages.) Many times in *Swan Lake* I needed to augment the corps with the big swans for the ensemble's first entrance in act 2, and bring out the cygnets and the big swans for the coda.

So it was difficult for us to take anyone who didn't have as close to a perfect balletic body as possible. We were looking for uniformity, for beautiful feet and legs. We were looking for dancers we could place everywhere. Our corps de ballet was not meant to look like New York City Ballet's, which functioned more as an aggregate of individuals who were rarely if ever in perfect synchronization. By definition, a classical corps is supposed to breathe and move as one body and one spirit. In Petipa's scheme, the corps members are multiple echoes, myriad refractions of Odette or Nikiya. And so it might happen that a girl with a rare individuality and talent but an imperfect body would be overlooked at a corps audition.

The girls at the Kirov were genuinely proud to be in the corps de ballet, because in Russia the corps is a star in its own right. The dancers understand that to create a perfect ensemble every dancer is crucial. If you lost one good corps member, the cohesion and synergy of the ensemble was weakened. But here in America, the dancers' mentality was such that to remain in the corps de ballet could mean that you were a failure.

Sometimes girls in the ABT corps didn't understand that at each rehearsal we were watching to see how they presented themselves. At times I would grab them in the hallway and lecture them: they were wasting their time, robbing themselves of a career. They were spiritless. In two or three years their potential would be gone. They had to understand that what they needed to love was being onstage and performing: it didn't matter if they were doing a solo part or putting in their time in the corps. It was still possible to feel like an artist and not simply an ant in an anthill. Even the most talented had to go through this routine before they could be promoted.

Coaching a corps requires infinite patience. In *Swan Lake* they were meant to dance in perfectly even lines, in exact unison, and often they would be uneven. By contrast, in *Les Sylphides*—one ballet in which the corps should not be even—it seemed they couldn't be anything but perfectly in formation. In the first act of *Don Quixote*, they all were supposed to walk casually just as though living some natural kind of freedom. The moment they were given this freedom, it seemed as though everybody walked on the same side, or two by two, doing exactly the same thing, or staying in straight lines—like sheep.

Stylistic distinctions were difficult to maintain. During seasons when both *Les Sylphides* and *Giselle* were in our repertory, I needed to keep reminding them that although they were wearing what was basically the identical costume in both ballets, the *Giselle* Wilis are dead, but the Sylphides are very much alive. The same ports de bras had to have a completely different look and feel. The *Giselle* ports de bras derive from the stiffly crossed arms of a corpse. In *Sylphides*, the identical port de bras had to be drawn softly to the body as though the Sylphides are covering themselves very modestly, with great femininity. I could show the dancers, and it was easy for them to copy me formally. They would keep their arms correctly, but it was difficult for their bodies to organically experience the movement intention.

At the same time, I thought that the *Giselle* Wilis needed a more lyric style than I saw when I first rehearsed them with ABT. On stage, they wore Dracula makeup and moved like man-hating viragos, dry as sticks. Over the years I coached them so that stylistically they resembled Giselle. Only she was saturated with love, whereas they were motivated by fury and frustration, their necks and backs held more rigidly than hers.

Sometimes people would tell us that our dancers looked like the Kirov and think they were giving us a compliment. Others would say the same thing and tell us we had lost our way. But in either case I disagreed. Ballet is, was, and always would be writing on water. It was impossible to perpetuate the same quality, the same mood from one performance to another, let alone graft one company's style wholesale onto the different bodies and different mentality of another ensemble with a different heritage and a different repertory. Even two companies with a similar academic foundation could manifest an enormous stylistic difference, as demonstrated, for one example, by the long-standing profiles of Russia's Kirov and Bolshoi.

I didn't want ABT to look like the Kirov. Neither Misha nor I ever thought of creating a copy. Our first priority was for ABT to develop its own style, a face that would be as instantaneously recognizable as those of other great companies around the world. If we had wanted to, it would have been quite possible to rubber stamp Kirov style on ABT, despite the vast gulf in training and psychology. One would just have needed to demonstrate to them exclusively Russian ways. American dancers were amazingly adroit at mimicry, which enabled them to dance all the many styles encompassed by ABT's repertory. I often watched ABT rehearse work by Merce Cunningham or Mark Morris and saw the dancers pick up quickly, by the process of external imitation, these foreign styles of dance with an impressive degree of accuracy.

Where classical ballet was concerned, no school in America offered the comprehensive training available to the Vaganova student. The closest was the School of American Ballet, which was set up primarily to feed dancers into New York City Ballet, although we sometimes hired their graduates as well. But SAB fell short in areas like acting and character dance, and didn't provide tutelage in academic subjects related to dance, such as music and dance history. And so the best way—really the only way—to maintain standards in a company like ABT was simply to leap past the methodical nine-year development of a style that was practiced in Russia and instead let the dancers absorb as much as they could from day to day.

In Russia coaches usually didn't demonstrate steps very much; they gave their corrections using only their hands or in words. But I understood from my first moment here that not only because of the language barrier but also due to the dancers' customary working habits, a lot of my teaching would have to be by demonstration. I had to show everything very clearly as well as explain as well as I could with the little English I knew at first. During Misha's *Don Quixote*, rehearsing the corps de ballet, I showed the steps precisely. It worked as well as could be expected. Without actually having to do anything technical, I could demonstrate the intent of the steps on demi-pointe. I was free; I believed in myself; I had good arms and style. But I always remembered that when Misha demonstrated choreography, dancers felt that they couldn't be as good as he was. Over the years I did less and less demonstrating. Each dancer before me had to feel that she would be able to absorb my knowledge but dance much better than I ever could have.

§ §

It was after our financially disastrous 1983 Met season that Misha agreed to work for a token one-dollar annual salary in return for not getting grief from the board about his time away from the company pursuing his own independent projects. He certainly had no shortage of offers to dance as a guest with other ballet companies; he made movies and worked on licensing deals. The ABT board had known all along that he wasn't going to shepherd the company exactly the way Lucia Chase had, but given our current problems they were at that moment out for blood.

Misha had originally agreed to choreograph Prokofiev's *Cinderella* for the 1982–83 season, but the dancer's strike delayed it a year. He wasn't really very enthusiastic about it, and might have wanted to use the delay to back out of the project, but ABT had already raised the money; the company needed a premiere and the money was earmarked. So in the fall of 1983, Misha collaborated with Peter Anastos, who had been one of the original drag ballerinas of the Trocadero troupe. I'd had a lot of fun working with the Trocks five years earlier when Peter asked me to stage for them *Giselle* act 2 and Petipa's *Harlequinade* pas de deux.

Despite Misha's successes with *The Nutcracker* in 1976 and *Don Quixote* in 1978, he remained nervous about choreographing. He didn't completely trust himself. But I think he definitely had choreographic talent. His body was so coordinated and so intelligent that when he moved alone to music, more than anything, his own body could guide and help him. *Cinderella* was, however, greeted with a negative critical consensus when it reached

New York, but I didn't agree. There was a lot of good material there. The male variations that Misha created were first-rate. Peter created the classical corps de ballet material, for the four seasons of act 1, and I think there were some problems there. Santo Loquasto's costumes and scenery were heavy and operatic, but the surface was still Broadway-glamorous. Some of the glamour was deliberately tawdry, to show that this court was vulgar and corrupt. When Konstantin Sergeyev choreographed *Cinderella* for the Kirov in 1946, the court had also been deliberately ugly, and I think that statement remained in Misha's mind. Perhaps Misha and Peter weren't entirely certain whether the purpose of the ballet was to appeal to children or to be directed at adults as well. But their *Cinderella* barely survived two seasons.

In the fall of 1984, Kenneth MacMillan joined ABT as Artistic Associate. As dancer, choreographer, and director, he had been associated with London's Royal Ballet for thirty years. He was one of the most prominent people in British ballet, and I don't know why he wanted to spend more time away from London. Perhaps he simply wanted to work with Misha. He was also good friends with ex-ABT ballerina Nora Kaye, now a member of ABT's board of trustees, as well as with Charles France. A few of MacMillan's works were already in our repertory. At the Kennedy Center in December, we premiered his 1965 full-length *Romeo and Juliet*.

Kenneth could be quite cruel, but he was also erudite and endowed with a magnetic intelligence—analytical, philosophical—and a potent charm. His dry British humor was great fun to be around. He caused a furor of ambition among our principal dancers, all of whom were jockeying—regardless of suitability—to impersonate the immortal lovers.

Makarova had returned to ABT in 1981 after disbanding her company. But she had already injured her knee in the summer of 1980, and she did less and less classical repertory. In 1982–83, she starred in a revival of the musical *On Your Toes*, and was injured by a falling piece of scenery at the Kennedy Center. She called me from her hospital bed, saying that she was ready to start working on *Giselle* again, but her knee injury permanently impaired her jump, and she never danced Giselle again. Earlier in 1984 she and Misha had been reunited in *Other Dances* during our Met season. Now she was returning to dance Juliet on tour and in New York.

Ten years earlier she had danced MacMillan's Juliet as a guest with the Royal Ballet. She complained to me that at the Royal MacMillan's choreographic text was cast in stone: "They put me in a cage!" She wasn't allowed to deviate one eyelash blink from the ironclad text, although years earlier MacMillan himself had made changes to accommodate Margot Fonteyn after creating the role on Lynn Seymour. An oceanic personality like Makarova's could never have as much space as it craved. She needed editing sometimes because she could go overboard, but if the container were too confining, she wouldn't be successful, either.

"Trust your instincts," I told Makarova, and referenced her own seven-year-old son: "Think about Andrusha, how he thinks and acts; he doesn't play a little boy; he *is* a little boy." In a role like Juliet, many ballerinas make the mistake of trying to simulate youth, when what they need to do onstage is free themselves from the burden of their life experience—and to rely on their own, ever-present inner child.

Her knee bothered her frequently, and when we rehearsed it was sometimes difficult for her even to walk. We had to find physical expressions to compensate for what she couldn't do. I never changed any of MacMillan's choreography, but with Makarova, and later when I worked on the ballet with other ballerinas, there were many steps that I tried to fill with new and different ideas. The ballerinas could do exactly what MacMillan had choreographed, but more naturally. They didn't have to be as egregiously realistic as he intended, nor rely on what were sometimes conventionalized poses of fear and convulsion.

The potion scene was the most difficult to believe in. Juliet's fear ricocheted her from one side of the stage to the other as she cringed at hallucinations. I changed the approach a little bit so that Natasha did less with her arms and didn't pummel herself so drastically, but still made clear the terror inside her. After drinking the potion, MacMillan's Juliet starts to gag as if she is vomiting. To me that was just gross, and I coached the ballerinas to look instead as if their heads were going limp from the effects of the drug.

Before the curtain in New York, I went to the company box and sat next to Misha. He hadn't been with us on tour, and so this was going to be his first look at Makarova's Juliet. He was sure that she would go overboard. But when Natasha appeared, Misha gasped, and grabbed my knee. "Oh, my God—she looks fantastic!" She embodied the true spirit of youth rather than its obvious mannerisms. Her spirit was so unfettered and her movement so innocent. Her vulnerability in the final scene reduced me to tears.

~ 27 ~

ferri and others

ABT's Kim Highton had a quality of isolation that reminded me of the Kirov's Alla Shelest, but unlike Shelest, her physical endowment was phenomenal. On the dark Met stage, I once saw her working by herself on Odette's act 2 variation. I've coached some ballerinas for years without ever getting them to articulate the phrase-concluding arabesque pose as beautifully as Kim. Regrettably, she never danced *Swan Lake* with ABT. Nor did she dance Nikiya in *La Bayadère*, although Makarova had agreed to cast her. Right after that, however, Highton was injured, and my understanding was that, being Christian Scientist, she didn't seek out medical treatment. She was away from the company for two years. When she did return in 1982, she was only in her late twenties, but it was somehow too late, psychologically, to reclaim the position that should have been hers. But during that last year with the company she continued to give some unforgettable performances in solo roles. Dancing Myrtha's lieutenant Zulma in *Giselle*, Highton was a paradigm of romanticism. She was naturally moonstruck, and she understood exactly what play of musculature was needed to give the illusion that her limbs had neither bones nor sinews. She wheeled into the renversés in her variation with an abandon that momentarily gave the Wilis the flavor of maenads.

ABT's Anna Spelman also had her own spellbound quality that was unique and mesmerizing. Spelman was among the dozen rather neglected young corps de ballet dancers who danced on a tour I led in the summer of 1984 to three cities in Israel. Heading the tour were Susan Jaffe and Deirdre Carberry from ABT, and Rex Harrington and David Nixon from the National Ballet of Canada.

No matter how talented, a dancer will find it difficult to retain the technical fitness and maintain the confidence for performing difficult solo variations when they dance only in the corps. Being warehoused there had brought more nerves and inhibitions in these young dancers than even I would have expected.

We began rehearsing for Israel during the final week of our two-month Met season at the end of June. We were due to leave for Israel mid-July. During our last week at the Met, I came down with an attack of kidney stones. Now the dancers needed to rehearse on their own, and that was, for most of them, a new experience and an intimidating task. It took a thick skin for a corps girl to announce her ambition by going into a free studio in early evening and trying out a solo. She was sure to be jeered at for the chutzpah of trying to rise above her station. In addition, most were too exhausted from dancing every night in the corps to think about expanding their repertories. And now, going into an empty studio and facing their own mirrored reflection without the guidance of an authority figure was daunting. I was out for about a week, then I began to rehearse them in the Pineapple studios in Soho, where I was then doing some moonlighting teaching. We pulled the whole thing together, not as thoroughly as I would have liked, but as much as possible in the time we had before leaving.

At ABT, Anna Spelman customarily danced one of the two demi-soloist positions in *Les Sylphides*. But even after she danced leads for me in Israel, it proved impossible to get her a performance of the Prelude solo in the same ballet. The fact that she would have given a revelatory performance did not carry as much weight as it should have. And yet Misha thought she was beautiful. While it was difficult for Charles to appreciate people who were not part of his little group, earlier that spring he had said to me that he couldn't take his eyes off her in *Sylphides*. But several other dancers performed the Prelude regularly, and they did expect performances. And unfortunately, it is the policy of ballet companies around the world that dancers who are not necessarily on track to become officially ranked soloists do not get assigned solos they would be great in. I'm afraid that's a particular bias of the ballet profession; it's in part due simply to laziness of administration and staff. It's also a function of economic considerations. That had been Lucia Chase's argument to me in 1977, when she didn't want to let corps members Cynthia Harvey and Julinda Menendez dance the flower girls in *Don Quixote*. (But of course both Harvey and Menendez were later promoted.)

ABT's Hilary Ryan did get to perform the same solo from *Paquita* that she danced on our tour. That December during our season at the Kennedy Center, Ryan danced it at a Sunday matinee, while in the evening corps member Jennet Zerbe made her debut in the very same solo. Two years earlier, Zerbe had joined ABT after graduating from the school of the Royal Ballet in London. I worked with both Ryan and Zerbe in New York before we left for Washington. We were fortunate to have enough rehearsal time. I wanted them to succeed so badly! In Washington, each one danced the demanding solo with technical security as well as high individual style. My heart sank when Misha, however, dismissed each one as being too tall, and put paid to any further attempts by either one. Hilary was able to dance it one more time. But she did hardly anything else of note with ABT until leaving the company five years later. Charles France liked Zerbe, and she did some major roles before injury forced her to leave ABT at about the same time as Ryan.

On the other hand, there were talented people who were pushed much too fast. Ricardo Bustamante came from the San Francisco Ballet in 1985, a few months before Robert La Fosse left ABT to join New York City Ballet. Misha was very angry at La Fosse for leaving, after we had spent an inordinate amount of time developing him. As a result, Ricardo was given too many lead roles all at once, and he hurt his knee badly during a rehearsal, trying hard to please Misha. Ricardo was able to recover. But Bonnie Moore was a wonderful talent who was so damaged by our team that she had to leave the company. I worked with her when she danced the *Swan Lake* White adagio with Misha in 1986. She wanted to be left alone, to develop normally, but she was being pushed way beyond what she was comfortable with. She was smart enough to know it wasn't good for her, but at the same time she was a very grateful girl and she couldn't say no. But she started to be very nervous and was frequently injured.

When Alessandra Ferri arrived from the Royal Ballet in the fall of 1985, she was twenty-two, technically weak and stylistically unpolished. In London she had starred in MacMillan's expressionistic repertoire. Kenneth and Misha had spoken of me highly to her, and she began work enthusiastically. But she didn't immediately understand that mechanics and artistry are indivisible: she would have to polish her style and sensibilities as well as her technical ability. At first, she would take from me but not

trust me enough to give back. It was one-way work; there was no reci-
procity between us. As she realized that I wasn't trying to superimpose
myself into her, to blur her identity, she started to make much more rapid
improvement.

I thought that the first act of *Giselle* would be easy for Ferri. She was
such an actress, and she already had enough technique for it. It was the
second act that I worried about. Alessandra wasn't by nature or physique
a romantic ballerina. She had strong bones, and her movements, her muscles, were heavy in spite of her light extension. To make her arms more
delicate, I reminded her not to bend her elbows, so that her arms never
flexed. Her arms and hands needed to rest naturally, while making sure
that they did not droop.

In the second act, love had to emanate from her without her face or
body trying to signal or generate emotion. It was a less earthy, less realistic approach than she had acquired dancing MacMillan's ballets. Yet she
understood, and she transformed herself. The musicality of her legs let
her discover the right style: everything in her movement was breathing,
living, sensitive. Alessandra's legs were a very sexual instrument, and they
introduced a muted erotic overtone.

It was the first act that wound up giving us trouble. At twenty-two,
she had difficulty imagining herself living in a time when a kiss could
mean as much as sex. Juliet was already her signature; Juliet, too, is vir-
ginal, but her passion is violent. I tried to bring Giselle closer to Alessandra's inclinations as much as I tried to get her to find the character. Her
Giselle could legitimately be a less fragile girl physically than Makarova's
or Kirkland's. Ferri's heart did not burst from a congenitally weak nervous system, but because she was prey to emotions so powerful that they
finally obliterated her. Finally, Ferri's first-act Giselle began to fructify,
until eventually she dispelled the modern girl with modern mentality
and behavior. The roughness was gone; Giselle's emotions were no longer
trumpeted.

If Misha was ever inspired by a ballerina, it wasn't visible to me. His
Giselles changed, yet his responses were the same. Working alone, Ferri
and I had slightly revised some mime exchanges between Giselle and Albrecht to reinforce her interpretation. But Misha never went along with
what we'd done. He just corrected us as if we had had a memory lapse, and

it was clear no appeal was possible. Ferri was furious. "Couldn't he even change one movement of his hand?" she asked me after rehearsal.

But it was wonderful to see Misha back in *Giselle*. He was dancing fewer and fewer classical parts. On tour in 1983–84 he danced only Twyla Tharp's pieces, while in New York he added *Les Sylphides* as well as *Other Dances*, made for him and Makarova in 1976 by Jerome Robbins. In 1984–85 he was off the entire tour making the movie *White Nights*, but then danced in New York a few Black Swan pas de deux as well as *Other Dances* again. In my opinion, he was taking himself out of the classical repertoire early, but my impression was that he didn't want to compete with himself.

Misha had decided that it was essential that Martine van Hamel dance Myrtha in these *Giselle* performances opposite himself and Ferri. But as far as Martine was concerned, she had finished with the role forever. Generally, ballerinas believe that if their part doesn't dominate the entire evening, it isn't worthy of them. But although Myrtha appears only in act 2, she is a crucial axis. Without her the second act does not exist. The ballet sags when the role is given to beginners, or to soloists who may be strong technically but whose personalities do not dominate. Myrtha *demands* each movement, each gesture the way only a ballerina knows how.

At the same time Martine was complaining to Misha that she wanted more rehearsals with me. He told her that Myrtha was the perfect opportunity. Somehow it all worked. We were in the studio and Martine was telling me how much she hated Myrtha. I told her that was a pity and tried my pitch about how great a role it is, a ballerina's role: "At the Kirov, a ballerina was always cast."

"I don't care," was her response. But the moment the piano started, she devoted herself to work. Technically, Myrtha is a role for a young dancer with no limitations. Martine was forty and her shape wasn't perfect, but maturity enabled her to give a better performance than she had as a young dancer. Her arms and upper body were more beautiful now because she floated them over her legs. Martine danced those performances with almost brutal implacability, and yet every movement glittered with femininity. I don't think Martine ever became reconciled to the role, but watching her was like seeing Myrtha reclaimed as a showcase for a prima ballerina.

~ 28 ~

how to dance

Sometimes critics accused our dancers of being over-rehearsed, when in fact just the opposite was true: in fact, they hadn't had *enough* rehearsals to let their techniques breathe. When our young ballerinas went onstage, they showed the critics and the public the lessons they had learned in the studio. But so often they had not achieved the freedom that made it possible for them to trust themselves and make breakthroughs on stage. Dancers learn things in performance they can never acquire in rehearsals. But each ballerina might perform these classical parts no more than five times a year—too much other repertory also had to be scheduled. Of course at the Kirov, where we danced almost exclusively the classics, a ballerina might also dance a full-length ballet no more than a handful of times per season, because the roster was so vast. But for our ballerinas—amid all the other repertory they had to contend with—a few performances a year was not sufficient to make them feel secure enough to take chances or risk failure in classical roles.

On stage a dancer isn't supposed to be preoccupied with worrying about technical errors. But too often our dancers were drilled by Misha and Charles that mistakes were not tolerated. If Misha saw a ballerina stumble in the rehearsal studio, he'd tell her, "Don't try three pirouettes, you'll have to do just two."

"She'll never be able to do it," he'd tell me, "and it will be embarrassing onstage."

When teachers asked me why my corrections worked, I would say that you had to feel the dancer's problems empathetically within your own body; otherwise it wasn't possible to give good corrections beyond the basics. As a student I'd somehow managed to perform the required sixteen fouettés at my graduation exam, but by the time I joined the Kirov I was never able to do them anymore, because my feet stayed weak. But one night during my Kirov years, I dreamed I was going to have to perform

Sleeping Beauty, and mysteriously my variation in the last act was going to include fouettés.

"Why fouettés," I asked my teacher Lidia Tyuntina in my dream, "when there aren't supposed to be any in *Sleeping Beauty*?"

She hovered at my side insisting, "You have to do them; remember!"

I was panic-stricken. "I don't even know the choreography," I told her. I couldn't remember a thing, but then I started to perform the fouettés—and I did them *perfectly*.

"Good, good," Tyuntina said, and the more she encouraged me the easier it became. My legs and arms knew exactly what to do; my body found the perfect coordination for this step. I spun ecstatically. When I got up the next morning, this same confidence knitted my limbs. I ran straight to class and tried fouettés, and they worked as well as they had in my dream. It was like a scientific exercise to understand how much the mind controls the body—in dance just as much as everywhere else.

In the United States, different ranks of dancers all took class together, although ideally it's a better idea to have separate classes for the corps de ballet and for the soloists and principals. You can give the principals a stronger class, whereas the corps de ballet needs simpler steps. Male principals need to do grand pirouettes and manèges of jumps.

The corps doesn't need it. It's good if they can do it for the experience, but it's more important to give the corps men and women small jumps to make their feet work better, as well as spend more time on port de bras to enhance style. You like to keep the personality of the principal dancers distinct and different; in the classical corps de ballet you need to unify their style into homogeneity.

At ABT, I started to teach a private class, at first for women only. The dancers asked me to, because they thought they weren't getting warmed up enough in company class. Later men joined us. On tour or at the Met, we didn't even have a studio. We usually had to work in some corner backstage. We didn't have music because the company wouldn't spend extra money for another pianist. I snapped my fingers to give a metronomic accent, difficult because at the same time I had to give them corrections. Sometimes after "and one," I would skip two counts, slipping in my corrections instead. Eventually I think that helped the dancers to become more musical, to produce the rhythm and phrasing of steps within themselves.

At first Misha didn't like the idea; he thought that the dancers couldn't survive without a full class with piano accompaniment, with center work and jumps across the floor. Yet Misha along with everyone else saw the improvement in my dancers. Their pointe work improved; their jumps were bigger. Three attitude turns was duck soup for them, whereas until that time, the two (really one and a half) attitude turns that Giselle dances in her act 1 variation gave just about everyone trouble.

I was against the ballerinas taking the entire class in pointe shoes, the way they did at New York City Ballet. Dick Tanner had defended that practice to me by saying, "Well, they have to dance on pointe, they never dance in flat shoes onstage." But when the dancers worked at the barre without pointe shoes, every little muscle in their feet was forced to work. The dancers felt their feet stretching all the way through. In a pointe shoe, the foot is caged and relies on the shoe for strength; the dancer can fake a pointed foot when all her foot is really doing is initiating a sluggish flex.

In Balanchine's choreography his dancers were always on pointe or demi-pointe; they rarely brought their heels down fully to the ground. Aesthetically it was beautiful: the ballerinas whizzed across the stage like Mercury, and the audience never saw their heels squatting on the floor. Physically it could be dangerous, because the Achilles tendon could weaken and lose elasticity, making it more difficult for the dancer to jump.

Nevertheless, I tried to merge Balanchine's approach with my Vaganova background. My students wore soft shoes in my class, either flat slippers or old pointe shoes they'd hammered the stuffing out of. At the barre I used more deep pliés, ensuring that the heels kept pressing down all the way to the floor, keeping the Achilles tendon stretched and working. But when we rehearsed, I tried to make them stay as much as possible on demi-pointe as preparation for pointe, not to sit into positions with flat heels.

I find one of the biggest mistakes teachers can make is to try to their make their class "interesting," by which I mean needlessly complicated or overchoreographed. At the same time if class is too dry and monotonous, the dancers' minds and their muscles are bored. Class is supposed to be simple, but composed of varied rhythms and energies. If the whole class is very fast, muscles will spasm and they can't respond, can't develop anything. Too much tension stays in the thighs and behind, and circulation to the feet is blocked; it stops at the knee. If too much of the class is slow, then dancers never learn speed and attack and their muscles became overblown.

I had come to disagree with some of what I had been taught at Vaganova. Tyuntina's warning that I would be in pain for the rest of my life pursued me when I began teaching. Ballet was not supposed to be torture. The dancer never needed to reach a point of total exhaustion in class. Legs didn't need to be ground into pulp; when muscles were ready, legs would rise easily. "Stretch your knee," we had been told constantly in school. But forcing the knee is another way to block circulation to the feet. The dancer needs instead to use the feet to stretch the knee. When the movement is initiated by the arch of the foot, the knee stretches into the optimum placement naturally, without needless strain.

But what gives freedom to the limbs is the strength developed in the lower back. There wasn't a single dancer in ABT who used his or her lower back completely correctly. Dancers trapped their tension in their shoulders and neck. That became their center, and as a result their gravitational stability was off-kilter.

"Your backs have to smile," I would tell the corps de ballet when they danced *Les Sylphides*. Even when they turned away from us, we in the audience would then be able to know that we were in the presence of scintillating, weightless, happy creatures. That's how expressive a back can be and should be. "Feel him through your back," I told the ballerinas as they rehearsed the White Swan pas de deux. If you are attracted to someone standing behind you, your entire body senses him. Just the same way, every time Odette turns away from Siegfried, as he supports her in arabesques or promenades, the audience must feel her muscles and nerve endings yearning, a tropism toward him like a flower to the sun. Otherwise these long, sloping positions are beautiful but empty, her limbs no more interesting than the arms of a clock.

Even more than joy or longing, the back gives maximum expressive potency to emotions of pain and sadness. It's an unwritten law of ballet, and anyone who intuitively understands movement will obey. In *Pillar of Fire*, Tudor turns Hagar's back to us before her sex experience and during her humiliation after. Her shoulders are hunched, her spine stiff: Hagar's back tells the audience everything about her pain and loneliness.

Or the way Fokine begins *The Dying Swan*. The swan is turning upstage; the music's quiet, tranquil, and she's moving slowly, perhaps even peacefully, you might think for a moment at first. But then her back catches our eye. We see how rigid it is. She's in pain, she can't breathe. You know all this and only *then* does she turn her stricken face to us.

Among the most important ways a dancer creates a character on stage is through her walk and her run. Everybody dances on the same level floor, but by the quality of run and walk the ballerina conveys the illusion that she is stepping across clouds, or on glass.

Runs on the ballet stage shouldn't have any resemblance to a jog on the sidewalk. But that's how many dancers approach them. Instead it should be as though the emotion were running, propelling the body. Otherwise it destroys the aristocratic image: aristocrats never hurry, they're never late. They set the clock.

Different ballets require different runs. In *La Bayadère* when Nikiya runs to Solor in the first act, passion and impatience pilot her. When she flees the palace after her confrontation with Gamzatti, hers should be a run toward tragedy that has the impact of a scream. When Giselle first reveals herself to Albrecht in act 2, her run across the rear of the stage is the passage of an entity that has become all spirit. It can take a ballerina years to perfect this moment. Runs soak up a dancer's individuality, and the more they have to give, the more their run will be a signature. In Russia I watched Galina Ulanova run ahead of herself, her legs sprinting in front of her body. Her torso leaned forward, as if her body were following her spirit. Her steps were so swift and tiny you could barely notice one foot darting in front of the other. Everything moved: her torso and head as well as her limbs. You never saw her heels crunching the ground behind her; her legs were always forward. In the United States, Gelsey Kirkland's torso was more static as she ran; her spirit was in her arms and, supremely, in her legs. Gelsey took a longer, larger, more vertical step than Ulanova's. She showed her flexed knees as one foot succeeded the next, and the transition had the flavor of a miniature emboîté. Kirkland's run was more ethereal, Ulanova's more palpable; both were incredible.

~ 29 ~

harsh beauty

In the fall of 1986, ABT went to Italy for the filming of *Dancers*, directed by Herbert Ross. Large chunks of the ballet *Giselle* were to be included as a parallel to the story of a young dancer's romance with a company director. Misha realized that the film would serve as the final record of his Albrecht. We spent an entire day filming his variation, as Misha requested retake after retake. Dancing Giselle and Myrtha, however, Ferri and Browne were sometimes given only one take to accomplish many of their most difficult passages. Sometimes I begged Herbert to give Leslie a couple of extra takes; sitting for hours in her dressing room waiting for a shot, she would get a little out of shape. I must say both she and Alex performed beautifully and even heroically given the shooting circumstances.

"Did you see this Anna Magnani with tears?" Misha asked me after Alex performed her mad scene. "What's wrong with her? Why real tears on stage? It's not a drama theater."

"She's emotional," I told him. "She feels it this way." He thought it was provincial and unprofessional. On stage I might have agreed. But for the intimacy of cinema it worked very well. And it wasn't pretentious at all: she was able to generate actual emotion onstage very naturally.

Before shooting the mad scene, Charles had gone into her room and probably supplied some of the unsolicited hair and makeup advice he liked to dispense. I went to see her after the take was finished. A picture on the wall was crooked, exactly where a large bottle of mineral water meant for Charles had landed. "I needed to get in the mood. I needed adrenaline," Ferri told me. "That was perfect!"

Back in New York Julio Bocca, age nineteen, had just joined ABT. He had a great technique and an infectious enthusiasm. There was something so exciting and irresistible about his energy that the audience was carried away in a kind of ecstasy. ABT patron Howard Gilman complained to me that he was trying to help Julio in the face of a resistant Misha. "Can you talk to Misha?"

"Howard, *you* can talk to Misha."

"No, I can't, he's not listening to me."

At that point I did go to Misha: since he didn't want to do full-length classical roles much anymore, why did Julio have to wait in the wings? But Misha said that 1) Howard wasn't giving ABT enough money to justify having his whims catered to, and 2) he hated the way Julio had inserted his tricks into Misha's *Nutcracker*, in particular a circle of jumps that mimicked a trademark of Bolshoi great Vladimir Vasiliev, whom Julio idolized. There was no denying that Julio was thrilling in it, and the public stood on their heads with excitement. Julio wanted to do it in every ballet. But what Julio did was circus-like, it was bad taste, Misha claimed, and of course he was right.

"Since he's your protégé," Misha said, "you go tell him he's not allowed to do that in my ballet."

"Julio, don't destroy my reputation!" I joked. The look he gave me told me that he thought we were just being party poopers. But it was important that he understood that he was pushing every movement and putting himself on the road to an early burnout. "Julio, you have to work now to put elasticity into your muscles and then you will be able to dance for a very long time."

I decided to ask Misha to come to Julio's rehearsal and work with him himself, and he did. Their relationship became smoother. Julio listened, improved; sometimes he came to take class with me. But rehearsing a classical role, when Julio had to stand or sit or perform a simple mime passage, it was very hard work for him and for me. He thought it wasn't necessary; he reminded me of Nureyev saying "I'm not a mime!" backstage at the Kirov in 1959. Today I still couldn't say conclusively whether he genuinely understood how important it was, or whether he wanted to prove to Misha that he was a good dancer, or whether he simply knew that he had to prepare those gestural and pantomime aspects or he was not going to have a performance.

Coaching Julio for Albrecht in *Giselle*, I didn't want to steer his energy and enthusiasm toward melodrama. We created his first act as if the flirtation was a game pure and simple. Julio's Albrecht was spinning a convenient, easy lie, a lie he thought no more than a prank. Giselle's world was a playground for him to escape to. But the game went much farther than he had ever expected. Giselle's madness and death brought his childhood to a close. From that moment it was a turning point in his character. In the second act, he evolved into a different person, a mature adult.

In *Giselle*, the partnering Albrecht must do throughout the second act is almost impossibly difficult. The flying lifts are especially difficult with a very long, loose, and supple ballerina like Ferri, yet Julio performed them perfectly. By the time they dance the coda, every Albrecht is exhausted, his breath coming in gasps, but nonetheless he must bounce Giselle across the stage in sauté arabesques that should look as though she is skimming along the ground on her supernatural momentum, pulling him along with her. Every Albrecht hates those lifts, but Dowell and Nagy had performed the passage heroically during the 1970s. In the eighties, Bocca, too, was willing to marshal every reserve of energy and make himself all but invisible to more poetically propel Ferri.

§ ℰ

Had Misha remained in Russia, he would never have become quite the superstar he did in the West. He would have been cast by physical type and not have danced certain important roles. He knew himself that he wasn't entirely right for Siegfried in *Swan Lake*, and that's why he only danced the role a handful of times at ABT. Even when he choreographed his own *Swan Lake* seven years later, he didn't cast himself. Nor did he ever dance the full-length *La Bayadère*, and he usually didn't give the role of Solor to other short danseurs. Danilo Radojevic, however, asked Misha for years if he could try the full-length role, rather than only the Shades scene he did when we performed it separately. Finally Makarova, who had the final say given that it was her production, said yes, and Misha had no choice but to accede.

During Ferri's first season I had pleaded with Misha to perform Solor opposite her in *Bayadère*. I think they would have been great together. But Misha didn't think he could embody Solor. "He's supposed to be tall and husky," Misha said.

"What about Danilo?"

"You think he's right for it?" Misha asked. I wasn't entirely sure, but there was no denying that Danilo worked in the studio with fantastic tenacity and in performance had a huge success with the audience. That is something that no artistic administration can afford to entirely ignore.

Originally, MacMillan envisioned casting his Romeo according to emploi. Although Misha had danced both Mercutio and Romeo with the Royal Ballet in London, when we had premiered *Romeo*, MacMillan thought Misha should be Mercutio. It turned out, however, that he never danced in MacMillan's *Romeo* here at all. Ferri fought for Julio as her Romeo, and after Bocca, MacMillan eased the casting restrictions. Every man who could dance the steps and had the right passion was allowed to do Romeo in our theater.

MacMillan needed money and was pressuring Misha to stage more of his productions. "Please speak to Misha," he asked me, "you have so much influence with him." That was news to me, but I did discuss it with Misha, who thought perhaps ABT should stage MacMillan's *Swan Lake*. We certainly needed a new production; we hadn't shown David Blair's 1967 production since 1984, two years earlier. But I had already seen MacMillan's *Swan Lake*, and I didn't like it. The women wore Empire-style dresses that made them look pregnant. The whole concept was so wintry that it reminded me of *The Nutcracker*. MacMillan then suggested the *Sleeping Beauty* he had previously staged in Berlin when he directed there in the late 1960s. But I was sure that we did not want that production, which was set in the old Russia of the Muscovites, with the style of the arms changed to Russian folk dance à la the Moiseyev troupe or the Russian ballet chestnut *The Humpbacked Horse*.

Instead, Misha asked MacMillan to stage a *Beauty* that would retain the French baroque-style port de bras that was the signature of the Kirov in this ballet. He told MacMillan that style would be my responsibility. MacMillan said he would be delighted to work with me. Before he signed the contract in September 1986, I was supposed to go to London to learn Kenneth's choreography. But I wanted to stay on vacation in the country and, anyway, I knew that I'd be able to learn his steps quickly when Kenneth came to New York to begin rehearsals. Charles France did want to go to London to shop for antiques, and so he went in my place and had a good time.

Soon after, we started to work in New York. "Show me how this variation is in Russia," Kenneth would ask me. "That's nice," he would say, and
then turn to Monica Parker, his choreologist assistant, and say, "How was
it in our version?"

Monica would show him exactly what he had staged in Berlin; she was
an excellent choreologist.

"Well, okay," MacMillan would say, "let's do halfway this and halfway
that."

Inevitably, the whole production turned into a hodgepodge almost immediately. Some arms were true to Kirov style. Some arms were an English view of Petipa's style as danced by the Royal Ballet, and some were
still Russian folk, as they had been in Berlin. For example, it was, for me,
entirely incongruous for the Lilac Fairy, with pointe shoes on her feet, to
perform a Russian ethnographic bow to wicked fairy Carabosse.

Rather than launching a movement-by-movement war, I soon gave up
on Misha's mandate about Kirov style. "It will be *your* name on the program," I said to Kenneth at one point. "Do whatever you want . . . Just tell
me what to do and I will do it!"

Where Kenneth retained what we can call the essence of Petipa's choreography, the production was good. Yet his musicality could be awful;
there were some nasty, ugly steps he mixed into this ballet's sublime in-
vention. In addition, the dramatic logic of this new *Beauty* was flimsy,
which was surprising for a choreographer who made so many narrative
works. MacMillan's Aurora was sweet and pretty and one-dimensional.
She didn't have any real character, nor any real relationship with other
characters on the stage.

Wooed by four suitors from around the globe in the Rose adagio, Aurora should be polite at all times, since she doesn't want to hurt the four
princes' feelings. She must manage to not show a preference, but rather to
react slightly differently with each one of them. But MacMillan told ABT's
Auroras to react exactly the same to each prince, to pay more attention to
the flower itself than to who was presenting it.

I started working alone with the principal dancers. When I came back
to watch a full-cast rehearsal of the Prologue, I saw that by now nothing of the French baroque style preserved at the Kirov was left. The arms
had reverted completely to Royal Ballet classicism, a square, boxy geom-

etry that is not my preference at all. But the principals working with me looked the way I thought they should look. I now realized it had been a mistake on my part not to go to London and work with Kenneth from the very beginning. If I had, I might have been able to save more of *Sleeping Beauty*'s authentic style.

As much as I found to disagree with MacMillan's production, however, I began to make myself believe in it. I couldn't have worked on it otherwise. It was virtually impossible to justify to dancers aesthetic decisions that I myself couldn't believe in. When Monica began demonstrating Kenneth's version, I was as uncomfortable as I could see the dancers were when they tried to do some of his torturous steps. But then I stopped reacting empathetically and began to make myself believe I could do it. I virtually hypnotized myself. "It can be very pretty. It will be an absolutely different aesthetic—English, but it's pretty, it's feminine. It's not necessary that it be exactly like it was at the Kirov, or the Royal when Fonteyn danced Aurora with them in Leningrad in 1961. I can take the Royal aesthetic as an axiom and still adapt it to my dancers. And maybe something very nice will come out." Without changing any choreography I tried to soften and polish the dry, harsh angles of Kenneth's choreography, to make the overall signature more elegant.

Unfortunately, before the production premiered in Chicago in February 1987, Kenneth was diagnosed with throat cancer and forced to return to London for an operation. Among our coaching staff, I continued working with the Auroras and Prince Desirés; Georgina Parkinson concentrated on Lilac and worked with Amanda McKerrow for Aurora, while Monica rehearsed the corps de ballet.

Whereas Aurora is the heroine in this fairy tale, the Lilac Fairy might be called a double fairy tale, because she is the leading fairy in a fairy tale. She is as much illusion as substance. She can fly; she can walk on air; she can assume any shape. Each attribute that the entourage of Prologue fairies present Aurora is but one color in Lilac's all-inclusive spectrum. You cannot give what you do not possess: to bestow these attributes the Lilac Fairy must herself exemplify them. More than anyone else on stage she is graciousness, generosity, sunny temperament, beauty. Whereas the King and Queen are intent on consciously molding an image of authority, *Beauty*'s fairies, most of all Lilac, are completely comfortable within their divinity. Lilac doesn't have to prove that she is a goddess. She doesn't have to prove anything.

In my day the Kirov administration often seemed to believe that Lilac required only technical prowess and a sweetly vague presence. But Lilac also received interpretations that made the role every bit as important as Aurora, which was as it should be. I saw Alla Osipenko dance Lilac many times over two decades, but my most vivid memory of her in the role is dancing at the dress rehearsal of Konstantin Sergeyev's new production in 1952. Tyuntina took our entire class to watch. Osipenko was nineteen and radiant with freshness and enthusiasm. By contrast, Alla Shelest brought a mature graciousness to the role. Inna Zubkovskaya had also brought star quality to her.

At first I thought Kenneth had miscast Susan Jaffe as Aurora. I told Kenneth she should be the Lilac Fairy instead, for Jaffe was beautiful, rather tall; she had the right capacity. But when I saw the awful, constipated variation MacMillan had made for Lilac I understood that in this production that role wasn't something worth fighting for. One particularly nasty sequence had her doing arabesque fouettés in place. It was going to be very difficult for anyone to look good in that variation. I explained the philosophy of the role to ABT Lilacs, the values she needed to embody. But the variation was so awkward that that we were forced to concentrate on technical difficulties, which hardly anyone could consistently surmount.

In the old days at the Imperial Mariinsky, Aurora's parents, the King and Queen, could be played only by very special artists because they were in a sense the most important roles, a mirror of the Romanov's own hierarchy. And even after the Revolution, the Kirov continued to show great respect for these roles. It was treated as a litmus test of the Kirov's noble style, and I'd often watched Sergeyev work tirelessly to ensure that every detail was perfect.

In the Kirov's production, royalty's gestures were never raised higher than the dancer's shoulder, for to do so would have been the equivalent of raising their voices, becoming strident, losing composure. And royalty never showed agitation or anger in front of the court. A king didn't turn his body away from its vertical axis. He was like a living statue. He didn't need to be polite. He kept his distance at all times. He might talk amiably to a subject, but no matter the affection he evinced he was still talking from the top of his position, implicitly giving commands. He was not sharing his soul. But at ABT, we couldn't afford a fraction of the time needed to reach the right level of distinction for these roles.

Petipa's choreography for the role of Aurora inevitably helped all ABT's young ballerinas to grow, to further their education. Petipa's steps in each variation demonstrate the academic dance at its best. More than *Swan Lake* or *Giselle*, *Sleeping Beauty* is a ballet of sparkling, clearly defined edges. Clean and definite punctuations are as necessary here as in Balanchine, but unlike Balanchine's choreography, what's never called for is a full, complete stop to a movement phrase.

Charles had discovered Cheryl Yeager in ABT's corps and promoted her during Misha's first season. She had beautiful legs, a high jump, and, as Charles said, a cute behind. Yeager improved dramatically by dancing Aurora. Her technique strengthened, her style became more polished. Her dancing became more feminine. As Aurora she was better than I ever thought she could be.

Christine Dunham had joined ABT's as a corps member in 1985, but she had already been a principal dancer at the Dallas Ballet. In MacMillan's production she first performed the Lilac Fairy and then Aurora. Her face and figure were beautiful, but her muscles rather stubborn and resistant. She needed much more basic work before she would be ready to try Aurora. Dunham herself understood that to some degree. She couldn't quite comprehend, however, why she needed so much work when she had already reached ballerina rank in Dallas. She was frequently injured, frequently in tears. I told Misha that Aurora could break her.

"But she's so beautiful," he said. Sure enough when she made her entrance onstage, she fell and pulled a muscle. "Witch!" Misha rebuked me. (But she recovered, and she really came into her own dancing Odette/Odile in Misha's *Swan Lake* a year later.)

Leslie Browne was born to do Aurora, but as it turned out she never got the chance. I did try to campaign for her—unsuccessfully. Ferri was fifth-cast Aurora and never got to do it at ABT. At this particular moment Ferri was unhappy with Misha and the entire ABT routine. All but deliberately, I thought, she had injured herself by going into a rehearsal without doing a warm-up first. She was out for several months.

Working on *Beauty*, I told Jaffe, "The minute you step into the studio, you already must feel that you're a very good person. You're gracious; you're generous. You're sweet and you're happy." Putting herself in the right mood lightened her movement. She developed a greater refinement and for the first time a real tenderness. I was thrilled when she received reviews unlike any I'd read for her before.

Yet it was Amanda McKerrow who was heiress apparent for ABT's premiere Aurora. *Beauty* demanded the clean, fresh precision Amanda could produce. Her body was exquisitely proportioned. Standing in a perfect textbook position, she could command the same engrossed attention aroused by a da Vinci study.

I hadn't worked with McKerrow very much, only on some variations, among them the waltz in *Les Sylphides*, as well as for Gamzatti in *La Bayadère*. Unlike so many others, she came to ABT already equipped with a sound and flexible body and technique. She could jump; she could turn; her back was pliant. Technically, she didn't need me as much as other dancers did. Stylistically, her arms were only not bad, but she arrived more ready to advance than practically anyone else in the company.

Unfortunately, when we premiered the new *Beauty* in Chicago, Amanda delivered a flat and limited performance of Aurora. Misha wasn't happy with her at all. On stage after the performance, Amanda told him through tears that it wasn't her fault; if she wanted him to dance it his way, he should have let her work with me. And so MacMillan gave preference not to McKerrow but instead to dark horse Jaffe for most of the opening night *Beauty*s on tour as well as New York. Georgina knew Kenneth well from her years at the Royal Ballet. She called Kenneth and told him that I was meddling with his ballet.

In Los Angeles, Leslie Browne was about to make her debut as Giselle. A few days before her performance, she walked into our *Giselle* rehearsal sobbing. She had come directly from a stage rehearsal of *Beauty* where she and a number of the dancers had been given a venomous dressing-down by Kenneth, who had just arrived in town. Our *Giselle* rehearsal was down the drain; she was too hysterical to be able to work. I walked to the wings of the Shrine Auditorium stage. MacMillan appeared from the auditorium followed by Georgina. He approached me with a glowering face and reprimanding finger. "You're not allowed to change my steps!"

And I shook my finger back at him: "How can you be so rude to the dancers? You've destroyed Leslie's rehearsal."

"How can you talk to me like that?" he demanded. Poor man, he was forced to whisper because of his throat, and I had gotten very loud. The dancers' ears were popping. John Taras, who had left New York City Ballet in 1984 to become associate director at ABT, suggested that we repair to an empty dressing room.

"What did I change?" I asked Kenneth.

"You changed the entrance." In Petipa's choreography, Aurora performed a beautiful jump in second position; MacMillan had made the same step short and pinched by adding a switch of the legs in demi-pointe. I hadn't changed it; I just had my dancers pass quickly through the most ungainly part of the sequence. They held the second position longer, moved quickly through the demi-pointe rather than sitting with their legs bent, then went immediately up into the jump. But timing is so important that a slight alteration can make the same steps look totally different.

"You ruined my ballet," Kenneth insisted. "I will sue you!"

"Really? If I ruined it, why did you choose my ballerina? And what about Petipa? If he were alive, don't you think he would sue you for destroying his brilliant choreography?"

Kenneth's wife Deborah started to scold me. "How can you talk to Sir Kenneth like that? It's so rude; how can you?"

I turned to Lady MacMillan. "Excuse me, who are you? Are you working in the company, and I didn't know anything about it?"

"I'm Kenneth's wife," she said.

"Yes, I know, but I didn't know we have a position like that in the company. It's a company meeting. What are you doing here?"

Kenneth was astonished. "She's my translator," he said.

"From which language to which?" I asked. "She will translate to me into Russian?" In actuality, Deborah was of course there to talk for him after his operation.

"He's a sick man," she said, "and you don't have pity for him."

I said, "You know, if a sick man doesn't have pity for the entire company . . . Everybody worked so hard and so well, and he came right before the opening and destroyed their mood. Show me exactly the steps that aren't there!" Well, it looked different, Kenneth insisted. It looked *better*, I told him, but the step was the same.

"You know, Kenneth, everybody, *everybody* is talking about you, how you appear and destroy art. Leslie Browne is supposed to have her first *Giselle* in three days. It's so important for her. You don't care. She is crying hysterically now; I had to cancel her rehearsal and there are only two more left before her performance. You're trying to tell me you're an artist, or you really care about people and the company?"

"How can you say that? Everybody loves me!"

"Kenneth, let's face it, everybody's talking about you this way. Not only me."

"Who is talking about me?"

"Everywhere you work, they fire you and people hate you."

"Who told you that? You weren't there."

"No, I wasn't there, but other people were there, and people told me who were there."

"Who told you?"

"Well, we're not in court. I'm not going to tell you names, when you will punish them. But even your closest friends."

"Who?

"Georgina, for example." Just that morning she had been badmouthing him to me.

"Is that true, Georgina?" he said poisonously. She was speechless.

"Okay, okay, wait a minute," mediator Taras said. "Let's be nice to each other. It's a very important premiere and let's find a way to be able finish that. Let's not fight anymore."

"Of course I understand we are all temperamental," I said, "and if Kenneth will tell me and the whole company that he's sorry—"

"No, never!"

"In this case, I'm taking myself out of this production," I told Kenneth. "I'm not going into any rehearsal studio. You can fix it yourself; you can do whatever you want. It's ready anyway; I've prepared three casts for you, and there's only one more week left on tour."

Misha was arriving in Los Angeles the next day. Taras said that he would conduct rehearsals in my place until Misha's arrival. Kenneth screamed at him that he was going to sue Misha personally, sue me, sue ABT.

"Are you happy?" I asked Georgina. But she had stopped speaking to me.

A day later I walked into the office to pick up the day's rehearsal schedule. Misha, Charles, Kenneth, and Florence Pettan were silent as soon as I appeared. Charles told me later that Kenneth had been in the process of demanding that Misha fire me.

"I can't fire her," Misha told Kenneth, "she *is* ABT." It was the biggest compliment that Misha ever gave me.

"Misha never said that about me," Charles later lamented to me with tears in his eyes.

Amid the sturm und drang over *Beauty*, McKerrow was dancing her first *Giselle* opposite Baryshnikov. In Los Angeles, their paths crossed in a handful of great performances. Like Misha, she was very disciplined. From Amanda, I would have liked to see something "wrong" that would still be beautiful: some degree of imperfection enhances a ballerina's individuality.

We had only three weeks between her first rehearsal and the night she stepped onstage in Los Angeles. But she remembered every single correction I gave her. It was exciting for us to open a new door in her. Misha came to rehearsals a few days before the performance. He never wanted or needed to spend too much time brushing up his old roles, and, in addition, at this moment his knee was bothering him. But it was very easy to bring them together. Amanda always wanted to make her partners comfortable. I don't know how close she could come to a partner spiritually, but that's not what Misha was looking for. Amanda could make any adjustment Misha felt he needed to bring the right kinetic and visual union. She was willing to experiment in the studio, but on stage she never did anything unexpected. Misha knew that, come the performance, Amanda would be there: easy, light, secure. She was all of that, *and* she was warmer and more vulnerable than I had ever seen her onstage. She was inspired rather than academic; her positions were filled with emotion. She even produced what in Russia is called "dance impressionism": an illusion of improvisation. If anything distinguishes romantic style from classical style, it is that, and as a result, romantic technique is even more difficult. There are many moments throughout the second act of *Giselle* where she must accomplish difficult technical things, but nonetheless the ballerina's very human body cannot look human at all. Instead she must convince the audience that she is a spirit with no more physical substance than a cloud.

During act 2, the Wilis hear Albrecht approach, and at Myrtha's order they disappear offstage to apprehend him, returning with their new victim whom they intend to force to dance into oblivion. But Giselle rushes forward to protect him. Myrtha points Giselle to the center of their haunted domain. If she is determined to share Albrecht's guilt, she must atone equally with him.

Giselle begins the pas de deux alone, raising a long, slow développé. Her leg whispers down to the floor and then rises again in arabesque. She promenades, her face turned down; ideally we believe her to be peering from a great height, perched in the sky. Her feet wing into entrechats six, which ideally will dazzle like shooting stars. Facing Myrtha, she bends down to the ground, a bow to her queen. She folds her arms over her body, as if covering herself from Myrtha's evil.

At the height of her développé the ballerina shouldn't hold her leg still even for a second, so that the eyes of the audience are not allowed to scrutinize any limitation in the range of Giselle's limbs. The illusion we want is that her leg could continue rising indefinitely; if she hadn't lowered it, her leg would have taken her off the ground. Giselle's limbs continuously defy the logic of human mechanics. For example, after bowing to Myrtha, Giselle's left leg rises in second position, lifting her torso with it—a reversal of the customary flow of human motion.

Giselle now has no weight. She is a like a feather, a bubble, a cloud that responds to every passing breeze, no matter how slight. Whenever Albrecht passes her, Giselle has to reflect, to echo, his movement. When his arms circle her waist in the pas de deux, he is restraining her from floating away, constantly trying to bring her back to him. We must be convinced that they are united, that they feel every step the other takes. Every time the Wilis separate them, she must remain connected by a loop of energy that circles back to him. "You see him with your back and *that's* why you turn," I told ballerinas. "His energy touches you inside."

Chimes announce 4 a.m. and the Wilis must disappear back to the tombs where they rest during the day. Albrecht has fallen spent to the ground, but he still lives. Giselle takes Albrecht's hand and places it on her heart, transferring her soul to his. In Russia and in the West, most Giselles then indicate with the raised arm and fingers pressed together that they are swearing eternal fidelity. That has always seemed wrong to me. Existing in the next dimension, a spirit doesn't have to swear to anybody or anything. I think what she is really doing is showing him the sun, and eventually I came across a photograph of Galina Ulanova in performance doing just that. I'm convinced that this was what Giselle was supposed to indicate originally, but because these gestures are so similar, the expression has become corrupted over time. Giselle is pointing him to light: "Take my love and forgiveness, and live your life." Giselle has not become a Wili. She began the initiation rite, but then her love took over. She has successfully defied Myrtha.

Leslie Browne finally danced her first *Giselle* on the closing night of that same Los Angeles season. That night bedlam ruled backstage at the Shrine Auditorium. Doors were slamming, sets dismantled, costume trunks loaded for the trip back to New York. Surrounded by chaos, Leslie had to create the unearthly stillness of life beyond the tomb. Her debut was the culmination of years of preparation and frustrated plans, but she was now in the best condition of her years with the company. No longer fighting her body, Leslie's emotions were able to take flight in movement. In LA she gave a great performance. Every moment in each act was true.

By the time the second act curtain had fallen on Leslie's debut, the Shrine Auditorium had become only too appropriate a context for *Giselle*. Backstage was like a ghost ship. Leslie and I walked past one empty dressing room after another. Most of ABT had already cleared out their things for the trip to New York. Leslie's feet weren't yet back on the ground; she seemed to still linger in the next dimension of *Giselle* act 2. And so I helped her pack. That night was a vindication for both of us.

Soon after we returned to New York, MacMillan consulted a lawyer who called me. They were planning a court appearance. "Do you understand ballet that well?" I asked the lawyer. "If I show you steps, will you know exactly what I'm talking about?

"Actually no," he confessed. Kenneth dropped the suit. It was a farce. But I was now back in the *Sleeping Beauty* production officially. In fact I had been continuing to work with my ballerinas "underground," as well as with McKerrow, after Misha and Amanda herself asked me to work with her for *Beauty*.

One day during our spring season at the Met, Jaffe and I were sitting together in the opera house cafeteria. Kenneth came to our table and asked if he could sit down. Susan was so tense she could barely swallow, and she left right away.

"I want to talk to you and I want to apologize. Will you accept my apology?"

"Sure."

"Can we have dinner sometime and talk about it and get past it?"

"Yeah, sure."

I finished lunch and we walked together to the stage where I had a rehearsal.

"Please," Kenneth asked, "could you walk across the stage with me?" He put his arm around my shoulders, and we walked slowly from one side of the stage to the other. We showed the company that we were friends once again. But sadly we were never really friends anymore.

~ 30 ~

glasnost

The *Beauty* tour had been the most grueling yet for me. I told Misha that I wanted some title that would protect me from another experience similar to what I'd just gone through with MacMillan, that would above all protect me from having to take orders from Charles. He was an extremist: a creature of unchecked Rabelasian appetites. And yet today I see so little passion in the field, even on stage, that I appreciate more than ever Charles's passionate love for ballet.

He was intelligent and educated, but from my point of view, his taste in dancers and choreography was often questionable—he was partial to ornate, pretentious kitsch as well as to white-bread blandness. And his decisions were invariably dictated above all by personal considerations. If one of Charles's favorite dancers wanted a stage rehearsal on a day off—forty-five thousand dollars worth of overtime per hour—he rubber-stamped their request. If a great or good dancer who Charles felt had been rude to him requested an extra *studio* rehearsal during regular working hours, Charles gave her a summary no. With people Charles didn't like he was rude, obnoxious, and dismissive—or he acted like they didn't exist. Susan Jaffe's career almost ended when she and Charles's favorite, Robert La Fosse, clashed over partnering problems during a rehearsal of *Other Dances*. Sorting the company into the select and the outcasts did terrible things to ABT morale.

I certainly didn't feel that Charles's professionalism or experience surpassed or even equaled my own. Despite the authority Misha vested in him, it was frequently galling to have to defer to Charles.

Misha and I were at a stalemate when, in the fall of 1987, I received a call from two American producers who had organized a United States tour of the Moscow Ballet, led by the great Bolshoi star Viacheslav Gordeyev. I would be the first Russian émigré to work again with a Soviet company. I asked, Were they *sure* they could get permission for an émigré to work with Soviets? They told me it was no problem at all; on the contrary, the Soviets approved of this as a demonstration of cross-cultural cooperation.

I had known Gordeyev slightly in Russia, when he was first married to the Bolshoi's Nadezda Pavlova. I saw them often at the home of a mutual friend, Vlad Kosten, a set designer in Moscow. The group that Gordeyev had brought here comprised members of his permanent ensemble and guests from companies across the USSR. They had worked together only for about a week before they traveled here, and they came to the United States without a ballet master. Since Gordeyev had to dance and attend meetings as well as rehearse, things had become a bit chaotic. It was he who suggested that I be contacted.

I said yes and came straight from the train station to the theater in Baltimore. Gordeyev was very happy to see me and took me immediately onto the stage and introduced me very cordially to the company. He asked me to rehearse the second act of *Swan Lake.*

I said, "Slava, let me watch it first, I don't even know which version they're dancing."

"We don't have any time; we have to do it," he said.

At first it was very tense. Many of the younger kids had never before been in the West. I stared into a sea of suspicious, admiring, and curious faces. Glasnost couldn't happen in the blink of an eye. Only a year earlier, the Kirov had performed at the Mann Music Center in Philadelphia. I went with Baryshnikov and Makarova to see them. Ninel Kurgapkina smiled and waved from outside the stage door, but she wasn't allowed to approach us. Irina Kolpakova received permission to sit with us in our box, but it was surrounded by a phalanx of KGB agents. As I was walking out of the theater during intermission, a hand yanked at my arm. It was an old friend of mine who was now coaching. "How are we doing?" she asked furtively. "We're trying to be good!"

To my amazement, what was most difficult for me during that first rehearsal with Gordeyev's dancers was struggling not to lapse into English. I thought it would be such a relief to be able to run a rehearsal in Russian once again, but I was nervous. I though it would be very tacky if I let an English word slip in. And yet some English expressions, such as "lower back," were not only perfectly specific but didn't have exact equivalents in Russian.

After company class the next morning, we began to feel more comfortable with each other. Dancers told me that my class felt good, but it was a little bit different from what they took in Russia. My combinations were now shorter and less grueling than the Russian school, to avoid making muscles heavy. I'd also added a lot more work on feet since I left Russia. The old Russian school had been scrupulous about this, but it had gotten a little lost in the present generation.

Working with Gordeyev's group also brought me closer to my son, since a friend of Alyosha's was dancing with them. Igor never forgave me for walking out on him, and too often Alyosha became the brunt of Igor's resentment. As soon as Glasnost dawned in 1985, I had sent an invitation for Alyosha to visit the United States for a month . . . which Igor quickly squashed. Now Alyosha had finally escaped Igor's jurisdiction and was dancing at a tourist hotel in Moscow, making a good salary.

I was toying with a plan to marry Alyosha off to an American woman, thereby allowing him to automatically become a U.S. citizen and resettle here if he chose—and I was sure that he'd want to. The younger sister of an American friend of mine was willing to have a go at it. She visited Alyosha in Moscow for ten days. But the KGB kept close tabs on exactly this kind of charade. Love at first sight wasn't going to cut it. Return visits needed to be made. A gradual blossoming of mutual ardor had to be simulated. The young woman, however, balked at the prospect of repeated visits to Moscow. For one thing, she found the food, even Russian delicacies, absolutely intolerable!

Now I tried extending to him another vacation invitation. Sometimes I had sent him letters and postcards from Europe via standard mail instead of with courier friends. This was good, because he had to produce these to prove that he still had a relationship with me in order to be allowed to leave the USSR.

In the meantime, I loaded up Alyosha's friend in the Gordeyev troupe with a VCR and a camcorder to bring to Alyosha. In Russia they would have gone for fifteen thousand rubles, which was what an average Soviet made over the course of a *decade*. To make sure that the presents actually reached their destination, I also bought Alyosha's friend as many gifts as I could. In the past, my presents wouldn't always arrive intact; the messenger would skim off something for himself en route.

Misha called me while I was on tour. "Please come back." My new title would be Ballet Mistress for the Classical Repertoire. Gordeyev let me leave his tour two weeks before the final performance to go back to ABT. The company and I had come a long way together during those six weeks. It was a very emotional parting. Gordeyev made a warm speech, the dancers gave me cute little gifts, and we all cried.

Glasnost continued when the Kirov's Altynai Asylmuratova danced Nikiya in two *La Bayadères* with ABT in New York in May 1988. In rehearsals, Altynai studied me out of a cameo-perfect face of olive-tinted skin. Her sense of humor was captivating, provided she felt relaxed in her surroundings. With people she didn't know, however, she froze. She would not let them come inside her life or see her emotions; a veil of Asian inscrutability would settle on her face.

Watching Asylmuratova I saw again that ballet training from the waist down had declined in Russia. Her legs were gorgeously shaped but not as responsive as they could have been. Her upper body and arms, however, were much better than our ballerinas: her back was beautiful and flexible, her arms emotional and free. But she was self-conscious, slightly defensive in rehearsal, because she could see that our dancers were more technically adept. Just as we had been in the 1960s, Soviet dancers appearing in the United States were still indoctrinated that their mission was to educate the heathen Americans in the fine points of the art. Altynai would ask me for corrections, listen carefully to my suggestions, and try to incorporate them. But if she didn't see a result immediately, she would move on right away. I didn't belabor it; it would just have disoriented her, especially since we had only a few days to work together.

Yes, the Soviet barricades were starting to topple. First Asylmuratova . . . and now my son! In June he let me know that he would arrive in New York in August for a month's visit with me.

In July I was on tour in Italy, directing a small group of ABT dancers organized by Alessandra Ferri. She had made great strides since joining ABT three years earlier and was now able to show just how wide the range of her talent was. She had worked very hard to strengthen her feet; in Balanchine's *Tarantella* she was fast and sharp and precise the way no one would have dreamed she could be just a few years earlier.

That summer, my friend Genna Smakov was dying of AIDS. He lived in the East Village, and every day after rehearsal at ABT's studios near Union Square I'd walk down to his place. He'd always been a great conversationalist, but now he was too listless to say much at all. The diagnosis was the diagnosis, but nevertheless to me it was if he had really been destroyed by the rigors of everyday life here. He knew the language and literature of eight different countries. He had taught literature in a Russian university. He wrote books here, translated other people's books, and still he couldn't support himself from literature or find a full-time job teaching. Through Alex Liberman he also became a consultant for *Vogue*, but he worried about what would happen after Alex was dead. After Genna was gone I couldn't help looking through his diary when I came across it in his apartment. He had written with painful honesty about his own insecurities and his limitations as he perceived them.

He was close friends with Joseph Brodsky, and their paths in the West were in some ways parallel as well as very different. Joseph never really wanted to leave Russia. The Soviets forced him into exile. For a poet to be removed from his sources, out of his land and language, was very difficult. His life here was not at all easy. He never had enough money. As a full professor at Mount Holyoke I believe he was paid twenty-five thousand dollars a year. After he won the Nobel Prize in 1987, he told me that the college offered him an extra sixty thousand dollars per year if he would agree not to teach anywhere else.

Looking back, I see that my perception of the Soviet Union was of something like a giant kibbutz. Some comrades lived better, some lived worse, but generally we didn't see the extremes of wealth and poverty that were visible in the West and, increasingly, in the United States. Soviet bigwigs certainly had many privileges: slightly bigger apartments, better food, dachas, but all of that could be rescinded at any moment without cause or notice. Their wives were not very chic. They did have cars, but their drivers were there to report every conversation overheard. Indeed, they were afraid to speak out loud in their own homes because they knew they were under surveillance at all times—as was, of course, so much of the Soviet Union. What began to bother me more and more as I lived in America was seeing people whose value to society was all but nil living in palazzos, while someone like Joseph, a Nobel Prize–winning poet, lived in a pleasant but cramped apartment. His Nobel earnings were not really sufficient for him to think about upgrading, but in any case he was very generous and not at all materialistic.

At ten o'clock in the morning on August 21, 1988, I got the news that Genna had died. As much as I'd known it was coming, it was no less devastating to hear. That afternoon I went by limousine to JFK to meet Alyosha. I was so upset about Genna that seeing Alyosha again was more bittersweet than it should have been.

"How is Genna?" Alyosha asked. He had adored him in Russia. I couldn't tell him that he had died; I couldn't spoil his first moments in America.

We came home and I started to recognize in the grown man who stood before me the sixteen-year-old he'd been when I left Russia. We picked up our relationship exactly where we'd left off twelve years earlier, but of course there were adjustments to be made owing to the fact that he was now an adult.

Friends of mine told him he was crazy to return to Russia when the month was up; he might never again be able to leave the USSR. I didn't want him to go back, but I didn't want to pressure him. But he wound up never returning; his vacation has now lasted twenty-four years.

~ 31 ~

peak

ABT's 1987–88 season broke box-office records on tour and in New York. Dick Tanner had left our rehearsal staff and gone back to New York City Ballet, where he kept a vigilant watch on the respective attendance at each company: their take versus ours, who was up and who was down. He regularly reported our numbers to me, and right now they were very impressive. When Dick asked me what we were doing right, I told him it was because the most valuable thing on the ballet market now was quality. Balanchine, Tudor, Ashton had each died during the 1980s, and we didn't yet have choreographers of comparable genius to replace them. We would go on commissioning new work, and we had just finally instituted our Choreographer's Workshop. But at least for now, the quality of the company could replace choreographic innovation. ABT was giving excellent performances of the classic repertory. Even *Les Sylphides*, the most elusive ballet for performers and audience, was now winning enthusiastic applause.

But ABT had not yet arrived at Olympus, not compared to what I knew the company could have been. The women in our corps de ballet could have had a better bourrée, lighter, easier. They had improved their upper bodies, but their legs were a little wooden, not able to produce sufficient melody in their muscles. Arms could improve through imitation in rehearsal, but improving legs needed the right class, special steps, a particular way of using the muscles. They couldn't be fixed only in rehearsal. The physical potential of our corps was better than its manifestation in movement.

I wanted them to be free enough to do more than simply execute steps, to really start to *dance*. They were imprisoned by their anxiety about making a mistake with a count or a step. But I told them that they would be one-hundred-percent professional *only* once they had stopped worrying about being wrong.

They were still learning how to dance *through* the music and still be musical. In *Giselle's* act 2 coda, merging into the travelling arabesques they were still stomping down on each beat like soldiers in lockstep. They had the same problem in their entrance to the second adagio in the Shades scene. But little by little they were lightening their musical grip.

Something that never ceased to startle me was the way that Americans counted every dance step they performed. As a result they rarely could produce movement that filled out the shape of the entire musical phrase. I kept urging them to listen more deeply, but no, they still had to have all their counts. The result was a needlessly choppy musical line.

At times during my years with ABT, I was coaching as many as seven lead couples in addition to the corps de ballet. If I had been working in Russia during the same period, I would have had one, two, or at the most three ballerinas. We would have worked for months on every detail of a role. That is not necessarily the best way to work; every body works on its own clock. Some dancers pick up ideas very fast and can get bored with too much repetition. Others need a long time to start to feel confident and comfortable and to be themselves in what they're working on. But at ABT we never had the time to indulge in that type of luxury.

To conduct a philosophical inquiry, you must be free to not think about time, to not have to rush, to not have to condense everything into one hour or forty-five minutes. You must abstract yourself from immediate realities. A story I heard once recounted a philosopher asking his master if he is now a true philosopher. Can he now, in effect, receive his diploma? The master calls a dialogue to order. They two talk and talk and talk. The master brings wine, puts out two glasses, and starts to pour. A glass over-flows. He continues to talk. The philosopher reminds him, "Master, it's spilling over."

"You're not a philosopher yet," the master tells him.

Truly, it took an advanced level of physical and emotional readiness for a dancer to be receptive to some of the deepest and most subtle ramifications of a ballet. Short of that, I could explain the point, message, or mood of a piece more simply. At ABT, we had to work for immediate results and ready possibilities. I told ballerinas that the *Bayadère* Shades was "a goddess piece." They had to embody a type of abstraction: they weren't supposed to produce the emotion of actual love, but at the same time an unconditional warmth and courtesy needed to be visible. And using those types of cues our ballerinas often gave very good performances.

One person speaks slowly, another one rapidly; someone pronounces each word distinctly, while someone else garbles them. Comparable distinctions in timing and articulation determine the kinetic personality of the ballet dancer. Details, timing, dynamics, phrasing affect the audience's emotions and enable it to see an individual. I looked for what best fit each dancer. What I wanted my coaching to do more than anything was to preserve each ballerina's personality, so that she looked like herself and no one else. It bothered me when I saw my personal mannerisms repeated on a dancer, but it happened when I worked on act 2 of *Giselle*. I was giving them a particular style for the arms, but only the most emotive and expressive characters were putting their own personality on top. However, I knew that the schooling and style I could demonstrate would be right. There wasn't always time to try to work them past my own style and coax from them a statement that would be correct stylistically as well as unique to them.

If I stopped even to have a sip of tea, ABT's dancers were instantly nervous that they were losing one minute of attention. They danced such a large repertoire, encompassing so many styles, that their bodies kept forgetting—not classical technique, but classical style. A lot of what I did was maintenance, correcting style and arms and quality.

Learning the Stanislavsky system was a tremendous boon to Russian dancers. Fingering imaginary objects the way mimes did, we learned to imagine our body recoiling from or warming to a phantom touch. Studying like this you could imagine anything; you could turn an empty stage into a force field. We learned that no matter how formal and stylized ballet is, classical ballet is body language. Somehow it was the hardest concept for American bodies to grasp as they stretched up and out without always thinking where, why, to whom.

ABT could have developed much more rapidly had we not always been strapped financially. Despite the significantly enhanced budget that Misha's celebrity made possible, we could never afford enough stage rehearsals, enough orchestra rehearsals. Ideally, we needed a separate character dance corps de ballet, like the Kirov and the Bolshoi had. For dancers whose repertory is primarily classical never really look good in character dances. For them, the particular sparkle, the upper body coordination required for the Polish Mazurka, the Hungarian Czardas is difficult.

A dancer depends on the music, but our dancers never worked in any kind of depth with our conductors. I hardly ever heard even a good orchestral performance; not one performance that I could call musically superb. Dancers often struggled with the tempo and phrasing that the orchestra was giving them. Rarely did ABT conductors come to watch the dancers rehearse, and even when they did they didn't understand what the dancers needed apart from wanting something faster or slower. The dancer and the orchestra need to be like one body, but in thirteen years with ABT I saw it happen only with Jerome Robbins's *Other Dances*, performed to Chopin piano pieces. The same pianist who was going to play onstage during the performance played for the studio rehearsals. The dancers were able to discover the appropriate cantilena, and in this case it didn't upset them if the performance tempo was a little faster or a little slower than what the pianist had played in rehearsal.

We needed to train our own conductors, to generate musical direction equal to what had been provided by Yuri Faier in the Bolshoi and Pavel Feldt at the Kirov, who were master conductors for ballet as well as opera. The music never suffered under them. At the same time the dancers felt like it was they who were generating the music. Later, conducting at the Kirov began to decline. Kirov ballerinas made the conductors accommodate whatever tempo they wanted to take, or to abruptly shift tempo in the middle of the variation.

I reminded the dancers to breathe. When they didn't organically incorporate their breathing into the choreography, their movement became like an unresolved statement. It made me uncomfortable watching them, and I was pretty sure that the audience felt the same way, without knowing why. Our conductors and pianists needed to do the same thing, but they still didn't understand how important it was when the music breathed. They played the scores without breathing, without respiration. They either didn't understand or didn't care that a little rubato applied to the last bar of the musical phrase would give the dancer the time and room he or she needed to fully resolve the phrase before moving on to the next.

Our auditions had become much more rigorous. San Francisco had countless schools, and yet when we'd conducted auditions during one tour season there, we had found only *one* girl we could hire. We found excellent dancers from Washington, where Mary Day and Hortensia Fonseca were doing good work, as was Sonia Arova at the Alabama School of Fine Arts. But the level of teaching in America still needed vast improvement, and perhaps the greatest stumbling block to ABT's progress was that we didn't have our own school. The School of American Ballet was the best in America. But they were creating dancers for their own company. The kids who came from SAB were very talented, but it was difficult for them to adjust to our style. At New York City Ballet, ballet meant dancing steps first and foremost. In Balanchine's repertory they were dancing all the time they were on the stage. So there wasn't any stigma for them to enter the corps at City Ballet. Whereas when they came to us they sometimes freaked out and left. In the Petipa ballets, and even in contemporary works like MacMillan's *Romeo and Juliet*, the corps de ballet was acting, walking around, as much as dancing. For the SAB kids it was a huge shock. Of course it was difficult for *most* dancers when they arrived in ABT to learn how to use their body performing mime and character dance. But if we had had our own school, we'd have been able to train them for our repertory.

In 1982, Misha had closed ABT's school. I never watched any classes, but something definitely was wrong, because no stars ever emerged from there. Unlike SAB, the classes were open to anyone who could pay, but there were also scholarships given to talented young people, some of whom joined ABT. Misha thought it would be easier to disband the old structure and start an entirely new one. But all the school really needed was fresh, good faculty. The basic organization was sound and we had a junior company in place there, which Misha also closed. He had made a mistake and I talked to him frequently about reopening it. I asked him once to let me start up the school again myself, but he didn't see how I handle both responsibilities, school as well as company.

All around the West Side, ballet studios were being demolished to make way for monster apartment buildings. Catty-corner from Lincoln Center were two buildings that had housed a bank and a movie theater. Around 1986, I told Nureyev about it and what a perfect location it would make for a new school. He was very interested. He asked me to send photos to him and find out as much information about them as I could. A friend of mine located the owner and negotiated a purchase price of eight hundred thousand dollars. But I was on tour with ABT and in and out of New York all the time. A year later I came to Paris and Rudi invited me for dinner with my old friend Genya Poliakov, who was now working as Rudi's assistant at the opera. Rudi asked about the status of the buildings.

"Oh my God, I completely forgot."

He let out a few curses. "Can you check?" I was startled at how seriously he was taking it. Back in New York I immediately checked and the buildings had by now been sold—another monster high-rise was going to be built. I was so embarrassed when I called to tell him.

"Cunt!" Rudi expostulated. "Think about it: you lost such a great place and a great opportunity." He had by now only five years left to live. He knew that he was ill and that's probably why he was so impatient. The school would have been a real memorial to him. I didn't know he was sick, but there were rumors. Everybody thought with his lifestyle AIDS was inevitable, but I thought and hoped that because he was so strong, so primal and animalistic, somehow he would be able to beat it.

In 1988, Misha finally began a new ABT school. He started teaching there, and he hired Marina Stavitskya and Alexander Filipov, both very good teachers. But what no one could have imagined was that this would be Misha's last year with ABT.

~ 32 ~

baryshnikov's swan song

It was just at that moment, when ABT was poised to consolidate the difficult construction of the past decade, that the company we'd built began to implode. After *Cinderella*'s critical drubbing in 1984, Misha was particularly gun-shy about doing more choreography. We urgently needed a new production of *Swan Lake*, and Misha was considering again commissioning MacMillan, who was still listed as ABT artistic associate. After MacMillan's *Sleeping Beauty* in 1987, I thought that was asking for another company ordeal; anyway, I'd seen it in Berlin and didn't like it. Charles was pushing Misha to do *Swan Lake* himself. Charles wanted him to choreograph more for the company, to be a more active presence in ABT. Charles did not want Misha monitoring what he did too closely, but he knew that without Misha around he could easily lose his position—which is what eventually did happen. I also believed Misha should do it himself, so long as he retained the foundation choreographed by Petipa and Ivanov in 1895 for the Imperial Mariinsky. He would be at least as good as anyone else. Finally, he agreed and asked me to be his assistant for the new production.

Pier Luigi Samaritani's sets and costumes for our *Bayadère* in 1980 were still the most resplendent in our repertory, and now Misha picked him to design *Swan Lake*. Misha went to Italy to work with Samaritani while I began rehearsing the corps. Stylistically, this ballet is more difficult than any other classical work. The women must imagine that they have no torso. They have wings, and they have legs, and their two halves converge at the waist. Once the ballerina imagines her upper body as a triangle of wings growing out of her lower back, then her shoulders, arms, and torso immediately lift and lengthen.

Their arms suggest the flight of wings, but I impressed upon them that they are still ballet dancers—not animal impersonators. They have to emulate the untamed spirit of a bird, the swan's flight as a metaphor for liberation.

Misha arrived in New York a week after I began working.

"They look wonderful," he said when he saw the corps rehearse.

"Not yet," I said. There was still a lot of room for improvement. The following week he started to choreograph a new fourth act, working with much greater speed and assurance than he had when he had staged *Don Quixote* a decade earlier.

In October, ABT performed for a week in Paris. Genya Poliakov relayed an invitation to me from the state ballet company in Vienna. Was I interested in interviewing for the post of artistic director? The troupe was to be radically overhauled. Yes, by all means, I told him. My work was always incomplete at ABT; now I wanted to bring my ideas to fruition rather than feeding them to the company and sometimes seeing them diluted. Yet I would never have wanted to direct ABT myself. I was convinced that the American body and brain had the potential makings of the world's best ballet dancers. But directing in America meant spending most of my time not working in the studio, but instead soliciting money from corporations, individuals, and the government. "You'll never leave ABT," Genya told me. But I did like the prospect of spending more time in Europe.

And yet I had invested so many years in ABT. The last ten years had been a difficult process of evolution, but now the entire company, from corps de ballet to principals, was in good, professional shape. Leave now and start again practically from scratch—did I dare? I felt guilty at the prospect of leaving ABT, Misha, and my dancers; I felt they all needed me. Still, the challenge was very attractive.

Swan Lake requires the ballerina to find within herself her most vulnerable and most seductive sides; if she can't find them within herself, she won't really be able to inhabit the role. "Look at yourself in the mirror," I told the ballerinas. "Look within yourself. Try to create the image you want to see . . . Don't copy me . . . Don't copy each other . . . Put your own personality and feeling on top of our structure in the studio . . . Surprise me!"

At the end of November, Misha flew to California with us for the first public viewing of his new *Swan Lake*. Orange County's Performing Arts Center was an appropriate forum for his extravaganza. From the leafy trees rimmed with pink and red impatiens on the plaza outside to the state-of-the-art backstage facilities, the very air seemed scented with wealth.

Before the curtain on December 2, 1988, I talked to the corps de ballet as they assembled onstage, impatient to perform after ten weeks of rehearsal. They could not think of themselves as cogs in a scaffolding supporting the ballerina; they were echoes of the Swan Queen, and each had to conduct herself with the pride and stature of a ballerina. They needed to participate in the drama. In their first entrance, they advance upon Benno, the prince's retainer, surrounding him in dissolving circles of piqué arabesques: these had to be feral blows struck at the stranger who invaded their domain. When Odette begs the prince's hunting party for clemency, they should construct the corridor down which she ran as if unfurling a red carpet for their queen.

From the auditorium, Misha and I watched Susan Jaffe and Andris Liepa lead the opening night cast. Liepa was a young principal dancer at the Bolshoi, the son of the great Bolshoi star Maris Liepa. Glasnost had brought him, too, to New York and to ABT. The burghers of Orange County adored *Swan Lake* and they loved the sumptuous new tableaus spread before them, complete with mechanical swans gliding across the lakeside. Baryshnikov and Samaritani produced a *Swan Lake* that was childlike in attitude and vision—a pretty fairy tale in which to lose oneself.

Rehearsing Jaffe in *Swan Lake*, I saw she could now do anything she wanted with her body. She danced incredibly in Twyla's pieces, making the knottiest circumlocutions of Tharp's vocabulary look effortless. But something crucial was still missing. A ballerina produces emotion through her body; the thoughts and feelings inside her are what color her movement. Susan's physique was perfectly toned, but she could manifest less expressivity than she was capable of because she had gotten in the habit of calculating too much.

At nineteen, Susan had been cool, calm, and collected making debuts in important roles. But as her standards rose she started to become more insecure. Had she really lost it or was she trying to turn herself into Gelsey Kirkland, I wondered as I watched Susie now, at twenty-six, try to nail down the same pirouettes over and over and over again. "If you only do two pirouettes instead of three," I told her, "it's much less important than being able to dance with joy and freedom."

Later in December we were scheduled to leave together for Russia. She would dance Kitri in *Don Quixote* as a guest artist with the Kirov in Leningrad. Susie's appearance would be in exchange for Altynai Asylmuratova and Konstantin Zaklinsky's upcoming performances with ABT in Los Angeles. The Soviets were going to allow exactly two ABT personnel to visit; rather than send Jaffe and a dance partner, Misha decided to send Susan and me. Susan did not have a regular partner in the company; she had last danced *Don Quixote* opposite Patrick Bissell before his fatal overdose in 1988. Misha thought Susie could dance opposite the Kirov's Farouk Ruzimatov. Her performances in Russia were scheduled for December 28 and 30, but, without asking our consent, the Kirov administration moved them up to the twenty-first and twenty-third. Jane Hermann, who was the Metropolitan Opera's director of dance presentations, arranged for Susan's visa to be shifted to December 14. But when my visa came through, it was for December 24, and so it was going to be impossible for me to go at all. I suggested Susan postpone the *Don Quixote* and instead dance two *Sleeping Beauty* performances already scheduled by the Kirov for the following spring. Her Aurora in *Beauty* was the best thing she had ever done. We could go together in the lay over between our seasons in Washington, D.C., and New York.

Tycoon and arts patron Howard Gilman was forming a new management company and wanted Jaffe to join, and so Howard was suddenly very much involved in our Russia discussions. Howard, Jane, and Charles all told Susie that she was being childish, capricious. She had to go to Russia by herself, they scolded her.

Susan was perfectly capable of traveling alone, but Russia would present unique challenges. She spoke only English. She would be making her debut at the Kirov in a full-length ballet without adequate time to acclimatize herself to the raked Kirov stage and its production. I didn't trust the Soviets; I thought she could have a very difficult time with them if she went on her own. The Kirov's director, Oleg Vinogradov, had graduated with me and he specifically asked ABT that I accompany Susie. But nonetheless there would be a lot of resentment toward her from every pocket of the Kirov.

Two days before her performance, Susan decided not to postpone her debut but instead go to Russia with her husband, Paul Connelly, one of ABT's conductors. Deliberately or not, the Soviets gave her a hard time from the moment her airplane landed. Jaffe was dragooned from the airport to a stage rehearsal conducted in Russian. Realizing that one day was not enough time to adjust, she tried to cancel the first performance. The Kirov sold tickets for foreign artists at double its customary prices: if she cancelled, they would have had to refund the accumulated till. The theater administration told her they would sue ABT if she pulled out of her first performance. (What she didn't know was that the contract was not with ABT but with the Metropolitan Opera.) Susie was so stressed that she injured her knee during the first act of her debut performance and had to withdraw. The theater officials were naturally dismayed, but no refund was obligatory. Two days later she performed the entire ballet and had a big success.

When Jaffe got back to New York she told friends that Russia had been a nightmare; she told me nothing until much later. She was angry that I had been right, and that didn't make our working relationship any easier.

When I saw Misha's new *Swan Lake* performed in the rehearsal studio, I thought he had done a very good job. In the third-act ballroom scene, he made good dances for four warriors and for three girls who wore hermaphroditic masks, capering through harlequinade posturing. Tchaikovsky's fourth-act dance of the swans is inspired by the Khorovod, a traditional Russian folk dance based on walking and stillness. In most *Swan Lakes*, this music sounds disjointed from the balance of the ballet. But Misha deftly used a serpentine patterning that recalled the second act waltz and thus effected a thematic link to the earlier lakeside episode.

What sank Misha's production were the costumes, the substitution of long tulle skirts for the traditional tutu, and the elimination of the black swan costume in the third act. *Swan Lake* hinges on the dualities of black and white, positive and negative, the dichotomies that are in all beings, all phenomena. Dressing the ballerina in both black and white creates a more legible statement of the ballet's theme, and black provides a more graphic characterization for Odile. Ballet is a visual art, after all. But Misha thought it was illogical: wouldn't Odile's black costume cue Siegfried that this swan was a counterfeit?

The long, bell-shaped costume, perfect for a romantic-style ballet such as *Giselle*, was ill-suited to Petipa and Ivanov's classical choreography and unflattering to every one of our Swan Queens. The skirt tortured our ballerinas and their partners, for it made it uncomfortable for the man to hold his ballerina in supported turns. *Giselle* contains no pirouettes and only a couple of lifts, but both the White and Black Swan pas de deux are built around pirouettes. Misha felt that by rehearsing with the skirt they would be adjusting and it wouldn't be a problem.

Later in February, one week after we opened our annual season in San Francisco, I returned to New York for a week's rehearsals with the Kirov's Asylmuratova and Zaklinsky. I was ready to teach them anything they wanted to adopt from Misha's new choreography, but although Zaklinsky performed Misha's act 3 variation for Prince Siegfried, Asylmuratova hewed entirely to the same choreography she danced at the Kirov. I almost had the feeling that husband and wife had decided beforehand how much they would, as a unit, be willing to integrate. We flew to Los Angeles five days before their first performance. There were four *Swan Lakes* before theirs, but Asylmuratova and Zaklinsky shocked ABT by not attending one performance. Perhaps they were simply overwhelmed. Altynai told me she was disoriented by the time change and the brutally hard floor of the Shrine Auditorium stage.

Asylmuratova was going to dance our *Swan Lake* wearing the tutus— both black and white—she had brought from Russia. Certainly, she wanted to look as good as she could. Misha had left the tour two days after the Orange Country premiere in December; he was now in New York rehearsing for his Broadway debut in an adaptation of Kafka's *Metamorphosis*. On the phone he had politely given her carte blanche, since she was a guest of the company, but he obviously expected her to do it his way. He was highly offended when he found out she wasn't going to, but he didn't want to confront her. He respected her artistry and they had a cordial relationship. Over the phone he asked me to speak to her. Altynai and I went to look at the skirt in the wardrobe room. "No," she said. The subject was closed.

Charles was almost apoplectic, preoccupied as always by costumes, hairstyles, makeup—all the tools of make-believe. One night he kept me on the phone until 3 a.m. bewailing Altynai's impropriety and demanding I take care of things for him.

"What if Misha tells her that if she doesn't wear our costume, she won't be allowed on stage?" Charles asked me.

"She will take the next plane back to Leningrad."

"It's unbelievable how hard all of you work here," Altynai said to me. At the Kirov, ballerinas danced much less frequently. Yet Altynai herself was exhausted after five grueling years as the Kirov's prima ballerina and ace in the hole. Although the Kirov's reputation had somewhat declined in the 1980s, she had been shown off like a hothouse orchid on back-to-back international tours and seasons in Leningrad. At the stage rehearsal in Los Angeles, she barely made it through the last act. But she was mistress of what I called the "Russian mannerism." In those days, a Russian ballet dancer, no matter how tired, projected her love for dancing every time she appeared onstage. Altynai's two performances enchanted glamour-happy LA with her sinuous arms, her ravishing face and figure, and vivid stage presence. She used her eyes like a sorceress, mesmerizing the audience with Odette's poignant distress and Odile's hypnotic seduction.

Not only was Altynai wearing the only tutu onstage, she was the one dancer whose costume or headdress sprouted plumage, for Misha and Samaritani had denuded their flock. Altynai looked as though she had wandered in from a different performance. I felt that she was somehow extending a gesture of solidarity to ABT's disgruntled ballerinas. Their loud calls of "Brava!" sailed above those of the packed audience, providing a calculated show of support for Altynai's rebellion.

~ 33 ~
end of an era

"It doesn't matter whether you do the premiere, Susie, what matters is how you dance." Jaffe sat on the studio floor unwinding after a rehearsal. Her long fingers were expertly manicured, but they were blanched, as though an icy fear was immobilizing them. I was sure that Jaffe leading the New York premiere of Misha's new production would only serve to draw critical fire. The critics would review her as Misha's chosen ballerina, and thus very likely she would become something of a scapegoat for the production's problems.

Susan eventually told him she would do the second performance, but Misha insisted she appear on opening night. For two weeks Misha let Susan decide who she wanted to partner her. Finally, she said she had decided on Ross Stretton. Stretton was a good partner, but Liepa was an even better one and had been Susie's outstanding Siegfried on tour. Misha then told me he wanted Ricardo Bustamante instead to partner her at the opening. But Andris was an assured actor, whereas Ricardo was still too shy onstage to project the easy confidence of a prince. Liepa's high coloring and fair hair fit the German background of the story, whereas Ricardo's jet-black hair and eyes made his relationship with Jaffe look like brother and sister.

Just ten days before the Met opening, Charles and Misha began a mad shuffle of switching casts. No one knew with whom he or she would be dancing.

"Listen, you really are a genius," I complained to Charles. "You've managed to make every single person in this company unhappy."

A day after Misha was championing Bustamante for opening night, he took away all of his *Swan Lakes* in New York. A day later Bustamante asked if he could at least have one. Misha now decided to give him two. Liepa's originally scheduled four performances had now dwindled to two. Stretton had originally been scheduled for two performances and now was given six. Charles was angling for Susie to dance with Jeremy Collins, who was a raw recruit, not yet ready to be what Charles wanted. Susan was resistant. Finally it was decided that Stretton would partner her.

Susan asked me to work alone with her for an hour on Sunday, one day before the opening. Over and over and over she repeated different passages until one hour turned into three. I didn't want to call a halt to it because if anything didn't work during the performance, I didn't want her to think that I hadn't given her the chance to prepare. I tried to make her feel comfortable, to help her relax—the more nervous she got the less anything worked. But she would put *everything* she had into her opening and I was sure that technically she would be very good. She was a fighter, and she definitely danced better under pressure. Indeed, Susan was very good the next night; I thought it was the best she'd ever danced *Swan Lake*. But when the reviews appeared two days later, the production itself was panned, and Jaffe's performance not overly admired.

Vienna had called a week earlier and asked me to come look over the company and meet Eberhard Waechter, who was going to take over direction of the opera house. He had been a star baritone with the Vienna Opera, practically an idol in his city.

I didn't tell Misha why I was leaving for several days. The morning I was due to fly out, he called to ask how I felt. "Horrible," I told him. "I need a rest. I need a change of atmosphere. I can't see one more ballet step. I haven't had one day off the entire tour," which happened to be perfectly true.

"I know, I understand," he said. "Everything here is so frustrating." I knew he was upset about the bad reviews for *Swan Lake*. Earlier in the season he had told me outright that he wanted to leave, but I hadn't paid any attention. He had threatened to leave numerous times before, and I thought that once again it was just a momentary whim.

I went first to Paris, where I stayed with Genya. Nureyev phoned him from the airport. "I just got in and nobody was here to meet me. I've been waiting a half hour for a car. I'm going home. I will hate everybody for two hours. Then I will come to the theater and I won't scream at anybody." That night we went to Rudi's for a wonderful dinner by candlelight. He had just bought several antique kimonos. I tried them on for him, enjoying their centuries of history but not their centuries of stale perspiration.

In Vienna two days later, I met with Waechter. He was blunt, but jovial, his manner both Continental and specifically Germanic. He was someone who knew how to wield power, and he knew as well that he possessed an innate charisma and power apart from the office he occupied. He told me that ballet there had sunk so far below the level of music that it was embarrassing. I was prepared for a state of absolute inertia wherein nothing could be changed, no one could be brought in and no one fired. But on the contrary, he told me that they needed to fire at least forty dancers and staff; otherwise there was no way to remake the company. I could bring eight outside dancers in soloist and principal positions as well as hire two new ballet masters.

I watched *The Sleeping Beauty* that night. The company was actually better than I had been led to believe, but overall they were in bad shape. "They've forgotten how to work," Waechter told me. His verdict was confirmed when I went to watch company class the next day. It began at 9 a.m. I told Waechter that that was the first thing that had to change. The dancers weren't rested enough from their performances; their muscles were still sleepy. At ABT class was usually about an hour before rehearsals started. If I taught company class, it would be at 10:30 a.m.; if it was just my own group, it would be 11 a.m. But sometimes when rehearsals weren't beginning until the afternoon, class might be as late as 2 p.m.

Ballet classes customarily last ninety minutes, but in Vienna they were never longer than an hour. It isn't enough time to make improvements. Waechter informed me that the unions insisted class be early because all work was supposed to end at 1 p.m., when a three-hour break began. Work resumed at 4 p.m. or 5 p.m. Could we change the schedule? I asked.

"Good luck," he said.

The next day I saw class once more and then met again with Waechter, who showed me an entirely blocked-in opera house schedule for as far ahead as 1992.

The company was in fact frighteningly well organized. Every single occurrence on the stage—rehearsals as well as performances—was accounted for three years in advance. Their season was September first to July first, and they received in addition two months paid vacation.

Waechter's assistant, Susan, drove me back to my hotel. She was Austrian. "I have to tell you," she said, "that Waechter wants you to take the job and isn't telling you about a lot of potential problems. It will be very difficult to fire people and make changes and bring in anyone from the outside." I had thought that he did sound too optimistic. But if she worked with me, she could liaise with the unions and the government as an insider.

Waiting in the wings at ABT was Jane Hermann. A year earlier during our Met season, Jane, who was then the Met's director of dance presentations, had asked me to bring her to Misha's dressing room. It was at that moment off-limits to her, but she wanted to resolve their differences. She told me that she had some good ideas to present to him. Misha looked at her and turned away. I told him in Russian that she thought she could raise some money from the Met to help ABT. Several months later, ABT's executive director, Charles Dillingham, left, and to my surprise Jane was named as his replacement. "It's very dangerous," I told Misha. Jane was going to be on his case as much as the board.

And I think now that Misha felt that ABT had slipped out of his control. Cut to the quick by the *Swan Lake* reviews, this time he made good on his threat, making his decision to resign during a meeting with the board of trustees a few days before his announcement. Board chairman Melville Strauss had reproached him for not communicating with the board.

"It's true," Misha told me later. The board also resented that he didn't help more with fund-raising. "I didn't do that," Misha admitted to me.

On June 21, Misha addressed the company. He told the dancers that he felt life was going too fast and his responsibilities were cheating him of normal life experiences. He told them he'd still be with them all next season. He'd spend much more time with them. He told whoever wanted to talk to him to please feel free—after nearly a decade of avoiding that kind of face-to-face communication. He'd be open to everybody. The company thought he was being honest, as well as contrite, and they applauded him. Misha said to me, "Charles will stay with the company, definitely, not in the same position, but Jane will find some job for him." But Charles saw the handwriting. He and Jane had always been enemies. For him the party was finally over. Very quickly, it was clear that she was in charge now, and before long we learned that she had been made artistic director as well as executive director—a dual appointment that was almost unprecedented. I was doubly pleased and relieved when I heard that Vienna was definitely hiring me.

A note was posted backstage at the Met during the last week of our season, instructing the dancers not to talk to Baryshnikov, Charles, or regisseur Susan Jones—only to Jane Hermann or John Taras. Taras was moved to a higher position now, but Jane was going to end what had become a costly sinecure extended to Kenneth MacMillan. And in less than a year, she would fire Taras as well.

Misha had been able to raise ABT's budget enormously. His name had attracted much more money than ABT had ever received prior to his tenure. Nevertheless, ballet cannot be a self-sustaining enterprise when it is entirely dependent on private contributions and the box office. There is always going to be a deficit, but compromising the quality of the company to save money was not the way to go. That, however, was exactly what Jane now planned to do. She announced that the principals would be given a shorter contract because not all of them would be asked to tour. She was going to cut back on rehearsal time. Unlike Misha, she would be happy to give anyone time off to do his or her own gigs. She had told everyone that she was a genius at fund-raising. But all she did was cut corners any way she could.

Jane ruined her relationship with Misha needlessly. I think she could have easily retained his support. Misha had asked Jane to keep Charles on staff at least another year, until his contract expired. But early in September 1989, Charles called me in tears. He was in his office at our studios, packing up his things. There'd been two meetings with Jane, one the day before and one earlier that same day. Jane told him she couldn't work having too many people in charge of the operations, and so she had to fire him. Charles had injured many careers, many spirits. Now he told me, "Ballet can kill you."

Misha was still the most famous name in ballet, a very glamorous name, and the rich wanted to be allied to glamour. Jane's dream was that Misha would stay on as a figurehead, so that she could continue to mine his brand for funds. But after she fired Charles, Misha declared that he, too, would leave immediately. Now she wound up having to pay Charles his entire year's salary *and* she lost not only Misha's name but his productions of *The Nutcracker*, *Don Quixote*, and *Swan Lake*. Before long the full impact of his decision had sunk in. "I don't know why Misha did it this way," Jane groaned to me.

Jane and the board still thought excitement came only with foreign guest stars. They didn't understand that we had had a banner season in 1987–88 with only Makarova and Asylmuratova dancing a handful of guest performances.

"You want to have the old ABT," I told Howard Gilman.

"Yeah, that was the best time," he said.

"You don't understand," I said, "you can never create the same thing twice; you can't go back."

But overnight it seemed as though ABT was a different company. A race to erase the prior decade and put the clock into reverse had begun.

directing vienna

Throughout the 1989–90 season I worked with ABT, while shuttling to Vienna on ABT's lay offs. I had two years paid preparation before my first season in Vienna. Once I actually assumed the directorship in the fall of 1991, I'd be required to spend six months there every year. Originally I had thought that I might continue to spend the rest of the year with ABT. But as the months went on and Jane began reconfiguring the company, I knew that I didn't want to be involved beyond my contract's expiration in the summer of 1990. Besides, Jane was pretty much determined to cashier Misha's team altogether; one by one we were eliminated. It also became clear that it would be irresponsible to spend only six months per year in Vienna since there was so much change I was planning on instituting. I changed my contract so that my presence was assured for each full season in Vienna.

There followed two full years of negotiating with the Austrian unions, who exerted absolute control over every opera house policy and routine imaginable. There were union representatives among the dancers who had to be appeased; there was also a national theatrical union. All parties had to agree with any change to any law, no matter how minor the change, no matter how ridiculous the regulation that would be abolished. Nationwide representatives from the dancers' union had to agree to a change with the musicians' regulations. People who didn't know anything about what we were talking about could still say no. Attempts had been made for years to reform the union laws. Nureyev, who was a great local favorite, both as dancer and as ballet master, had nevertheless warned me that it was hopeless.

But I was lucky: I was a complete outsider but came with a reputation, and I could tell that the union officers were intimidated by me. I immediately took advantage of that. I didn't threaten; I just told them in no uncertain terms what I needed. Sometimes they had arguments to give me and sometimes they had no answer at all to justify regulations that were indefensible and often just plain stupid. When I later told the nationwide head of all unions that I couldn't believe it had taken me the entire two-year preparatory period to bring about some changes, he corrected me. Two years was a blink of the eye. He himself had spent years trying to make some changes, without being able to make all parties agree.

In the fall of 1990, I was in Vienna to decide which corps de ballet dancers I was going to retain and which would not have their contracts renewed at the end of that season. I would teach class for three days and then decide. I had already drawn up a tentative list, but I actually wound up keeping some I originally thought I was going to fire. Knowing that a new director was on her way had already motivated the company to begin to improve.

On my first day teaching I deliberately came to class seven minutes late to defuse some tension. It was the company's day off. On the rare occasion when class was given on a rest day, it was usually scheduled later in the morning. Especially for me, I guess, they kept it at 9 a.m. I think some outgoing administrators hoped that nobody would show up. The dancers themselves thought that I'd overslept, but when I appeared the entire company was in place at the barre. There was hardly a sound in the studio. They were naturally apprehensive since they knew what I was there for. My class was different, because they were used to having their own teachers and their routine, and this was a new person speaking English. But they worked very well. I taught for ninety minutes, and even though I gave them an easier class than I did with ABT, it was more difficult as well as longer than what they were used to.

I forgot one step: after two tendu battements at the barre, I omitted jeté. Only later, back in my hotel room, thinking over the class that I'd given, did I discover that the missing card was jeté. The next day I came to class and apologized. Nine in the morning in Vienna was three in the morning New York time, and I'd just arrived.

"Did I forget yesterday to give you jeté?"

"Yes," they told me, but they weren't sure . . . Maybe in my class I didn't give jeté at all! I tried to make the atmosphere a little bit easier.

"Today we won't miss this step!" I assured them.

By the third day I could see they were already improving. But the end of that third class was when I had to talk to each of the sixteen dancers I asked to remain at the end. Firing people is really an assistant's job. I had fired people for Misha on more than one occasion. But Susan refused to do it for me. Probably for the dancers, however, it was better that I spoke to them myself. It was more personal, and I tried not to undermine their belief in themselves. They could understand from my class that technical standards were going to be more rigorous. I told them I was looking for a little bit different type of corps de ballet. I needed to have people of more uniform height. One dancer wasn't physically what I was looking for, another was limited technically.

In a situation like this, you immediately start to think about their families, about the lives they had already built in Vienna, the many ramifications. At the same time, I had to enforce my own professional judgment or it would be impossible to build a new company. I kept every single one I thought had the potential to significantly improve. In their current condition, eighty percent of the company was substandard.

Some had tears in their eyes and yet they remained composed. When another woman broke down, I thought that I would, too. But they even thanked me for explaining my choices. I told all of them they shouldn't lose their time to dance. They of course would dance in Vienna for the remainder of the season. I invited four girls to come back to the auditions I would hold the following April.

At a press conference soon after, local journalists and critics asked how many dancers I had fired and why. Some thought that I wanted to import as many as forty dancers from America. I told them I wanted to bring good dancers and I didn't care where they came from. At the end I said, "Thank you for coming here, it means you're really concerned about the company and I'm very happy about that. It means we will—we hope—have support from you."

By the time I moved to Vienna in September 1991, union regulations about the dancers' work routine had been completely revised. I had expanded class to an hour and a half, in addition to an extra thirty minutes after class for dancers to work on variations with the teacher. I pushed back the start time of their daily class one hour to ten. Previously, the corps dancers worked after class until one in the afternoon. After that they had a break of five hours, and then worked in the evening for a couple of hours more. I changed the schedule so that the corps now worked until four, while soloists and principals were free after class and began their rehearsals at four. The entire corps was in hysteria. How were they going to do their shopping? At five o'clock the grocery stores closed. But actually it was more professional and thus more comfortable: their working day wasn't broken, and they really could concentrate, and then spend evenings when they weren't performing with their families. The dancers were older than American corps, and many had children. The principals could rest in the daytime, and when they came to their rehearsals they would have to do a warm-up. It meant that they had to do virtually a second class each day, and so they, too, couldn't help but improve.

Now I ensured that class was included as part of every dancer's working day, so that they had one less hour of rehearsals per day, but it became mandatory that every dancer take class every single working day. Probably half of the company was angry about that, because for years they'd been skipping a full class and only doing a warm-up in the morning instead. Since the company regulations hadn't changed in twenty-two years, the dancers were still paid what they had been decades earlier. The incredible reality was that Vienna, a rich opera house, paid the ballet corps less than did any other state company in Europe. I increased their salary forty percent, and then called a company meeting. "Now you owe me. You have got to work and show me that you deserved a raise." I also secured a new stage floor for the theater and refurbished the studios. They were beautiful and light filled; they just needed a new color, since they had been painted a depressing dark brown. I changed them to white.

We were opening the season with Frederick Ashton's *La Fille mal Gardée*. Rehearsing the ballet every day for two weeks, I made the dancers improve their speed. The critics noticed an improvement in the quality of the company instantly. Tasting success, dancing for larger audiences, the dancers began working with some degree of elation.

Soon after that, I staged two galas featuring international stars from American Ballet Theatre and New York City Ballet. Judith Jamison was conferencier. David Parsons performed his strobe-lit solo *Caught*, and Maya Plisetskaya made a special appearance from Russia. A couple of Vienna's own principal dancers also starred, and the full company performed a waltz from *Der Fledermaus*, the women on pointe.

By now, Nureyev was attempting to launch a new career as a conductor. He had asked that I allow him to conduct at least some portion of the two galas. But this was my first artistic statement in Vienna. (*La Fille mal Gardée* had been taken into the repertory by the preceding administration.) Rudi may have considered himself a musician, but the fact is he was not. I thought it would implicate me as neither objective nor professional, interested only in exploiting his name. Waechter declined Rudi's services on my behalf, and Rudi denounced me in the newspapers as a "a fascist . . . a dictator!" But the next time we met, he said, "Listen, bad publicity is sometimes the best kind." At the first gala I spied him looking around to make sure that nobody could see him as he pulled himself step by step up the stairs; he was already terribly stricken with AIDS. It broke my heart. He saw me and straightened up instantly. We kissed each other. "Ah, such red lipstick, like a vampire!"

Everyone who danced in those two galas was, I think, excited, and felt some sense of responsibility for the success of the entire program, not simply their own excerpt. "This is the level we want to have in this company," I told the native dancers about the guests. "Watch them, study them."

Probably Rudi took it as a further affront that later in the season my first new production was *Don Quixote*, replacing a 1966 production he'd done. It was established in the Vienna repertory but was not to my taste at all. It was typical of Rudi's productions, featuring luxurious costumes and scenery that overwhelmed the stage and the dancers. In a way he was right to fashion the ballet that way for Vienna because the company's technical level was never high enough to let the dancing itself become its own spectacle. But I wanted a young, fresh production, a complete contrast to Rudi's. The stage would be open. The costumes were by Edvard Erhlich, inspired to some extent by Yves St. Laurent's folkloric couture. The backdrops designed by Dmitri Strizhov were neo-Cubistic, reminiscent of the ones Picasso created for Massine's *Three-Cornered Hat*.

The production was energetic. I condensed some of the more sluggish parts and made the gypsy dances for corps and soloists more difficult. I made Cupid's role a little bigger; at the final curtain she led Don Quixote to his land of dreams. For most of the ballet, however, the Don was a more tragic figure than he usually becomes in this comic romp. For his act 1 entrance, music director Robert Luther interpolated a Minkus passage he'd uncovered and had orchestrated evocatively. I tried to make clear that the Don's apparitions were visible only to him.

When the curtain fell on opening night, there were boos as well as bravos. The reviews were mixed. One critic, an unconditional Nureyev partisan, vented her hatred for it in no uncertain terms. The audience loved it, however, and the run was completely sold out.

"Don't you feel like Don Quixote yourself?" the minster of culture, Rudolph Sholten, asked me. And yes, trying to put high-level ballet on in Vienna did often seem like tilting at windmills. This was particularly true when, not long after the *Don Quixote* premiere, Waechter suffered a fatal heart attack while walking through his beloved Vienna woods. He was only sixty-two. I mourned him as a boss and a friend.

He had been fully committed to placing ballet on an equal footing with opera, and treating it like a serious art. His successor, Iolan Hollander, didn't believe in the ballet's upgrade but wanted to reduce it to subordinate position once again. I could have left at the end of that first season, and I certainly contemplated doing so. But I had signed a separate contract to produce for them a new production of *Giselle* the following season. After that, for my third year in residence, I was planning a new *Swan Lake*. Waechter and I had already discussed it.

My first year I hired four new principals and four soloists from abroad. The second year I also hired Vladimir Malakhov, who had graduated from the Bolshoi school in 1985. He jumped divinely and had unusually elegant and shapely legs to a degree that wasn't at all common in men at the time. He was also hyperextended, which was something very rare in men at the time. He was definitely something different. While I've always appreciated dancers who are textbook perfect, I've also always loved to see people who are a little extreme. He immediately became a sensation with the public.

Working with different companies and coaching various versions of *Giselle*, I realized that something always bothered me about the way the production was designed. When the first act is awash with vibrant autumn colors, the spectator is often distracted from what is most important: Giselle's transformation from happy and trusting to mortally injured by life. I wanted to tone down the panoply and make color function symbolically.

"Please just do it normally," Waechter had said. "I don't want them to bite you." He wanted a good-quality conventional version that wouldn't incite any controversy. At that moment I thought, okay, I wouldn't upset him and I would do it his way.

After his death, however, the point was moot, although I continued to debate with myself. Ultimately I remained convinced that I was right to want to do something more adventurous. And this was why I had left the United States, I reminded myself, to test out my vision, my ideas, rather than always answering to another director.

I worked with scenery designer Ingolf Bruun and costume designer Clarisse Priun Miylunis to create a monochromatic *Giselle* set in the Biedermeier period. The scenery was black and white and gray, a silvery frame. Each principal was dressed in a quintessential shade. Spotlights provided accents to echo the costumes. Hilarion's costume contained about a dozen different greens, which blended to form one deep, complex shade. (The opera house boasted an excellent costume workshop.) His fellow villagers were dressed in gray with just a tinge of green. Giselle was in blue, the color of the cosmos. Her girlfriends in the waltz were in pale gray with a daub of the same blue—they were lit by Giselle's radiance. Dressing Albrecht in gray made particular sense because in the first act he is inchoate. His character is developed through tragedy. But his costume, too, was brushed with a tinge of Giselle's blue, a nascent acknowledgment of his spiritual debt to her. The aristocrats were in black and white and gray; Bathilde's ruby-red dress provided the only saturated color on stage. She was swathed in red—not only her dress but her gloves, shoes, trim. Although Bathilde is a victim, too, her costume acknowledged that she is also an avatar of all the worldly temptations to which Albrecht surrendered in act 1.

In the second act, Albrecht is never costumed in black, because his love for Giselle remains forbidden even after her death. He's not allowed to show the world that he is grieving for her. In Vienna, Albrecht's jacket was midnight blue; it was as though Giselle's first act blue had deepened to register his psychological growth.

I retained the Russian text of *Giselle*, descended from Petipa's revisions of the ballet in St. Petersburg during the late nineteenth century, fifty years after the ballet received its premiere in Paris. However, I choreographed a pas de quatre in place of the peasant pas de deux.

It's always bothered me that the peasant couple appear almost as guest artists to dance their pas de deux. Usually, Petipa doesn't jar us like that. When he staged divertissements, they were full-blown interpolations, like the wedding celebration in the original *La Bayadère*, with its parade of short diversions. But *Giselle* is no extravaganza. The story is so intimate, so intense, that it hurts to lose Giselle and Albrecht for so long. So I divided the peasant music among Giselle, Albrecht, and the lead peasant boy and girl. The peasant couple danced their entrance, then the adagio became a duet for Albrecht and Giselle—the music fits her character so beautifully. Then the peasant boy danced his customary variation, as did the girl. In the coda, I gave the boy's music to Albrecht, choreographing a very difficult variation to showcase Malakhov's personality—he was at that moment the finest Albrecht on the stage.

The peasant girl danced the first phrase of her original coda variation; Giselle supplanted her for the second phrase. Both couples danced alongside each other in the concluding measures. They all finished with bows to each other. It was a friendly competition that became a celebration of dance.

I could of course schedule as much rehearsal time as I wanted, and the Vienna opening was one of the rare nights when I was completely satisfied with my own work. All the little transitions that prepare us for Giselle's breakdown were newly legible. I asked Luther to quicken the first-act tempi, so that the second act would seem even more otherworldly. And then when dawn drives the Wilis back to their tombs, to slow the music even more so that they seemed to be melting off the stage.

There were tears in my eyes watching Brigitte Stadler and Malakhov dance the second-act pas de deux; they were two souls in complete accord. After the final curtain, the dancers and production received a forty-two-minute ovation, the longest ever recorded in the opera house log. Once again I was convinced: only when we don't do it justice is *Giselle* ever outdated. In fact for me it is the perfect ballet, taking us from the earth to the sky.

I was still too young, I thought, to become a time-server in the Austrian bureaucracy, given that Hollander didn't feel that ballet deserved equal footing with the opera. And so it was that after *Giselle*'s last performance in late spring I left Vienna for good.

epilogue

It seemed as though virtually from the moment I'd arrived in Vienna, I began to miss living in the United States. "Why do you want to come back to America?" Waechter had asked me. "You will understand how wonderful life is in Vienna." Back in the States, on more than one occasion during the 1990s, I would ask myself if indeed it would have been better to stay a while longer in Vienna. Little could I have imagined what was waiting for me in America. Ballet was changing. It was increasingly about cutting costs, taking shortcuts everywhere possible.

If I thought my old job at ABT was waiting for me, it was time to think again. Jane Hermann had been fired as artistic and executive director in the spring of 1992. Later that year, Kevin McKenzie, who had been one of our principal dancers, was named artistic director. We'd worked well together during his dancing years at ABT; he even wrote me a note once thanking me for my coaching. He danced at my Vienna gala in 1992. But ABT coach Georgina Parkinson and he were very close, and there was no way she would have ever permitted him to rehire me. Indeed, my name had become verboten in the company, as ABT's mood was, for now, anti-everything to do with Baryshnikov and Russians.

I was restless and rootless: I lived in Philadelphia, then bought a house in Princeton, New Jersey, then came back to Manhattan. I was always working. It was fun in 1996 to choreograph a short film version of *Little Red Riding Hood*, directed by David Kaplan and starring Christina Ricci. In 1997, I staged a new *Swan Lake* for the Princeton Ballet. Dancing Odette/Odile with them was Suzanne Goldman, who had been in the corps of ABT and danced on my tours to France and Italy in 1981 and 1984. Her career had taken off after she left ABT. I hired her as a soloist in Vienna during my first season there. In *Swan Lake*, she'd never looked so sleek and never danced so well. I coached at the Dutch National Ballet, taught at my old friend Genya Poliakov's s school in Florence. I staged *Don Quixote* at

Philadelphia's University of the Arts and taught ballet to modern dancers in the city's Philadanco company.

But my greatest satisfaction during the 1990s was working with my son Alyosha. Like most parents, I worried about the insecurity of a career in ballet, but he became an excellent teacher and coach. Ten years after his arrival here, we began staging excerpts from the Russian classics together for the senior students of the Nutmeg school in Torrington, Connecticut, where he was teaching. And I enjoyed watching him on stage as Drosselmeyer in their annual *Nutcracker*. He alternated with Momix artistic director Moses Pendleton, whose daughter Quinn was studying at Nutmeg. Both Alyosha and Moses were very interesting in the part, and distinctly different from each other. Moses was more grotesque; Alyosha was more psychological. After Vladimir Malakhov became director of the Berlin Ballet in 2002, I was pleased to be able to arrange for both Quinn Pendleton and Dominic Hodel, another good student of Alyosha's, to join the Berlin company.

I couldn't have dreamed in 1995, when I returned to Russia for the first time since 1976, that today I would be living on the Fontanka Canal, several blocks from where I grew up. I was coaching Molly Smollen, a talented young dancer who had just left ABT, for her participation in the Maya Plisetskaya competition, held at the Alexandrinsky Theater, part of the Rossi Street complex that included the Vaganova Institute. One night during my three-day stay in what was again called, after Glasnost, St. Petersburg, I went to see *La Bayadère* at the Kirov. I was standing in the lobby when suddenly Ninel Kurgapkina was running across the lobby toward me.

"What are you doing here?" she cried. "How is it possible? You made a huge career. Good for you!"

The next several years were momentous for the Kirov. I think it was in large part because of the dancers' exposure to new, Western ideas about training and style. The dancers slowed down and studied the videotapes that were now available to them. Of course this cut both ways, because not every Western practice was worth imitating. At the Paris Opera, Sylvie Guillem had, during the 1980s, initiated a gymnastic emphasis on extension that threatened to wrench the body's silhouette out of any classical alignment. But it was a gimmick that she deployed with intelligence.

It worked for her. Her liberties were now being adopted uncritically by the new Kirov generation, as was apparent in New York in November 1997, when a gala was held to mark the 125th anniversary of Diaghilev's birth. Prominently featured were rising dancers from the Bolshoi and the Kirov. It was startling to watch so many of them outdo each other in the ultimately pointless process of trying to get her leg up as high as possible.

Three months later, however, I was impressed by the advanced boys' class I saw young Kirov soloist Viacheslav Samodurov teach when the Vaganova Institute performed at the Brooklyn Academy of Music. He had incorporated into his class new influences, among them an emphasis on passé that derived from the French school. Passé helps the dancer turn out, helps her feel where her hips are supposed to be, makes the feet work. There was a good energy to his class, a good musicality; Samodurov understood how to use the old school as a base but at the same time add a fresh, modern rhythm.

A year later, in April 1999, I went to St. Petersburg to see the premiere of a revival of *The Sleeping Beauty* staged by Sergei Vikharev, a dancer in the company who was committed to rediscovering the Imperial aesthetic. He worked with a choreologist from the Stepanov notations that recorded a 1903 revival of the 1890 original. Vikharev's production was a refutation of everything my generation had been brought up to believe was the right way to make classical ballet relevant and contemporary. The pantomime was back, the musical cuts restored, the pomp and pageantry out in force. At the theater, I bumped into any number of old friends and colleagues who hated what they saw, but I was enchanted. There was controversy about how accurately Vikharev had been able to restore the choreography, given that the notations were incomplete. For me that was irrelevant. If the entire thing had been concocted by Vikharev himself, it would still have been magnificent. By contrast, the 1952 production by Konstantin Sergeyev in which I'd danced at the Kirov looked anemic.

A unique opportunity had now been bestowed on the Kirov. Except for Moscow's Bolshoi, no other company had the personnel to do these ballets justice on this scale. I thought that it was vital that the theater retain as much as they could of its Imperial inheritance, the masterpieces created on its own stage. But it could also retain the revised, Soviet-era productions in which I'd performed during the 1960s. It would be conceptually interesting for the company to include both the Imperial legacy and the Soviet revisions.

Studying the company in depth, I saw technical improvements achieved since I'd last watched them in St. Petersburg and New York in 1995. I didn't like the way the Kirov let the dancers' hips rise when they extended their leg. But now, by using muscles under the buttocks, their legs were turning out without the hip rising. Their lines were improved, and their extensions became easier—that was a mixed blessing, however, because the hips were now able to provide more effective support.

When the Kirov came to New York that July, their all-Balanchine program was just as exciting for me as *Sleeping Beauty*. Ten years after dancing its first Balanchine ballet, the Kirov was now poised to do his style justice. I watched *Symphony in C* from the wings of the Metropolitan Opera. Gianandrea Noseda conducted almost at the speed of New York City Ballet. The dancers were swearing when they came offstage, but they managed to keep up. Best of all was *Serenade*: they understood Tchaikovsky's music. Their movement was correct, and they were able to generate Balanchine's crisp attack but maintain their own lushness as well.

Noseda's tempi were obviously maintained at the behest of Valery Gergiev, who liked speed. Since 1995, Gergiev had surmounted the entire Kirov institution colossus-style. Formerly there had been an overall executive director, and then individual leaders of ballet and opera—separate but equal. Now, ex-Kirov principal dancer Makhar Vasiev was titular artistic director for the ballet. But while on tour his title was director of the ballet company; at home in St. Petersburg he was merely "company manager." I chatted with him a number of times during the New York season. Vasiev was open in conversation and at that moment rather insecure in his position. And I was naturally charmed when he told me that Baryshnikov had said to him that I was the most valuable of the ballet masters he'd employed at American Ballet Theatre. After some years of considering the Kirov stodgy, I thought that it could be sensational; it could set the world standard. Watching them at Covent Garden in London a year later, I remained convinced.

In March 2000, I found myself discussing the company with Gergiev in his hotel suite in Manhattan, where he was conducting at the Met. He didn't understand that Vikharev's *Sleeping Beauty* had enjoyed a great success in the West.

"Tell me the truth, which do you think is better?" he asked—Vikharev's or Konstantin Sergeyev's *Beauty*.

I said Vikharev's definitely, but they could maintain a curatorial approach and perform both productions. He was evidently surprised and confused, because, as he told me, "everybody" at the Kirov was opposed to it. Indeed, a lot of the ballet staff had insisted it was Sergeyev's 1952 production that should have been shown in New York the previous July. When the Kirov had last performed Konstantin Sergeyev's *Beauty* in New York, in 1989, it hadn't been critically acclaimed, but logic wasn't the strong point of the naysayers.

In the fall of 2002, I spent two months working at the Berlin Ballet at the invitation of Vladimir Malakhov, who had just become artistic director. I clocked in a great deal of studio time with both Polina Semionova, who had just graduated from the Bolshoi school the previous spring, and with the Kirov's Diana Vishneva, a permanent guest in Berlin. Malakhov had hired Semionova as a soloist upon her graduation. She had all the requisite physical equipment and aptitude; it was a question of shaping her in the right way.

Age twenty-six, Vishneva represented something of a new type in Kirov ballerina, by virtue of the fact that many of her best performances were in Balanchine repertory. She had great attack, good proportions, a strong technique, an exciting temperament; she was very pretty and alluring onstage. She also had raw edges that needed smoothing in the classical repertory, where she could be too staccato. Sometimes she seemed like a tall soubrette when she needed to convince us that she was a grand ballerina.

The Kirov's dancers now performed a much wider repertory than what was permitted in my years dancing there. Not only for Vishneva but indeed for many in the new generation, it was the classical aesthetic that often posed more of a stylistic challenge than did Balanchine or new work by contemporary choreographers.

As it turned out, Vasiev was adamantly opposed to Vishneva dancing at the Kirov one of the pinnacles of the classical repertory, Odette/Odile in *Swan Lake*. And so it was in Berlin that she had made recently made her debut in it. Malakhov showed me a tape of her Berlin performance and asked me to work with her on it. Certainly, at first glance it wasn't something she was ideal for, given that she was an allegro technician par excellence. But a ballerina who had contributed as much to the Kirov's success as she certainly had the right to try something a little risky. She had infinite capacity for hard work, which is always gratifying for a coach. Like all dancers, her spiritual batteries needed to be recharged from time to time, but she retained corrections and ideas very well.

In the spring of 2004 I went to Japan, where I coached Vishneva and Malakhov in a new film of *Giselle*. That spring I moved into the apartment in St. Petersburg I'd purchased a year earlier. The city was now so much shinier and more international than when I'd lived here that it was like some place I'd read about but never visited. I had come to love New York so much that I didn't think I could be happy living somewhere else, but it turned out that I'd now spend more time in St. Petersburg than anywhere else.

I was attending Kirov performances with some frequency. In 2000, I had been quoted in *Ballet Review*: "The Kirov has brought classical ballet standards back up. Now they have to continue, to clean, to refine, and I hope standards everywhere will rise." But only four years later, instead of continually striving for improvement, complacency had taken hold. Progress was starting to slow. As I watched the Kirov now, it was not quite the same company that had looked so triumphant, so invincible only a few years earlier.

Gergiev had announced to the press in December 2003 that he was going to replace Vasiev, but hadn't followed through with that threat. He did appear to be concerned, however, about the state of the ballet. He said he wanted me to get involved in the company. How deep his commitment to the ballet was I couldn't have said. In my youth the Kirov delivered great ballet that profoundly entertained and sometimes moved its audiences. Demand for ballet tickets was always fierce, whereas opera frequently played to near-empty houses. Gergiev had turned that around entirely. The opera was internationally renowned. Hopefully he could understand that the ballet could not lag behind; in a great theater they both had to be of the highest quality. It wasn't a question of ballet now competing with the opera—they were two different species.

Gergiev asked me to join the post-Glasnost successor to the old Art Soviet committee, a consulting body comprising delegates from the theater's performing roster and artistic staff. He took me to a meeting where one by one nearly every ballet coach present complained about Vasiev. There was blood in the water after Gergiev's announcement the prior December that Vasiev would be replaced. His wife, Olga Chenchikova, an ex-Kirov ballerina now company coach, was also present. She of course did not complain; rather, she sat like a stone. (I would imagine that she had a great deal to say that night at home, however.)

Very much on Diana Vishneva's mind that fall of 2004 was her upcoming debut season with American Ballet Theatre in New York the following spring. Two years earlier, she had danced a single Juliet with them. Now she would dance Kitri in *Don Quixote*, Giselle, and Balanchine's *Ballet Imperial*, initiating her as a kind of permanent guest with ABT. I'd helped Vishneva's manager, Sergei Danilian, plan her appearances, and I was going to go with her to New York and work with her there. Most important for her, she would also dance with ABT Odette/Odile in *Swan Lake*.

In New York, Vishneva and I rehearsed in a rented studio at City Center, paid for by patron Theresa Khawly, who underwrote Vishneva's ABT appearances. Vishneva's debut *Don Quixote* was very successful, despite the fact that her nerves hadn't allowed her much sleep the night before, and so were her two *Ballet Imperials*. Now we were beginning to work on *Swan Lake*. Her two performances were a month away, but she was going to be dancing in Japan for much of June. Ethan Stiefel was scheduled to be her Siegfried, but he was now recovering from an injury. He said he probably wouldn't be sufficiently recovered to perform with her, but they were rehearsing nevertheless. Vishneva and I, and Vishneva and Kevin McKenzie, discussed the possibility of various other ABT principal men.

There was certainly no love lost between me and McKenzie by this point, after all the years he had allowed Georgina Parkinson to keep me out of my old job. In no uncertain terms, they had attempted to obliterate my imprint on the company.

But much of my resentment had by now dissipated. Nevertheless, I certainly couldn't agree with much about the way he was running ABT. I had thought for a long time that he should be replaced, and he probably knew that.

Soon after Vishneva arrived in New York, she asked McKenzie if I could watch her rehearsals in the ABT studios, and he balked. Now after the success of her opening performances, he was allowing her to bring me in. But it was without any special emotion that I went back to the Met to rehearse.

Vishneva and I looked in at the big studio in the Met basement where I had led so many corps rehearsals, then walked over to the smaller studio down the hall. The tension was unbelievable from the moment I walked through the door. I said hello to Stiefel, but I didn't approach him. Kirk Peterson, who had been a leading dancer when I arrived at ABT and was now one of the company's ballet masters, came over and kissed me. At that point Stiefel walked over and we chatted. I felt so uncomfortable. Everyone present did. Irina Kolpakova was leading the rehearsal; she had joined ABT as a coach just as I was leaving. I said something to make Irina relax. She invited me to sit next to her in the center of the studio, but I preferred to sit off to the side, by the piano. Stiefel hadn't yet recovered enough to attempt any of the lifts, and he was short for Vishneva. To compensate, she tried leaning on him and squeezing herself down into plié, so much so that Kolpakova asked her, "Why are you sitting in plié?" I gave Vishneva and Stiefel some corrections about the partnering.

By the time Vishneva came back to New York from Japan, Stiefel had bowed out of *Swan Lake*. Angel Corella was interested in doing it with her but then suddenly had to make a trip to Paris. Maxim Beloserkovsky and she tried working together. That came to a quick halt. Days before the performance, McKenzie told her that she would dance with Gennady Saveliev, a soloist who didn't dance a lot of classical leads. Saveliev did his best and they were okay together. Her interpretation was already much improved since Berlin. In the White Swan scenes Vishneva was generating more warmth and tenderness. As the Black Swan she was too cool, perhaps trying too hard to be noble and thus sacrificing some needed erotic heat. Lacking preconceptions about the role that seemed to rule in St. Petersburg, the New York audiences and critics had no trouble accepting her in his ballet. Already good, she was now ready to go farther.

Finally there was *Giselle*, which was beset by tribulations so as to make everything that had come before seem inconsequential. Vishneva's partner was scheduled to be Malakhov. He was stricken with appendicitis. Then Vishneva herself spent two days in the hospital with a virus. When she was released, she wasn't sure whether she was up to *Giselle*, but McKenzie told her she would have to be. She finally danced it with Corella, with very little time to prepare. Their performance was certainly not on par with the *Giselle* she'd filmed in Japan a year earlier, but nevertheless I was gratified to see it featured on the front page of the *New York Times*.

Vasiev was still insisting that he would never let Vishneva dance *Swan Lake* at the Kirov—period. But Gergiev had decided that not only would she dance it but she would do so on opening night of the new season. The Kirov traditionally opens with *Swan Lake*, and this year's Odette/Odile was going to be Daria Pavlenko. Supplanting Pavlenko was only going to create additional animosity toward Vishneva. I told Gergiev that I was all for Vishneva finally getting to do *Swan Lake* with the Kirov, but rather than jam it down the company's throat, it would be better to wait until December. That way, I could spend all of November working with her and her partner, Igor Kolb. There was certainly going to be resentment from the administration, since Vishneva customarily worked with Vasiev's wife, Olga Chenchikova. Now I would be coaching Vishneva, although I wasn't a regular member of the coaching staff. Having lived so long in the West, I was an outsider as far as most of the company was concerned.

"No, why wait, December is too far away . . ." Gergiev wanted to open the season with some kind of new, fresh statement. "All Vasiev's young protégés look the same. I can't even recognize them on stage." Soon after, Gergiev's assistant, Marta Petrovna, relayed the message that he had promised to pay for Vishneva, Kolb, and me to rehearse in the studios of the Berlin Ballet, far from prying and censorious eyes in St. Petersburg. "Think about it and I will call you back . . . I will tell him."

I thought about it. It still wasn't a very good idea: it was still better to wait until December. Gergiev, however, was insistent when he called me again soon after. And so, by the beginning of August, it was agreed that Vishneva would dance *Swan Lake* on the opening night of the season, September 21.

Berlin was now out, unfortunately, because its studios were going to be fully in use during a busy rehearsal period. We had to rehearse in St. Petersburg, but it was fine at the end of August when we worked alone without even a pianist. As the company returned to work in force, however, it was clear that the administration was prepared to incite an amount of venom—against me, against Vishneva—that I wouldn't have thought possible.

There were other dancers who interested me. I watched Yulia Bolshakova, eighteen or nineteen at the time, rehearse the Black Swan pas de
deux for a Kirov benefit. She had extraordinary physical capacity but
was still a child who didn't know what she was doing or why. But appar-
ently she did know that she was supposed to utilize her extension to the
maximum biological possibility. Unbelievably, she had already danced the
full-length *Swan Lake* not only at the Kirov but at Covent Garden during
their season the prior summer. Twice in 2005, I saw Alina Somova dance
Odette/Odile at the Kirov. Somova was a year older than Bolshakova. She
utilized her extension to the max—and then some.

The ballet administration was now infecting the ranks of the Kirov
with the party line that Vishneva's performance was going to stigmatize
the company's name and reputation. But the idea that it was all right to
let any teenager contort her way through Odette/Odile on the Kirov stage,
but letting Vishneva dance the role was somehow going to violate hallowed traditions was nothing less than delusional.

One ex-Soviet ballerina who was now company coach actually went
to Vasiev and asked why I was rehearsing there and she claimed that we
were changing choreography. Yet it was ludicrous for anyone in the theater to talk about changes in choreography, since administration favorites
were given carte blanche to make any adaptation they or their coaches
chose. Indeed, I tried to restore some steps from the Sergeyev version of
Swan Lake in which I had danced during the 1960s, so as to bring Vishneva's performance in accord with Kirov tradition.

As the opening approached, I was exhausted from the negative energy;
it was much more systemic and engulfing than I could have imagined possible. Vishneva's nerves were getting worse by the second as she realized
that the entire company was expecting failure. In company class she felt
like a leper. I was actually fearful that someone was going to put something slippery on the stage. But nothing like that happened. Nevertheless
she danced with the wings of the theater packed with not entirely sup-
portive colleagues as well as students from the school.

On that opening night her Odette was outstanding. She had polished
and improved many details. Her line was classical and elongated. Everything about her performance was stylistically correct; her energy had the
right kind of humility. She was truly a tender and loving creature, more

gentle, significantly more sensitive and sensual than she'd ever been. Her Odile was better than in New York, but still too aloof for my taste. Better that than vulgar, however.

A second performance is often somehow more treacherous than a debut, because opening-night adrenaline is gone. Vishneva's second *Swan Lake* was no exception. This time, however, her partner, Igor Kolb, was much better in the studio and on stage. I wasn't thrilled with him partnering her in her debut, but she insisted that he would be the best. He turned out to be defensive in rehearsal and soggy on stage.

"My mistake was listening to you," I told her. But this time he was less defensive during the rehearsal process—and I was more blunt. "It's your business," I told him when I gave him a correction. "If you don't want to do it, don't. But what you're doing here looks ridiculous." He listened and incorporated what I said.

Vishneva, however, was feeling a little out of sorts on her second evening. She was agitated in the wings, and she brought that energy onstage with her. Her line wasn't as good as the first performance. I wasn't happy with her second act, the first lakeside scene, which had been the best part of her performance four months earlier. Her variation was good, but Noseda played the act too quickly. Her Black Swan was better than usual. In the final act, the second lakeside scene, she was excellent. I didn't tell her everything I thought until some time later, and she was upset. She didn't feel it was a bad performance, but for me it was lacking the magic of her debut.

With ABT in New York that spring, she danced *Swan Lake* opposite José Manuel Carreno. He was an expert and seasoned partner, not at all intimidated by her—perhaps her best *Swan Lake* prince to date. She did everything nicely, she was very strong technically, and nothing was overdone. She certainly did prove that she could do justice to this role.

On four occasions I coached Vishneva for guest appearances at the Bolshoi in Moscow. For me, the Bolshoi was a welcome change from the Kirov. The entire atmosphere was more open. The fear that permeated and paralyzed the St. Petersburg dancers wasn't visible to me as I walked these hallways and worked in these studios.

Dancing Aurora in *Sleeping Beauty*, Vishneva's Desiré was Malakhov, with whom she was very familiar and comfortable after a half decade of performances. Her *Beauty* in Moscow was a peak moment in her career and mine. Of all the Auroras I coached in my life, Vishneva's came most satisfyingly to fruition: it was the first and only time in my life I saw on stage an Aurora with a distinctly different character in each act. Raissa Struchkova, the now-elderly ex-Bolshoi prima, came onstage after the performance and told me exactly the same thing.

During the Kirov's International Festival in March 2006, artist Mikhail Chemiakin invited me to attend with him the premiere of a new ballet that he had designed. During the applause at the end, Vasiev alighted into the company box and we were face-to-face. He said nothing.

"Makhar, congratulations," I said. "I want to tell you that the festival was better than last year."

"Thank you," he replied, but not very pleasantly. We were forced to stand right next to each other. It was uncomfortable.

"Makhar, are you still angry with me?"

"Me? No, I'm not angry with anybody."

"That's nice to know, but don't you think it wasn't very polite to never come to my rehearsals, or never tell me hello?"

"Well, it wasn't my project. Who invited you?"

I controlled myself with great effort. "You don't know? Gergiev."

"Gergiev has nothing to do with the ballet."

"Really? What is most important is that I didn't try to make trouble for anybody and I didn't start any intrigues. I just wanted to do what is interesting for me. Diana worked with me in New York, and naturally she wanted to continue to work with me. There was a lot of information there for your company and your ballet masters." The dancers had largely forgotten that there was a story behind this ballet. It wasn't just steps or a chance to flaunt extension.

"By the way," he told me, "all the ballet masters said that they didn't like it and it was an entirely American version."

It was too bad, I told him, that his ballet masters didn't even know anymore what was American and what was Russian. And in all likelihood they did not. Perhaps they were not only duplicitous but truly confused. What is authentically, indigenously Russian, and what is the crossbred product of Western influence, whether one or the other cultural perspective is more valuable—these questions have been debated in Russia for centuries.

I see in the family I still have in St. Petersburg the possibility of an improved Russia. My warmhearted and stoic cousin Nina is a retired engineer. Her daughter Elena makes clothes; her granddaughter Nadezda recently graduated with high grades from law school. Elena and Nadezda take great care of Nina; they are civilized and caring people. The young generation seems both saner and kinder than mine, than what has come before.

§ §

Ballet itself today faces shortages in funding and media interest. By its very nature it cannot ever be a profit center. It is not suited to being put on in stadiums. It's a very expensive art. But American companies get virtually nothing from the U.S. government and must endlessly importune private patrons and corporations. This is increasingly true around the world. Boards today are largely made up of people without any knowledge of the field. But they have given money and they expect to be listened to.

At ABT, I saw the way that Lucia Chase had to take dancers into the company who weren't even good enough to be in the corps de ballet but nevertheless had to be given solos. Their parents had contributed money to the company. Even Balanchine had to do that at New York City Ballet. It was not Balanchine's or Lucia's fault. It was America's fault.

Support for ballet has now waned, however, even in countries where governments have traditionally supported it. Today the very relevance of the art form itself is questioned, but I believe it still can be a unique, meaningful artistic experience for the audience. But something so stylized must be seen at its best, or it really shouldn't be seen at all. The funding problems ensure, and are the result of, an equivalent decline in standards of artistry. Too many very young dancers now take on important roles for which they are neither physically nor interpretatively prepared. There is too much adoption of a sports mentality, something that should remain distinct and foreign from ballet. Sports is concerned above all with competition, while ballet is, or should be, concerned with so much else.

Today dancers are overscheduled and overworked. Companies exploit the resources of stamina bestowed on the very young; when they falter, they are discarded in favor of the next crop. In my youth at the Kirov, a ballerina usually had all the time she needed to work on a role; now there is barely any time at all anywhere—for anyone. Desperate to make as much money as they can before their bodies give out, permanent guest stars go directly from one gig to their next one across the ocean, without downtime to rest their muscles or their souls. Companies arrive in foreign cities the night before they are due to open a new season. As often as not, what we see on stage tells us exactly the cost of tactics such as these.

Ballet's artistic support system is imperiled as well. There aren't enough good ballet masters working. There is a lack of authoritative, knowledgeable, and dedicated artistic directors. Criticism that I read is frequently unprofessional. It hurts me to realize that the art form in which I've spent the past sixty years could very well disappear entirely, at least in a form recognizable to me.

I have a lot of respect for modern choreographers who are trying to update and refresh the balletic vocabulary. They are expected to give us a new message that will keep ballet contemporary and topical, but what is greeted as innovative one season may look like yesterday's news a year later.

And yet ballet has always been the most fragile and ephemeral of performing arts. Virtually my entire career has been a question of work that disappears almost as quickly as it's been achieved. Sometimes for days, sometimes for weeks or even months we prepare in the rehearsal studio a performance that may eventually surpass what's gone on in the studio or may just as easily, to my everlasting frustration, not live up to it. Then we start again: the ballerina now dancing perhaps with a new partner, on a different stage, in another city, following the baton of an alternate conductor, contending with muscles and a mental state that are always mercurial. Today we do have video to record highs and lows of performance. And yet so many ever-shifting variables go into determining the caliber of a performance that its quality will always be as fleeting as life itself. In some ways that is sad. In some ways, every moment working creatively becomes all the more valuable, knowing how short-lived the end product may be.

In 2014 a new arts center named for Diaghilev is scheduled to open in Moscow, the centerpiece of a vast new development on the Moscow River waterfront. It is the brainchild of bass-baritone Mikhail German. Mezzo-soprano Elena Obraztsova will oversee the opera company there, and I have been asked to direct all the dance that's programmed there: classical, popular, and ballet featured in opera. It means building an artistic operation from the ground up, choosing the dancers and rehearsal staff. It will be an enormous challenge. After the project is launched, I want to continue as consultant. Dance remains, after all these years, something I am happy to give my heart, soul, and energy to.

~ AFTERWORD ~

The transitory nature of any human experience is what is responsible for one's desire to put it into words. This goes for encountering a mountain as much as for observing a bird in flight. For even if the observed phenomenon appears to be permanent, the observer is not. The less verbal an experience is, the greater is the impulse to articulate it. On the whole, nature's reticence is the mother of art. The book you hold in your hand proves this in more ways than one.

The ability of the performing arts to engender literature about them, from reviews to monographs, equates them with a force of nature. In the case of ballet, this stands to reason, because of the volume of muscular exertion alone involved in every production. By and large, the length of a review does not depend on the production's success or failure: favorable or negative, it reflects first of all that production's purely physical, non-verbal reality.

In other words, any writing about dance is, by definition, retrospective, like the dancers' own sweat. Yet this is due not so much to the passing, transitory nature of that reality as to its non-verbal aspects. For what a dancer's movements call forth are precisely verbs of motion hitherto uncoined.

It is the absence of these verbs, of words adequately denoting what is happening in front of our eyes, that negates the possibility of retaining it and causes what we loosely call a sensation or emotion. The latter of course can be described or defined, but very much after the fact. At best, that would bespeak the subtlety of our hindsight rather than what indeed transpired on the stage or the dancer's own sense of what he/she was doing. In a certain sense, dance is the negation of a coherent response to it, let alone in writing.

But if dance were only the quest of motion to generate the verbs, that would be fine. The trouble is that dance has its own pantomime vocabulary for most known human emotions including incomprehension. And, quite apart from having its own language, dance in itself is a language—

more or less in the same way that birds in flight or mountain ranges are. What prevents one from reading it is that the letters are consistently in motion within the confines of the music that provides them, as it were, with a page.

A better simile perhaps would be a wind-tousled palm tree resembling a Chinese character that is constantly changing its calligraphy and meaning. For every dancer paints their part with their own unique set of muscles and agility, thereby changing, quite unwittingly, the story. He or she adopts the music rather than adapts to it. Moreover, no dancer can ever see him or herself dancing; therefore, what a dancer "reads" is not what a dancer "writes."

This difference is ballet's very oxygen: literally the air through which movements of a body travel into the static viewer's iris or vice versa. Yet there is only one person in the theater who breathes this air fully, who is simultaneously on the stage and in the stalls. This person comprehends both the reader and the writer, representing the very language they are trying to master.

What distinguishes this book from the rest of ballet literature is that it is written by such a person: by a ballet master. To continue with our metaphor: it is a book by language about its writers and readers. A rehearsal master's mind, as well as body, is the nexus of this language's grammar and transcription, of each movement's and gesture's semantics, etymology, synonyms, antonyms, allusions, multiple meanings, abuse, bowdlerized forms, of their past, present, and, with luck, future. It is also an extraordinary encyclopedia of bodies, for no dance can be repeated twice, even by the same dancer.

A dictionary of steps, the rehearsal master is not only the one who can tell the dancer from the dance; she is the one who puts the dance into the dancer. For this reason, a rehearsal master may indeed (as the author of this book did) refuse the career of a ballerina herself, for that would mean confining dance to only one body. Elena Tchernichova has elected to dance in them all, and that's what you see when the curtain rises. The way you see the letters of the alphabet coalescing into sentences when you open a book.

In other words, to the art of classical ballet in this country, Ms. Tchernichova is what memory is to conscious life. In the course of her thirty-five-year professional career she indeed has danced in them, and all over the place: in Russia, Italy, France, England, Germany. For the last decade alone, on these shores, as the classical ballet headmistress at the American Ballet Theatre she coached, among hundreds of others, such dancers as Gelsey Kirkland, Martine van Hamel, Leslie Browne, Alessandra Ferri, Natalia Makarova, Cynthia Gregory, Cheryl Yeager, Susan Jaffe, Mikhail Baryshnikov, Anthony Dowell, Fernando Bujones.

Yet what's most important about this graduate of the famous Vaganova Ballet School in Leningrad and the Moscow Art Institute of Choreography, with many years spent in the Kirov Ballet Theater, is that she brought the great tradition of Russian ballet to the American scene not to turn its wild sweetbriar into an old-fashioned classical rose, but in order to produce a qualitatively new blossoming species. What Ms. Tchernichova was and still is after is not grafting but fusion, and this is what sets her apart from her older compatriots Markova and Danilova. The wilting of that rose alone makes this book timely: both in the minds of its readers and the flesh of her current charges Ms. Tchernichova is to be on stage in the future. In a sense, this volume is classical ballet's insurance policy.

What distinguishes ballet among the arts is that its material is human flesh. The victory of its potential over its limitations is essentially what dance is all about, and a rehearsal master is the one who makes this victory possible for a dancer. A great value of studying classical ballet, especially when one is young, lies in the effort of converting one's complete concentration on something entirely abstract and formal into something entirely concrete and physical. This conversion requires an extraordinary, "unnatural," painful, exacting effort. It could be convincingly argued that this conversion is indeed a paradigm of artistic creation, enacted through the clumsy and dense material of one's own inertial body—a material quite unlike paint or marble and in which one feels the alien-ness of its objectivity, of its very purpose, in the strain of one's every movement.

This experience gives the lie to many a sloppy theory one hears of art as being purely "expressive," "confessional," "natural," "direct," or "spontaneous." A part of the pleasure of watching dance is of course in seeing the very effortful made effortless—but it is only a part, and a small one at that. The larger significance of witnessing the victory of one's potential over one's limitation is the pride and its attendant hope for our species. That's what our sensation of beauty is all about, that's what our exclaiming, "It can be done!" is all about.

Art is not natural in the sense that it reflects nature; Art is natural only when it overcomes or extends nature. "It can be done" is what Art says to nature, who until that very moment, has been saying, "No, you cannot." This book, then, is more about Art than about nature, since it tells you about how it gets done. Yet, by the same token, it is a book about nature: about its potential to evolve into Art.

Since no human being belongs in either category squarely, this book's audience is bound to be large. What guarantees its size also is that every victory of our potential over our limitations—that is, each work of art—increases the margin of our freedom. This is what dance is all about, and what Ms. Tchernichova's book is after. Mountains are free in their finality, so are birds in their flight. We can observe both, but as a model for imitation birds seem to be more tempting. That's why classical ballet involves swans and nymphs and sylphs—creatures with a lower margin of gravity than ours.

Ms. Tchernichova was born and grew up in the town that is justly regarded as the cradle of the Russian Ballet. Situated by the sea, this town often falls prey to foul, capricious weather; in cold seasons, it is incurably damp and foggy. There are only two swans in that town (dwelling, in summertime, in the Summer Garden), and as for its nymphs, well, they are more likely mermaids. Yet every child in that town, long before sinking into a seat under the Mariinsky (the Kirov) Theater's cupola, knows quite a lot about ballet from watching the droves of seagulls suddenly emerging from the fog that envelops the embankments and vanishing into it again, as unexpectedly as they appeared. There are no soloists among them; they are all corps de ballet. Therefore, they'd rather merge with the curtain than take calls.

In this respect they resemble this book's author; but that's what a real ballet is.

JOSEPH BRODSKY

Elena Tchernichova and Joseph Brodsky were close friends and fellow artists-in-exile in New York. He wrote this afterword for an earlier version of Elena's autobiography, which formed the basis for this volume, in 1991. He died, in Brooklyn, in 1996.

~ INDEX ~

NOV   2013

Northport-East Northport Public Library

To view your patron record from a computer, click on
the Library's homepage: **www.nenpl.org**

You may:
- request an item be placed on **hold**
- renew an item that is overdue
- view titles and due dates checked **out on your card**
- view your own outstanding fines

151 Laurel Avenue
Northport, NY 11768
631-261-6930